Contents

Sensing Disaster

Sensing Disaster

LOCAL KNOWLEDGE AND VULNERABILITY
IN OCEANIA

Matthew Lauer

UNIVERSITY OF CALIFORNIA PRESS

University of California Press
Oakland, California

© 2023 by Matthew Lauer

Library of Congress Cataloging-in-Publication Data

Names: Lauer, Matthew, 1970- author.
Title: Sensing disaster : local knowledge and vulnerability in Oceania /
    Matthew Lauer.
Description: Oakland, California : University of California Press, [2023] |
    Includes bibliographical references and index.
Identifiers: LCCN 2022038186 (print) | LCCN 2022038187 (ebook) |
    ISBN 9780520392052 (cloth) | ISBN 9780520392076 (paperback) |
    ISBN 9780520392083 (epub)
Subjects: LCSH: Traditional ecological knowledge—Solomon Islands. |
    Tsunamis—Solomon Islands. | Hazard mitigation—Solomon Islands. |
    Disaster relief—Solomon Islands.
Classification: LCC GN671.S6 L38 2023 (print) | LCC GN671.S6 (ebook) |
    DDC 577.099593—dc23/eng/20220914
LC record available at https://lccn.loc.gov/2022038186
LC ebook record available at https://lccn.loc.gov/2022038187

Manufactured in the United States of America

32 31 30 29 28 27 26 25 24 23
10 9 8 7 6 5 4 3 2 1

Acknowledgments

First and foremost, I must acknowledge the people of Roviana Lagoon and Simbo. Many thanks for your kindness and generosity in sharing your lives with me and your patience with my unending questions. In order to acknowledge the insights and contributions of specific individuals, I have not changed their names in the text unless it was a sensitive topic or my interlocutor requested it.

From the early days of my research in the village of Baraulu I would like to thank Selena, Sam Peke, Jimi, Rihia, Billy, Fiji, Paqo, Joe Lamia, Jacke, Tomi Roe, and Pastor Jon Lingi for my first introduction to Solomon Islands life. Thank you for graciously accepting me into your village and your homes and teaching me so much about your ways of being. I would also like to thank Lawson and Winston for assisting my students during their extended research trip across the Western Province conducting interviews about the tsunami. I am also grateful to Mathew Sasae, Henry Nangu, Loti Gasimata, Rhody, and Joana Pina, the leaders of Roviana Conservation Foundation in Munda, for our memorable discussions about resource management. *Leana Hola!*

On Simbo I would like to thank all the clan leaders including Goldie, John Siqo, Arelo, Samson Elly, and Lawrence for their inspiration, kindness, and endless patience as they taught me their histories. Other influential leaders also deserve recognition; they include Obed Joi, Stewart, Harold, Isaac Vula, and Belshazaar. I would also like to thank the entire Valusa Fishing Group, Dovala, Getson, Rona, Idisi, Jackson, Jeremy, John, Johnny, Junior, Laniusi, Lawrence, Russell, and Tonny, who kept diaries of their fishing outings and catch over an entire year. Idisi, Rona, and Qetson deserve special praise for taking me on numerous fishing outings and providing endless instruction about the intimacies of the ocean around their island. Over the years a number of people have helped my students and me as translators and coresearchers; they include Sampson, Darrel, and Kati. In Tapurai, Daniel Tuke and Amos were thoughtful teachers and generously shared their insights about the tsunami and the reconstruction. In Meqe, I am most indebted to Gideon Tuke, his wife Vasity, and their delightful family for their generous hospitality and loving support. I am grateful for our friendship and the many nights of laughter we have shared over the years. In Lengana, Nickson Sione has grown to be a dear friend and has made much of this research possible through his keen insights and tireless companionship. His father Stewart has also been infinitely generous with his time and instruction. I also want to thank Nickson's father-in-law Aseri for our memorable walks to Ove volcano and through his ancestor's territory. His enactment of his clan's history will always remain in my heart.

On Ghizo I want to acknowledge Ruta Pina and Kerita for assisting Savanna Schuermann during her MA thesis research in Titiana. Over the years I have received unwavering support from all the premiers of the Western Province. The staff of that office in Gizo always received me with open arms. In Honiara the support of Rence Sore, the former permanent secretary at the Ministry of Environment, Climate Change, Disaster Management & Meteorology, was crucial, as well as that of Tim Ngle, the undersecretary of the Ministry of Education, who grants research permits. I also would like to thank the Solomon Islands National Disaster Management office staff, Danny Ruel, Augustine, and Alex, for teaching me about their inspirational work as a growing cohort of professional disaster experts. I am deeply grateful to Lawrence Kiko and Grinta Ale'eke from the Solomon Islands National Museum, who have supported the archaeological work on Simbo, especially Grinta, whom I had the pleasure to work with and learn from while we conducted fieldwork on Simbo during two field seasons in 2015 and 2019. Many more people in the Solomons have helped make this research possible, and I regret that I cannot mention them all here.

This book has been nearly twenty years in the making, and its intellectual filaments spread across not only the Solomon Islands but also the United States and parts of Europe. I am deeply grateful for all the productive engagements and supportive encouragement my colleagues and friends have provided over the years. During my graduate studies A. F. "Sandy" Robertson's and Francesca Bray's careful mentorship has left an indelible imprint on my thought, and I thank them for their dedication and thoughtful guidance. Many thanks to Rebecca Zarger, Glenn Davis Stone, Roy Ellen, Courtney Carothers, Rick Stepp, and especially Mark Moritz for their feedback and insights that helped me refine some of the ideas presented here. We all participated in a lively 2012 session of the American Anthropology Association in San Francisco called "Knowledge Boundaries: Conceptual and Methodological Challenges in Studying Indigenous Knowledge." Another conference in 2013 organized by Christopher Filardi and Eleanor Sterling at the American Museum of Natural History in New York was particularly invigorating. I was an invited speaker along with Simon Albert, Senoveva Mauli, Patrick Pikacha, and Christopher Filardi, all of whom provided constructive comments that deepen my arguments. Jerry Jacka and I co-organized another productive conference session during the 2017 AAA meetings. Our discussions about resilience are reflected here, and I want to thank Jerry as well as Jeremy Spoon for their feedback and their friendship. I also must mention the 7th International Conference on Environmental Future, held in 2018 at the East-West Center on the University of Hawaii campus in Honolulu. The conference brought together island scholars from around the world and was intellectually invigorating. In particular, I would like to thank Konai Helu Thaman, Randy Thaman, Edvard Hviding, and Tamatoa Bambridge for their stimulating conversations and constructive critiques. Finally, I would like to thank the disaster scholars Roberto Barrios, A. J. Faas, Ryo Morimoto, Heather Lazrus, Mitchell Sedgwick, Susanna Hoffman, Elizabeth Marino, and Qiaoyun Zhang for their comments on an early draft of chapter 6 that I delivered at the 2019 AAA meeting in Vancouver.

At San Diego State University, many thanks to my former students Chelsea Hunter, Douglas La Rose, Ben Nugent, and Luke Campanella for assisting in the fieldwork on Simbo. Savanna Schuermann, who conducted her own independent fieldwork in the Gilbertese community of Titiana, provided many insights into that community's experience with the tsunami that I draw on here. I also want to acknowledge Dr. Todd Braje for his friendship and the many, many invigorating discussions about the Anthropocene. I also would like to acknowledge his student Hannah Haas for teaching me about archaeology.

Many thanks to University of California Press editor Stacy Eisenstark for her keen editorial advice and also to Naja Pulliam Collins for guiding me through the publication process. I also would like to acknowledge three anonymous readers for devoting their precious time and providing valuable feedback to improve this work.

Brief passages in chapters 2 and 3 originally appeared in "Oral Traditions or Situated Practices? Understanding How Indigenous Communities Respond to Environmental Disasters," *Human Organization* 71, no. 2 (2012): 176–87; "Changing Understandings of Local Knowledge in Island Environments," *Environmental Conservation* 44, no. 4 (2017): 336–47; and "Indigenous Ecological Knowledge as Situated Practices: Understanding Fishers' Knowledge in the Western Solomon Islands," *American Anthropologist* 111, no. 3 (2009): 317–29, coauthored by Shankar Aswani. Brief passages in chapter 5 and 6 originally appeared in "Calamity, Kastom, and Modernity: Local Interpretations of Vulnerability in the Western Pacific," *Environmental Hazards* 13, no. 4 (2014): 281–97, and "Governing Uncertainty: Resilience, Dwelling, and Flexible Resource Management in Oceania," *Conservation and Society* 14, no. 1 (2016): 34–47. I want to thank the publishers for granting me permission to reprint them here.

Fieldwork for this book was funded primarily by a National Science Foundation Human Dimensions and Social Dynamics Program (BCS Award #0827022). A number of small grants from San Diego State University supported my field endeavors in 2014 and 2015, and the California Academy of Sciences funded my last field trip in 2019. San Diego State University also granted me a one-year sabbatical in 2020–2021. I am truly grateful for the support of these organizations.

Of course, this book would not have been possible if not for the unflinching support of my parents Don and Carol to be an anthropologist and pursue my dreams. My father accompanied me several times to the Solomons, where he assisted with the research and where we discussed under the dim light of kerosene lamps the topics of this book. He has left a deep impression on the people of Simbo and Roviana for his loving engagement and deep respect for their ways of being.

I wrote much of this manuscript during the tumultuous days of the pandemic, and I would be remiss if I did not acknowledge the loving patience and maturity of my daughters Cora and Hazel. As I locked myself in a bedroom and worked on this manuscript, Cora suffered through second grade as an online learner. Thank you, sweet petunias! Finally, I owe so much to my loving wife, the remarkable woman Eden Epling. She accompanied me many times to the Solomons, and her photographic memory and keen anthropological sense of things are written into the ideas and words that follow. You have always been there for me. Gracias mi amor. I dedicate this work to her and my family.

All royalties from this book will be returned to the Simbo people for purposes of community well-being.

Notes on the Simbo Language and Solomon Islands Pijin

The Simbo people speak an Austronesian language that is part of the Northwest Solomonic branch of Western Oceanic.[1] It is closely related to the well-documented Roviana language spoken in Roviana and Vonavona Lagoons of New Georgia Island as well as Hoava.[2] Because of precolonial alliances and intermarriage with the Roviana people and the influence of the Methodist Mission who adopted Roviana as their lingua franca, many Simbo elders understand and to some extent speak Roviana.

There is no published dictionary of Simbo, and at least three different orthographies have been applied to the language. A. M. Hocart created the first systematic orthography, and later the Methodist Mission introduced a slightly different system when they extensively studied the closely related Roviana language spoken on New Georgia. The British Solomon Islands Protectorate adopted the Methodist orthography for many of the languages of the Western Province including Simbo, although the influence of a distinct Seventh-Day Adventist orthography gained traction in the regions where that denomination was adopted, such as Marovo, Rendova, and Kolombangara. Today Simboans employ all three of these orthographies to write their language, and there are many inconsistencies.

In this text I have adopted a modified version of the standardized Methodist orthography of Roviana and attempted to apply it consistently to Simbo (except for official place-names). The vowels of Simbo are similar to Spanish and are pronounced as follows:

a   as "a" in "father"

e   as "é" in "café"

i   as "ee" in "feet"

o   as "o" in "bone"

u   as "oo" in "boot"

The pronunciation of the following denoted consonants is like their English equivalents: k, l, m, n, p, r, s, t, and z. In all New Georgia languages, voiced stops are prenasalized:

b   pronounced as "mb" as in "member"

d   pronounced as "nd" as in "pond"

j   pronounced as "nj" as in "banjo"

q   pronounced as "ng" in "linger"

In addition to the "q" there are two other "g" sounds, and distinguishing them in everyday speech is perhaps one of the most difficult aspects of the language for English speakers. These sounds were also represented differently in the Hocart, Seventh-Day Adventist, and Methodist orthographies and continue to be a source of confusion:

g   is a voiced velar fricative found widely in Melanesian languages and referred to as the Melanesia "soft g." There is no clear equivalent in English. Spanish, however, has a similar "soft g" in words such as "agua."

ng   is a voiced velar stop, pronounced as "ng" in "singer." In the standardized Roviana orthography this was written as "ŋ," which has been dropped by many for the more keyboard friendly "ng."

Importantly, I do not adhere to this orthography when writing many well-known place-names in the western Solomons. On official maps and documents the names of many islands and towns in the region adhere to different orthographies than I present here. To avoid confusion, I have kept the official spellings, which include Kolombangara (rather than Kolobangara), Munda (rather than Muda), Ranongga (rather than Ranonga), Rendova (rather than Redova), and most conspicuously Simbo (rather than Sibo).

English is also spoken well by more educated Simboans, although most people have only a moderate to rudimentary grasp of the language. Much more prevalent and spoken by nearly everyone is Solomon Islands Pijin, although it is rarely used between two native Simbo speakers. Solomon Islands Pijin is an English-derived pidgin that has its roots in Pacific trade jargon spoken in the nineteenth century by Melanesians brought to, and in many cases forced to work as laborers in, Queensland, Australia.[3] Today Pijin is critical for communication in the Solomon Islands between speakers of the nearly eighty distinct languages spoken across the archipelago. Whenever possible I write Pijin words using Jourdan and Maebiru's orthography and constructions. In addition to the standard Spanish vowels a, e, i, o, and u, there are two other vowels that will be familiar to English speakers:

ae   as "i" in the English word "bite"

ao   as "ou" in the English word "fountain"

For clarity I italicize Simbo terms and underline Pijin terms. I employ this convention only on their first use.

The name "Simbo" has an interesting pedigree and deserves comment. Early Europeans referred to Simbo Island and the language as "Eddystone" after the rocky pinnacles near the southwest coast that were thought to resemble Eddystone Rocks off the southern coast of the United Kingdom. In 1908 the British anthropologists A. M. Hocart and W. H. R. Rivers, who conducted ethnographic research on Simbo, employed this exonym for the island and the language, as did Peter Lanyon-Orgill, a linguist who made a brief visit in 1946.[4] Sometime prior to independence the island and the language became known as Simbo, as that was the term used by Harold Scheffler, an anthropologist who, in 1960, conducted nine days of research on the island.[5] Simbo is now the island's official name, and it is used by Simboans to identify it and the language to outsiders. The endonym of the island, however, is Madegugusu (or Madegusu), and this continues to be employed by the Simbo people in daily conversation with each other. The translation of Madegugusu is "four countries" or "four districts," and it refers to the island's four primordial divisions. The term "Simbo" refers to just one of these four districts. It is unclear why Simbo rather than the name of another district became accepted in the twentieth century both as the official name for the entire island and in the local vernacular. Even more confusing is the fact that the Simbo district is also its own small island, separated from the main island by a saltwater lagoon, and is referred to as "Nusa Simbo" (Simbo Island), which among Simboans tends to be shortened to just "Nusa" (Island).

Glossary

Simbo and Solomon Island Pijin terms and expressions that appear frequently. Other Simbo or Pijin words are glossed in the text.

ababa	general term for fishing
bangara	chief, clan leader; usually a man
bubutu	cognately organized descent group, community. I gloss it as "clan."
bulo poata	term used to describe a person who is destructively "in love with money," "money crazy," or "obsessed with money"
gasaru	deep water reef
geto	war canoe
gila	sign, mark, indicator
gusu	place, homeland, district, country
iama	term for "priest" prior to Christianity. The iama performed important practices such as consecrating new skull houses and carrying out the mortuary practices of cleaning skulls and disposing of bodies. In many cases iama were captives from other islands.
inaru	pre-Christian shrine dedicated to the propitiation of isu (skipjack tuna)
isisongo	household property; a direct product of the land that is produced through the labor of household members and their immediate grandparents. Note how it contrasts with peso (land, ground).

isu   skipjack tuna (*Katsuwonus pelamis*). In Pijin it is referred to as bonito.

kastom   tradition, custom, traditional. Usually refers to and celebrates pre-Christian practices such as mutual sharing and reciprocal exchange. Other uses include kastom stories (origin stories, myths) and a kastom person (someone who knows and applies pre-Christian practices).

lotu   Christian service, Christian faith

Madegugusu four places; endonym used among Simboans when they refer to their island

mana   power, efficaciousness

manja   hatchet

mola   dugout canoe

mulongo   sense, interrelate, perceive. Normally used in the verb form *va mulongo.*

nunu   earthquake

paile   canoe house, meeting hall

pajuku   form of land sale no longer practiced; involves the exchange of shell money to the landholding clan both as a transfer of wealth and to appease the land and all its imminent historically constituted ancestral relations

pazu patu drop-line fishing; an important fishing technique in which a hook is weighted by a small rock and dropped to depth

peja   strong, seasonal, northwesterly wind associated with the cyclone season from January through March; tends to pick up quickly

peso   ground, land. Like gusu, peso connotes the ancestral beings and essences imbued in the land that impose on the living. Note how peso contrasts with isisongo.

pinamanga respect, respectful relations

tabuna   pre-Christian shrine or sacred space

tamasa   spirit being, especially the Christian God

tioni   people

tomate   general term for spirit being

varivagana mutual sharing of goods and labor; connotes love and empathy between those who share and the intermixing of human and nonhuman substances

vunagugusu original or "bottom" clan of a gusu

Prologue

Monday, April 2, 2007, was a cloudless day without a hint of wind. From the village of Tapurai on the northern tip of Simbo, the forested profiles of Ranongga and Vella Lavella Islands filled the horizon. The seas were calm too, which is always welcomed, since Simbo is frequently battered with northwestern squalls or southeastern trade winds, making the 20-kilometer trip to Gizo, the district capital and center of commerce, a rough, dangerous journey in the small, open skiffs used to make the crossing. A local boat had already departed from Lengana, the largest settlement on the island, for Gizo. It was heavily loaded with passengers and their cargo of sweet potatoes, bananas, coconuts, and the profitable eggs of Simbo's famous megapodes. The tranquil ocean had attracted a group of men in their dugout canoes to leave the protected lagoon between Nusa Simbo and the larger main island to fish the two reefs called "man reef" and "woman reef," which lie a few kilometers off the southern tip of Simbo. Others were already fishing for pelagic species such as rainbow runner or kingfish around Patuia, a group of rocky pinnacles that jut up from the ocean off the southwest coast. Inland, women and their daughters were heading out to their gardens to engage in the endless task of tending the swidden garden plots.

Monday was also a full moon. That meant *boka* (*Serranidae* spp.) fishing would be good since they aggregate during full moons and spawn in some of the passages and reef drops around Simbo. Like most adults on Simbo, Daniel, the pastor of the United Church in his village, knows the distinct locations of these aggregation sites, and he decided to go fishing using a handline technique called *pazu patu*, a drop-line method in which a baited hook is attached to a stone with a strip of coconut leaf and sunk down to the deeper reefs a few hundred meters off the coast. Aided by a cloudless sky and clear midnight moon, Daniel loaded his dugout canoe with several fishing line coils, spare hooks, palm-sized stones, and a dozen small squirrel fish he had caught the day before and would use as bait. Like most fishers on Simbo, he would use only his bare hands to handle the line. Loaded and ready, he quietly paddled off alone from Tapurai's sand beach into a moonlit sea.

The people of Tapurai, Daniel's village, were excited to be hosting a bishop from the United Church. It was the first day of Easter Holy Week, and the bishop had spent the night and would be giving the sermon that day in the small church tucked up against the hill at the back of the village. Daniel's section of the village would be serving the bishop breakfast, so he left early, around midnight, to fish through the early morning under the clear moonlight and hopefully provide fresh fish for the morning meal.

The fish were biting. Floating in water 10 or so meters deep, he was able to haul in two large boka, plenty for the breakfast meal. Although it was already after daybreak and he needed to get back to the village to prepare the meal, he tried his luck once more and dropped a baited hook into the cobalt-blue water, letting it sink to the rocky reefs below. Just as he tugged the line to release the stone and free the baited hook, a large fish took his bait. Calm yet excited to have a fish hooked, he gently but firmly hauled in the line by grasping it and alternating one hand at a time while pulling. As he fought the fish, he heard the trees rustling a hundred or so meters away on shore. "What's that?" he wondered. After a few minutes, and still methodically pulling in the line of the large fish, he noticed something odd—the ocean under his canoe and all around him started bubbling like a "pot of boiling water." Just at that moment the fish broke loose from his line. That is when he knew "something was not right." He had fished the waters around his village his entire life and yet had never seen the ocean bubble in that way. Impulsively, he coiled up his line and started paddling toward shore. As he gained a clear view of his village. he was astonished and horrified: the fifty or so tightly packed houses, including his own, had been reduced to rubble.

Around the east coast of Simbo another fisher, Dovala, was paddling his dugout inside the narrow lagoon near Qaqo village. This part of the island has a barrier reef a few hundred meters from shore. It protects a shallow, iridescent blue lagoon where fishers will target snappers, triggerfish, and other reef fish that hide in the coral heads and other rocky features that dot the lagoon bottom. With his line in the water, Dovala noticed his canoe swaying as if a large fish were bumping the hull. This sometimes occurs when fishers visit the offshore reefs to catch pelagic species and sharks pass too close to their canoes. But Dovala was inside the lagoon, where there are no large sharks. He also noticed as he gazed into the crystal-clear water that coral heads and rocks on the bottom were rolling around. It dawned on him that it was an earthquake when he heard the palm trees on shore swaying violently back and forth.

He had heard stories from the elders that waves can sometimes form after earthquakes, so he coiled up his fishing line and paddled toward shore. As he paddled, the shoreline seemed to recede as water began rushing inland underneath the coconut palm groves that fringe this part of the island. Suddenly the current switched directions, and water backwashed away from the coast, forming two waves a meter or so high. He was able to paddle through the first wave, plunging the bow of his canoe up and over the foam, but the second wave was larger and caused him to capsize. Now in the frothing water, the current was fierce. Somehow he was able to find his dugout canoe and hold on to it. Gripping the canoe with all his might, he was washed around for what seemed like an eternity. As the ocean began to settle down, he ditched his canoe and wrapped his arms around a nearby coconut palm. Soon after, the seawater drained away, and he found himself dangling in the air 3 or 4 meters off the ground, clinging to the coconut tree midway up its trunk. He was soaking wet, terrified but alive. A few hours later he joined his family on high ground above the lagoon. They had witnessed his horrifying struggle unfold.

Durie was paddling her canoe toward Lengana, a village on the west coast that sits deep inside a protected bay and a few hundred meters from the seaside. When the earthquake hit she "saw the hills and trees shaking violently and the ocean water 'boiling' around her." Fortunately she was close to the coast, so she held on to the mangrove trees. "'After the quake, I continued to paddle along the coast and didn't think much of it. Suddenly, I heard a loud sound, similar to that of a raging wind. I looked up at the sky expecting to see dark storm clouds, but the sky was very clear. I was terrified. I didn't know what was going to happen, but I was afraid it was the end of the world.'"[1]

Then Durie saw the monstrous ocean wave rushing toward her. Frozen in panic, she didn't know what to do. She stood up, held on to the roots of the mangrove trees, and facing the tsunami, she waited:

> After a couple of seconds, the massive wave hit me, throwing me off my canoe. Even the mangrove trees were uprooted and thrown ashore. I didn't understand what was happening to me. I did not feel anything and fell unconscious. . . .
>
> Regaining my consciousness, I found myself under a pile of debris—tree branches, leaves and logs. Only my head sticking out, my whole body was buried under the mud. I could not move. The next tsunami wave, luckily, carried the debris away and I could free my arms. I saw that my arms were cut open, bones protruded out and I was bleeding heavily. Still, I dug my body out of the mud and dragged myself towards the village. All the while, quakes continued to shake the ground, and large rocks were rolling down the hills. Narrowly avoiding the rocks, I made it to my aunt's house. I asked for some water. As soon as I drank, my body collapsed. My aunt and other villagers carried me to safety.[2]

Joni was inside his house in Tapurai when the ground began to shake. Like most dwellings on Simbo his house sat on short stilts and was made from sago palm leaves, woven onto battens and layered to create the walls and the two panels of the gabled roof. The quaking started slowly, gently swaying back and forth. Then it began to shake more violently, jerking in different and uneven directions. One man said it felt like the island was "a basket hanging from a post, blowing in the wind." The movements rapidly became so strong that Joni was thrown to the floor. When it stopped, he stood up and felt a little dazed. He walked outside and was surprised to see people sprinting toward the hill behind the village. Confused, he stayed put for a minute or two, then he heard a roar, like an approaching helicopter, emanating from around the rocky point to the north of the village. Suddenly a huge ball of foamy ocean appeared, swiftly wrapping around the point and plowing over the beach into the village. He ran for his life toward the hill. But the frothy water was too fast, and it overtook him. Joni remembers how violent the water felt on his body as it engulfed him, banging him against debris, tearing open his left arm. As he was swirling in the mayhem all he could think about was his wife and three young children. Luckily he was an experienced diver, and he had the ability to hold his breath for several minutes underwater. Only a handful of men on Simbo specialize in free dive spearfishing the reefs and passes around the island and have learned to conserve their breath as they lie motionless on the bottom waiting for fish to approach.

At one point his head popped up above the surface, and he was able to take a deep breath. After several minutes, the tumbling and churning slowed. He felt his body come to rest on hard ground. As he gained his bearings, he realized that he had been deposited on the sand beach near shore. Stunned, bleeding, and soaking wet, he was stark naked. The wave had torn his clothes completely off.

Tuma was preparing food in her cookhouse. Like most of the women in Tapurai that day she had not left the village earlier in the morning, as she typically would on Monday, to tend her household's garden in the hills of the island. Simbo women travel to their household plots several days a week to weed, plant, and tend the sweet potatoes, greens, cassavas, or yams that form the staples of Simbo meals. Rather than adhering to the typical rhythms of daily life, Tuma, like many women on that day, was helping prepare food for the bishop. When the quake struck, she was sitting on the floor squeezing the white meat of freshly grated coconut through mesh into a metal basin that would be used to cook fresh fish. Like many others in the village, she shouted "Nunu!," the Simbo word for earthquake, as the earth shook. Having felt numerous earthquakes in the past, she hunkered down on the floor to avoid falling.

When the quake stopped, all she could think about were her twin girls. So violent was the shaking, she feared that they might have been hurt. The two young girls had left the house a few minutes earlier. As she called out, they came running toward her, unharmed. Soon after, a neighbor who had been on the beach during the quake ran by, yelling that the sea was

Figure 1. The destroyed site of Tapurai, a village of fifty households, ten days after the disaster. (Photo credit: Hermann Fritz.)

coming up and that they should escape to the hills behind the village. She tightly grasped her children's hands and ran.

From the safety of the hill just behind Tapurai where the church sits, many villagers watched in horror as their village was destroyed and some of their brethren were swallowed up by the sea. The rushing water that swept over the village arrived from three directions in three separate waves, the biggest one raging around the point to the north of Tapurai. The center area of the village was the last section to be inundated as the walls of water converged, bouncing against each other. This caused the water to rise quickly, lifting the leaf houses and sweeping them away. The fierce current formed a deadly swirl of timber, sheets of corrugated roofing, and other debris.

Nearly every dwelling was torn apart, leaving the village strewn with wreckage (see figure 1). Eerily, a few houses remained almost fully intact and were pulled out into the sea by the current. One house floated to a shallow area of the island's magnificent, turquoise lagoon, where it came

Figure 2. An intact thatch house that was lifted by the tsunami and floated out into Simbo's lagoon, where it came to rest. The photo was taken ten days after the tsunami, by Hermann Fritz, a researcher from Georgia Tech University who visited the island to record the physical effects of the tsunami. (Photo credit: Hermann Fritz.)

to rest with only the leaf roof visible above the water's surface (see figure 2). The sea floor underneath the house was a jumble of rubble that was a vibrant coral reef before the tsunami.

When the water drained from the village site back to sea level, most of those who had been swept up by the water lay on the ground among debris, exhausted and unable to move. Worried about their loved ones and fearing that the water would rise again, some of the men ran to the survivors and carried them to the safety of the church. Of those retrieved, a dozen or so were injured, and several were no longer breathing. A few were bleeding and had suffered major injuries, but all told only seven people perished in Tapurai

Of the seven individuals who died, only one elderly woman succumbed while trying to reach the hill behind the village. The others were all seen either returning to their houses after reaching high ground or staying in them after being encouraged to flee. As one man explained: "I was with Luka when the earthquake struck. He went out on the veranda after it was over and sat down. He said he was dizzy. We saw the water starting to rise and people were yelling to run away. He didn't run away; he ran inside his house. He sat down on top of his wooden box where he stored his money. His mind was inside of his box. . . . I yelled to him that we should run. He didn't say anything. He just sat there. I ran away." Luka's body was found later in the debris. The tin roofing material of his house had struck his forehead, splitting it open and killing him. In another case, a husband and his wife argued over what to do after the earthquake. The wife pleaded with her husband to run and leave their money inside the house. The Friday before he had just collected 10,000 Solomon dollars from a bank in Gizo. He rejected his wife's pleas, and he was caught by the water and killed. The wife ran away in time and made it to safety. In another case, a woman brought her child to the hill and ran back to her house to retrieve the money she had saved up from charging villagers to watch DVD movies at her house.

What surprised almost everyone was the behavior of children. Except for one small baby who was in the arms of her mother, no children had been caught by the tsunami. As one man explained:

> One of our biggest surprises was that somehow the children knew. Normally the kids of Tapurai go to the beach and play in the early morning. Some paddle around in dugouts canoes, others bodysurf, others just play on the beach, while others swim or float. But for some reason that morning not many kids were down by the seaside. We [the adults] thought that most of the children died [from the tsunami], but that's not what happened. Only one small child died, who was being carried by his mother but slipped from her hands and fell in the water. . . . The schoolteacher was surprised that the students knew to run. She was from another island and had been assigned to Tapurai and she didn't tell them to run, they all just ran like crazy. From fear they sensed (*mulongo*) to run. Some adults told the children to run, but most children just ran on their own to the hill. They didn't even run to their house first and look for their parents. They went straight to the hills and scampered up them.

That Tapurai's schoolchildren survived unscathed is even more surprising considering that the primary school was located on the beach at the northern end of the village, the first area hit and in the most vulnerable position for incoming waves. The schoolteacher, a young woman from another island, explained how she directed the students to hide under their desks during the earthquake. She had been trained to do that. When the shaking subsided, she was stunned but unharmed. As she pulled herself out from under her desk, the schoolchildren, without any prompting for her, stampeded out the school building door. Confused and unaware of what was happening, she followed behind the fleeing students as they ran toward the hills.

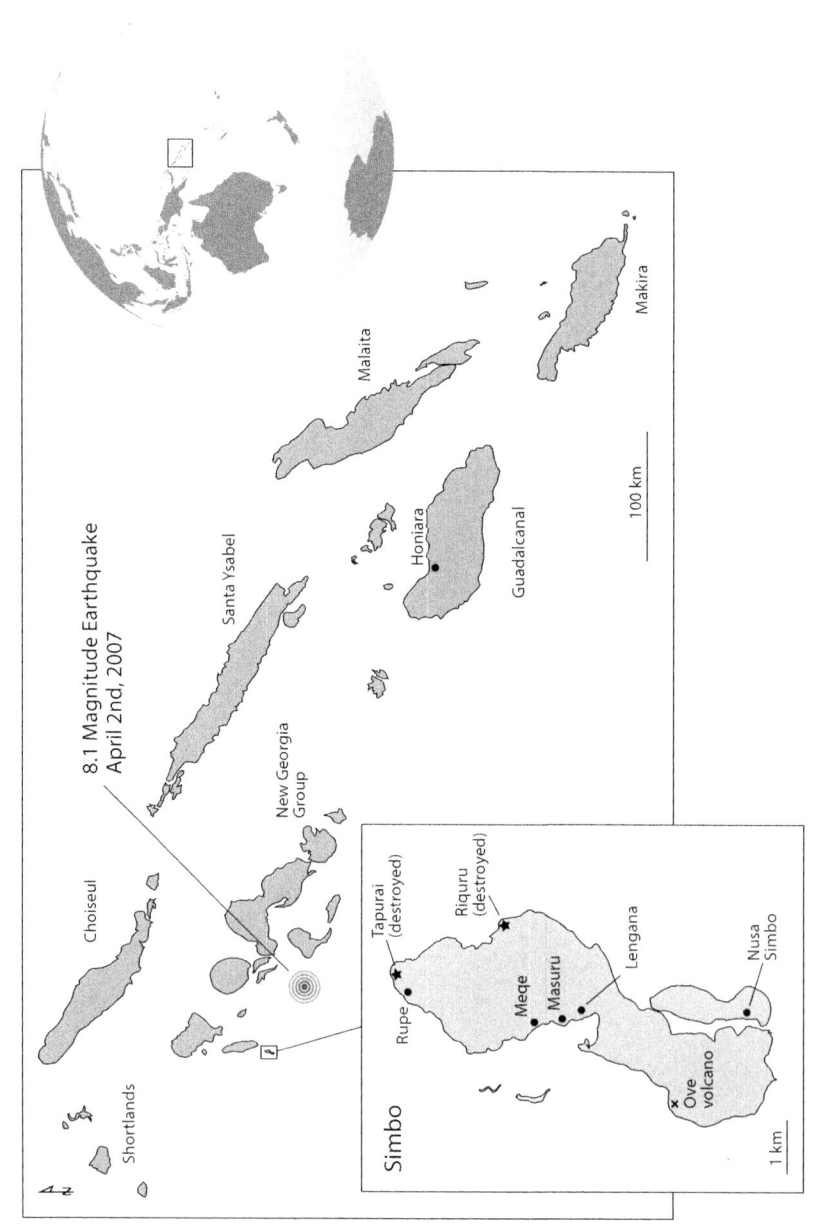

Map 1. Simbo and the Solomon Islands, with Simbo inset.

Introduction

The scenes in the prologue, reconstructed from survivors' narratives, describe one of the most terrifying phenomena ever experienced by the people of Simbo, a small island of some 13 square kilometers and twenty-seven hundred people lying in the New Georgia Group of the western Solomon Islands (see map 1). On that Monday morning of April 2, 2007, at 7:39 a.m. local time, Richter scales around the world measured a magnitude 8.1 earthquake that shook the seafloor just 50 kilometers southeast of Simbo. According to geophysical models, a massive block of the Pacific plate, the part of the earth's crust responsible for the Pacific Ocean's infamous Ring of Fire, lurched over 20 meters.[1] In this region the Pacific plate rides on top of three local plates, with the fault line passing through an 8-kilometer-wide passage between Simbo and Ranongga, a larger island to the north. It is the only place on earth where two islands sit so closely together on either side of an active fault line.

Within seconds the earthquake lifted the southern half of Ranongga nearly 3 meters out of the water, exposing large areas of live coral reef. Simbo, sitting on the subduction zone across the fault line, sank just over half a meter (see figure 3). In addition to the lifting and subsiding of coral reefs, the quake caused significant damage to structures on

Figure 3. Children playing on Simbo's main wharf in 2011. The earthquake caused Simbo to sink more than half a meter, so the wharf became partially submerged during high tides. It was rebuilt to be above sea level by the national government several years later. (Photo by author.)

the surrounding islands as well as triggering thousands of landslides.[2] On Simbo large boulders were dislodged and rolled down the north flank of Mt. Patu Kio, the 300-meter-high volcanic cone near the center of the island, causing a landslide.

The slippage of the earth's crust displaced an enormous amount of ocean water above it, sending powerful shockwaves through the water away from the earthquake's epicenter. The geophysical models, informed by field research completed in the area just after the quake, suggested that slippage occurred in such a way that most of the energy was sent north and west, generating an ocean surface wave that spread out in that direction.[3] Within approximately three minutes the energy released from the ocean floor reached one of the closest islands in its path, Simbo. As described by the survivors, a series of waves slammed into the island, causing near total destruction of two villages, Tapurai and Riquru, on the northern end of the island.

Just a few days after the tsunami, international teams of geoscientists visited Simbo to conduct post-tsunami reconnaissance; they measured the tsunami's "run-up," an estimate of the maximum size of the wave. Using survey instruments, the scientists documented freshly disturbed foliage many meters up the hillside on the northern end of the island and estimated that the wave had reached 12 meters in height. All told, these three-story-high waves impacted four other islands in the western Solomons (Gizo, Ranongga, Vella Lavella, and Choiseul) and were felt as far away as eastern Papua New Guinea. Across the region, fifty deaths were attributed to the tsunami, and two people died in earthquake-induced landslides.[4]

Despite the calamitous destruction of Tapurai and Riquru, miraculously only nine people perished. In an astonishing human accomplishment, nearly all the villagers fled to high ground before the waves slammed into the island. Their response was unaided by any modern response or emergency alert system. As a marginalized, economically poor island in a country known for an inept and corrupt central government, Simbo lacks even basic signage like the blue-and-white "tsunami evacuation route" or "tsunami hazard zone" signs that often dot beach areas in US cities like the town where I live, San Diego. Formal disaster monitoring infrastructure or an alert messaging system had not even been pondered as a possibility in much of the Solomons, nor had experts ever visited Simbo prior to the event to increase tsunami awareness or develop disaster preparedness and mitigation strategies.

The Simbo people's spectacular achievement of fleeing to safe ground gains even more weight when compared to that of thousands of people involved in the most devastating tsunami ever recorded: the 2004 Indian Ocean earthquake and tsunami. It was the first tsunami to be captured in detail on video, and it brought the word "tsunami" into the broader global consciousness. The catastrophe is thought to have displaced nearly 21.7 million people in areas close to the epicenter, such as the island of Sumatra, Indonesia, and the western coast of the Malay Peninsula, but also as far away as Sri Lanka, Somalia, and even Madagascar.[5] In total more than fifty thousand victims are estimated to have died, many thousands of whom not only did not flee the approaching water but instead were attracted to the strange movements of the ocean and gathered on the coastline and beaches.[6] Some even went out and explored the exposed reefs and rocks as the incoming waves loomed across the horizon.

There were, however, a few miraculous survivors. The media as well as disaster experts and scientists studying the disaster reported how a handful of Indigenous groups—the Moken in the Surin Islands of Thailand; the Ong, Jarawa, and Sentinelese of the Andaman Islands in India; and the Simeulue Island peoples of Indonesia—escaped unscathed by reaching high ground before the tsunami struck.[7]

Amid so much calamity and death, these Indigenous groups were championed for their capacity to respond without a modern alert system. The narratives and writings that emerged from the academic literature and media outlets brimmed with admiration. In most cases, their successful response was explained in rather unproblematic terms: these Indigenous peoples' "ancient wisdom" and "connection to nature" had enabled them to escape the impending tsunami. One newspaper article commented, "The Moken did not have expensive advanced technology to warn them about the killer waves. They survived merely because of their close relationships with and observation of nature and because they heeded their ancient wisdom."[8]

In fact, as I discussed this book project with scientists, professionals, colleagues, friends, and family, their reactions were similar, in that many *expected* Indigenous peoples like Simboans or the Moken to respond effectively. But as my fieldwork unfolded and I listened to numerous accounts of the tsunami, I found that the Simbo people had quite the opposite interpretation of their own behavior. Rather than expecting that they would respond adequately, many Simboans were puzzled, indeed surprised, at their own capacity to flee. Many had no explanation at all for their own individual behavior, and there was certainly not a self-evident explanation to which everyone gravitated. For many on the island the most fascinating and difficult to explain reaction was of their own children. As described in the prologue, Simbo children were some of the first to run to safe ground without even consulting their parents. Not only did Simbo children avoid death; so did the animals. I was told repeatedly that not one single dog, cat, pig, or chicken was caught in the tsunami. Even a large sow and her small piglets who were penned near the water's edge broke free, clambering over the barricades and escaping to safety.

Although the tsunami experience in many ways exceeded Simboan categories of judgment and understanding, it also engendered a number of different theories and explanations. As will become clearer in the following pages, I was inspired to employ the English word "sensing" in the title of this book during a conservation with a close Solomon Islander associate who described the tsunami experience as a case of mulongo, a term found in a number of the languages in the western Solomons including the Simbo language. I gloss the term in English as "sense, anticipate, interrelate," although as I listened to descriptions of mulongo it became apparent that it involved domains of Simbo life that the English equivalents failed to convey. Mulongo is not just the capacity to sense that something is odd or extraordinary; it also involves the correct judgment to act appropriately.

In the disaster literature mulongo might fall under what scholars refer to as "Indigenous ecological knowledge."[9] Indeed, within anthropology and the social sciences and natural sciences more generally there has been a dramatic surge of interest in Indigenous ecological knowledge that is linked to theoretical and empirical advancements in disaster research and environmental scholarship more broadly. The global community is increasingly coming to recognize the disconcerting trend that disasters are becoming more frequent and expensive.[10] From the Indian Ocean tsunami to massive hurricanes like Katrina, Sandy, and Maria, or China's Wenchuan earthquake and Japan's "triple disaster" (earthquake, tsunami, nuclear), there has been a sharp increase in the number of disaster events, and although improvements have been made in decreasing the overall lethality of disasters, the economic, social, and political disruptions they cause are growing.

Many in the scientific community link the growing intensity of extreme climatological events to the greatest existential threat our species has ever grappled with: climate change. The relentless uptick in average global temperatures, which now appear on a path to exceed 2.0 degrees Celsius above preindustrial levels, portends a future with increasing extreme floods, wildfires, and storms. Couple this with the realization that we are entering the sixth great extinction event and the widespread lack of political will to wind down the burning of fossil fuels, a future of more dislocation and suffering looks unavoidable.

Moreover, the idea that planetary geophysical systems such as weather systems and oceanic currents are now linked to human activities has compelled a major rethinking of what we consider "natural." There is even some evidence that earthquakes might now be influenced by anthropogenic climate change.[11] Rather than understanding "natural" processes impervious to human affairs, many are now proposing that we understand the planetary system as a human-nonhuman imbroglio that requires new analytics and approaches rather than those developed by the conventional distribution of labor demarcated by "natural" science and "social" science.

With the frequency of disasters increasing and environmental degradation reaching planetary proportions, the knowledge and practices of Indigenous peoples have come to be viewed by some as valuable and untapped resources that provide insight into mitigating global environmental ills. A wide range of experts, including ecologists, natural resource managers, and other natural scientists, argue that Indigenous knowledge and practices are important for understanding ecological hazards, reducing disaster risk, and mitigating vulnerability.[12] Indigenous ecological knowledge has emerged as a key resource that is now embraced by major international organizations such as the Intergovernmental Platform on Biodiversity and Ecosystem Services and the Intergovernmental Panel on Climate Change (IPCC).[13] Indeed, the concept of Indigenous ecological knowledge has circulated widely enough in policy and academic circles that it is commonly abbreviated IEK.

It was through the IEK literature that I became familiar with disaster responses in Indigenous communities. Nearly 6,000 miles away in my office in San Diego, I read the case studies and literature reviews about IEK so as not to arrive on Simbo blind, as Lieutenant John Shortland did in 1788 when his Royal Navy convict transport ship, the *Alexander*, chanced upon the island, which at that time was unknown to Europeans (for details about this see chapter 3). But when I finally arrived in Simbo and listened to the survivors' accounts of their disaster response, I found myself in a situation that Anna Tsing describes as a "productive misunderstanding."[14] Many of my Simbo interlocutors could not understand why I expected them to respond appropriately to a tsunami, and many were clear that they did not have IEK in the form that the academics or laypeople expected. There was only weak evidence that Simboans had "ancient wisdom," or what social scientists call "intergenerationally transmitted knowledge," about past tsunamis. My Simbo associates and I both found ourselves in a state of misunderstanding. Rather than rushing to mobilize IEK and explain Simbo's response, I instead listened closely to survivors to explore and possibly bring into view those aspects of their response that initially may not have been obvious. Thus, one of the threads running through this book, and central to any good ethnographic account, is not just to understand more deeply the Simbo people's miraculous achievement in sensing an approaching disaster and acting in time to save their lives but also to destabilize and render more explicit our own assumptions and expectations about Indigenous disaster response.

Undoubtedly the widespread acceptance of IEK both in scholarly writings and among disaster mitigation experts is a positive turn. Yet as I discuss in chapter 1, much of the bureaucratic, scientific, and popular writing on IEK in disaster research and environmental-oriented social and natural sciences accepts the validity of IEK only when it can be verified through peer-reviewed scientific knowledge collected by experts. Indeed, the rise of interest in IEK within the wider scientific community has in large measure relied on this asymmetrical positioning of science and local, nonexpert knowledge.[15] The implicit effect, arguably, has not been to facilitate a space for the possibilities of IEK and other modes of being more generally but rather to further entrench scientism, where science is assumed to be the ultimate arbiter of any knowledge claim.

I not only trace the emergence of IEK as a concept in the scholarly literature; I also direct my attention to the ways in which it is mobilized and put into action by disaster experts. In chapter 6 I detail tsunami preparedness workshops conducted on Simbo eleven years after the 2007 disaster that were carried out by staff from the Solomon Islands National Disaster Management Office. Through my interviews with Simboans who attended these workshops as well as the experts who carried them out, I learned that the workshops explicitly embraced IEK as valid and relevant to developing mitigation plans and escape routes for tsunami-vulnerable areas of Simbo's coastline. But the knowledge gleaned from Simbo survivors was limited to that which could be rendered legible through participatory mapping exercises. These kinds of interventions are now common practice among disaster experts, yet they are predicated on a specific formatting of IEK that has specific effects; most notably it implicitly flattens radical difference by presupposing that knowledge can be reduced to *cognitive information*. The Simboan survivors who participated in these workshops, many of whom had fled the tsunami without the aid of a formal evacuation plan, were invited to participate and communicate with outside experts as if they were reservoirs of data who hold precious rational abstractions. IEK, when put into action this way, has had the capacity to traverse across and enroll many scientific disciplines and bureaucratic structures and has served as a mechanism to circulate extracted information from Indigenous peoples.

Although these kinds of participatory capacity-building workshops may have the potential to subvert bureaucratic structures and enable Indigenous modes of disaster response, they simultaneously, albeit inadvertently in many cases, may be vectors for encroaching state control. In the case of community-based disaster resilience strategies carried out on Simbo, aspects of their IEK, such as the presence of ancestral power imbued in the landscape and their communication with animals and other nonhuman existents, leaked out of most accounts of their response that left the island inscribed in notebooks, maps, tape recorders, cameras, and GPS receivers to ultimately circulate globally as data in scientific papers or, in the case of the United Nations Development Programme (UNDP), a children's book about the disaster published on its website. In other words, the widespread embrace and deployment of IEK has resulted, at least partially, in what Tuhiwai Smith describes as Western social and ecological theory oppressing Indigenous peoples through erasure, although this epistemic imperialism is far subtler than in the past, when Indigenous peoples and their modes of being were explicitly deemed inferior.[16]

Taking up Smith's call to decolonize our methodologies and strive for epistemic democratization, my contention is that all knowledge, Indigenous or otherwise, is best understood as emerging from *situated practices*. Rather than emphasizing a priori distinctions between scientific and Indigenous, fact and belief, rational and irrational, empirical and spiritual, we should instead expunge these labels from our analytic vocabulary and focus on keeping in view all the local knowledge production conditions and practices. For this reason, I chose "local knowledge" for the title of this book rather than "Indigenous ecological knowledge." This book is an invitation to follow closely how Simboans associated and tied together a heterogeneous mix of human and nonhuman entities, discourses, and materialities when discussing their response to the tsunami, with the intent to register those aspects of Indigenous knowing and being that are often overlooked, even by those whose intention is to respect and support Indigenous peoples. At the same time, if you have already decided in advance that the "knowledge" underpinning Simbo's response is only that which can be caught in the net of scientific knowledge, then you should put down this book, since the Simboans' experience and the repertoire of elements they invoke to comprehend their successful escape do not fit neatly into that definition of knowledge. Rather than seeking an ultimate, comprehensive explanation or theoretical crown that resolves various understandings of Indigenous disaster response, here I develop an account that is intended to multiply our inferences and reflexively engender new questions and complications.

PLACE AND MELANESIAN LIFEWORLDS

If our intention is to develop a deeper understanding of Simbo's experience by registering dimensions of the tsunami disaster that typically are out of view, we first must take the time to listen to how Simboans describe their world. Over the years and the dozens of visits I have made to Simbo, my Simboan friends have frequently spoken to me about land, sea, animals, fish, and spirit beings in ways that challenged my assumptions about the nature of these entities. I heard countless stories about the land and the coral reef ecosystems that surround Simbo and how they are populated by existents that are regularly encountered, listened to, and communicated with. Indeed, it is these aspects of Simboans' IEK that continue to be openly dismissed by Western science and remain provincialized as merely "cosmology" or a "mélange of truth and inaccuracy" when the arbiter of truth remains unreflectively in the hands of scientists.[17]

The experiences related to me by Simboans parallel what Melanesians have for a long time been expressing to anthropologists and others who are patient enough to listen: that the islands and the reefs around them, their *place*, are composed through the regenerative process of interrelating and intermixing of humans, ancestors, land beings, and sea beings.[18] As Kwara'ae (Maliata) scholar David Gegeo noted about place: "It's in our blood."[19] In the Simbo language, the English word "place" could be glossed as *gusu*, which is similar to terms in other Oceanic languages like *voana* (Fiji), *ahupua'a* (Hawaii), and *fenua* (Society Islands), all of which denote "place" as not only a demarcation of what we call biophysical areas of land and sea but also local history, habitation, people's identities, and a multitude of nonhuman beings.[20] Yet as Tongan anthropologist and author Epeli Hau'ofa noted, landscapes and seascapes are entangled "maps of movements, pauses, and more movements," but "this intimate association between history and the natural landscape . . . [is] the basis for oft asserted and maligned notion that we are spiritually and mystically related to the land to which we belong."[21]

In chapter 2 I expand on these themes and describe the intimate relations Simboans have with the coastal waters and coral reefs around their island. Like the vast majority of Solomon Islanders, local seafood provides the bulk of the Simbo people's protein. Starting as young children, Simboans spend countless hours swimming, fishing, and paddling canoes as they learn to relate with their island's coasts and marine habitats. But their intimacy with the ocean extends far beyond these activities; it is central to the composition of their history, their understandings of the afterworld, their ancestor spirits, their totem beings: their "lifeworld conditions."

To grasp how people experience and bring place into being, scholars have formulated helpful approaches that conceptualize place as a fundamental form of embodied experience and posit that humans are centrally beings "in-place and em-placed."[22] Tim Ingold went further and entered ontological ground by theorizing place as "dwelling," which starts from the premise that inhabiting a landscape or seascape is inseparable from experiencing it.[23] Approached this way, there is no external position by which to contrast humanity with a biophysical world, since people and their landscapes and seascapes emerge through place rather than existing independent of and prior to it.

Importantly, in Oceania place is not created without contestation. As we dwell in and compose our place, this process inherently involves relations of power and politics.[24] Organisms, from simple to complex, may contribute to each other's mutual development but also may block and subvert each other's existence. Predators hunt, tsunamis destroy, people harvest crops, beings make other beings sick. These ongoing, everyday experiences of dwelling in the world are inextricably linked to relations of power and politics both between humans and between humans and non-humans. Indeed, ethnographers become entangled in these power-laden emplacing processes, as I was during a dispute between two clan leaders (see "Researching and Learning" in this chapter).

Simbo placemaking struggles tend to center on land "ownership." Similar to many locales in Island Melanesia, land on Simbo continues to be under what conventionally has been known as "customary tenure," whereby social groups rather than individuals or the state lay claim to the land and its resources. However, these concepts of ownership are premised on capitalist logics, which treat land as a mute biophysical surface upon which contingent "rights" are overlaid. Indeed, the colonial and postcolonial dispossession of Indigenous lands was grounded in theories of property that legitimized expropriation and the alleged superiority of Europeans.[25]

As Simbo recovered and rebuilt after the tsunami, these issues of ownership erupted as villagers clashed over land. In chapter 5 we learn about these disputes, and I argue that they were not just about the meaning of land or "rights" to resources, but about what Simbo land and place *is*. In other words, the contestation was not political in the modernist sense, where land plays no role and humans make decisions about who owns what. Instead, these might be better understood as "cosmopolitical" disputes over the island's future and which beings would be included and which might be disposed of.[26] To grasp the significance of these disputes during the reconstruction, I approach land as ontologically multiple, as a relational and a material-semiotic assemblage that is composed and stabilized through specific epistemological practices or modes of ordering that are fraught with moral and ethical implications for the humans and nonhumans involved in its composition.[27]

Disasters have long been theorized as "revelatory crises" or "triggers" that expose deep-seated tensions or core debates and social formations among those affected.[28] But I reveal how, when approached as an assemblage, the Simbo tsunami did not just render the implicit explicit; it was also generative. It imposed new entities (e.g., tsunami waves) and elicited novel practices (e.g., escape to the hills) among survivors, which were then interpreted through local concepts, being transformed in the process. Moreover, the Simbo tsunami provoked responses from national and international agencies that mobilized the global humanitarian aid apparatus. When this occurs, survivors become entangled in the projects, practices, concepts, and discourses of disaster experts and international aid workers. In this sense, disasters are not merely events but sites of production where new entities and concepts have the possibility to reshape the constellation of actors—human or nonhuman—involved.

I argue that in times of disruption we need to attend to those questions and debates Indigenous communities have about their futures by maintaining some level of critical distance from concepts that foreclose alterity and hence the ability of communities like the Simbo people to live their lives as they see fit. Arguably, we need to heed the call of scholars who advocate for expanding our "forms of noticing" toward the distribution of agencies and relations that were previously bracketed as "beliefs" or relegated as ontologically mute objects.[29]

BEYOND THE TSUNAMI

My account of the Simbo tsunami builds on the anthropology of disasters, a field of study that has produced enormous insights into the nature of calamities.[30] Anthropologists have helped reveal how modern catastrophes like the Simbo tsunami are unruly hybrid objects, entangling the past and present, the objective and the subjective, the global with the local, and the natural and the social.[31] The unruliness of disasters is especially evident in attempts to characterize their temporality. While many accounts, known broadly as "hazards approaches," assume that a perturbation is the start of disasters, anthropological analyses have made gains by historicizing calamity, wherein the hurricane, tsunami, or technological malfunction that triggers an event is understood as somewhere in the entangled middle rather the beginning of a disaster. These interpretations have helped reveal how catastrophes emerge through a meshwork of social and ecological relations that preexist and precondition the triggering event, the response, the aftermath, and the recovery. In other words, the timing of a calamity, its assumed starting point, is not neutral or ahistorical. A tsunami, earthquake, or toxic spill does not "come out of nowhere" to hurt people; instead a calamity is *produced* by a specific yet heterogeneous mix of material, technical, and discursive elements that generate different axes of *vulnerability*. In an Anthropocene age in which human activities have left their traces across the earth system, the "biophysicalness" of the biophysical triggers such as hurricanes, earthquakes, and tsunamis must be put into quotes because that descriptor is inadequate. Even these phenomena are no longer outside of human relations; they are thoroughly inside of them.

For these reasons, the historical processes discussed in chapters 3 and 4 are not "background" information that "contextualizes" the tsunami; they are interwoven into the macramé of the Simbo disaster. As you will read in chapter 4, socioecological preconditions not only contributed to Simbo's miraculous response to flee the tsunami; they also, tragically, played a role in the deaths that occurred. As the survivors' narratives in the prologue described, not every Simboan escaped the deadly waves. Nine people lost their lives.

As you can imagine, this was a horrific and troubling outcome of the catastrophe. Simbo is a small island community tied together through kinship, with a unique language spoken nowhere else in the world and a three-thousand- or possibly thirty-thousand-year history of Simboans' inhabiting their island. But the loss of life was compounded by the well-known and widely discussed fact that it was most certainly *avoidable*. Nearly everyone on the island told me that those who perished were not killed by the tsunami alone. Rather, the earthquake and waves were refracted through a well-known and long-standing phenomenon already operating on Simbo that contributed to the deadly outcome. They were gripped by a particular condition that is referred to in the Simbo language as *bulo poata*, which could be translated as "money crazy." More broadly, the troubling response of those who perished was interpreted through the idiom of kastom, a neo-Melanesian Pijin term found throughout the region that celebrates the opposite of bulo poata, those pre-Christian practices of mutual sharing and reciprocal exchange that produce empathy and love among Simboans.

Thus, to understand the island's vulnerabilities and the local interpretations that arose to comprehend them necessarily requires an analysis
of the immediate biophysical perturbation *and* the long-term processes
of Simbo's entanglement with capitalist relations and colonial processes.
In the Simbo disaster the wave that struck the island and the response
and recovery are inseparable from earlier shifts in settlement patterns and
resource use, colonialization, Christianity, and increasing entanglement
in capitalism. Thus chapter 4's principal aim is to trace how pre-tsunami
social-ecological relations shifted through time, generating a new repertoire of contemporary vulnerabilities, including the anxieties that now
abound on the island about modern currency, capitalist relations, and the
perceived erosion of Simbo life. However, I not only use vulnerability as a
conceptual resource to help explain the Simbo disaster; I also engage with
it critically. I ask: "What does vulnerability help reveal?" "What might it
displace?"

SITUATING VULNERABILITY

Vulnerability has emerged as a key organizational analytic within disaster
studies and more recently in the global environmental change literature.[32]
Yet there continues to be widespread debate about whether the sources
of harm engendered by a severe biophysical perturbation are exogenous
or endogamous to the community or society in question. Critical scholars
working with the tools of political ecology assert that extra-local processes
of colonialism or neoliberalism produce vulnerable communities or individuals through historical-material processes.[33] Mark Schuller's account,
for example, of the horrific 2010 Haitian earthquake unearthed the long
history of Haiti's underdevelopment and especially the rise of humanitarian nongovernmental organizations (NGOs), which in the decades prior to
the earthquake had divided up the country into their own semi-sovereign
fiefdoms, undercutting the ability of the state to mitigate the disaster
or effectively coordinate the aid effort.[34] Other scholars have employed
Foucauldian-inspired analytics of governmentality to evince how the vulnerable internalize and willingly conform to exploitative social norms,
ethical standards, or environmentally destructive activities.[35]

In contrast to these critical approaches, an influential body of literature broadly known as "resilience thinking" theorizes vulnerability as a condition of communities who lack certain adaptive capacities or institutional structures as they grapple with shifting social and ecological dynamics.[36] Resilience approaches tend to be more conservative and managerial in that they do not challenge existing power structures and forms of inequality. Instead, they transvalue political contestation and power asymmetries as potential engines of innovation if managed and harnessed toward productive sustainability solutions or disaster management mitigation efforts.[37] As noted by Nigel Clark, these managerial framings of complex human-environmental dynamics often are incapable of engaging the potential of radical alterity like that we might find in Melanesia.[38]

Vulnerability and resilience, however, do more than just provide analytic concepts for researchers to make sense of catastrophes. These concepts are transformed from bullet points on PowerPoint slides by disaster experts and humanitarian practitioners into actions as they carry out projects. From this starting point, I do not approach vulnerability in chapter 5 as an underlying condition waiting to be explicated by outside experts, but instead describe the ways in which vulnerability and resilience as concepts have been mobilized to address disaster mitigation and preparedness. I trace how islands like Simbo are interpreted as "vulnerable isles" that need outside interventions to render them more resilient.

On Simbo, the island's vulnerable status motivated disaster experts to visit the island eleven years after the tsunami to conduct disaster preparedness workshops. By detailing ethnographically these workshops carried out on Simbo, chapter 6 helps to illuminate the process of how vulnerability has seeped out of academic papers into the offices of disaster experts in bureaucratic and state structures and eventually arrived on islands like Simbo. During this movement and mobilization, vulnerability takes on a particular intellectual shape and undergoes important discursive shifts that have practical consequences. International disaster institutions, in large measure, have recast vulnerability in ways that downplay the exogenous structural determinants and instead emphasize building local capacities and resilience to live and cope in a world of growing social environmental risk. I argue that construing vulnerability as an internal condition of communities like those on Simbo enables external actors to declare that the vulnerable themselves need capacity building while also rendering wider structures of dominance and power unchallengeable.

Simbo's experience with vulnerability when mobilized by disaster experts is part and parcel of a larger effect of expertise itself, in which experts must compose an object that they can master in order to assert their authority over laypeople.[39] When disaster experts actualize vulnerability as an endogenous condition of communities, it then can be ameliorated through manageable strategies such as "participatory disaster mitigation" or "capacity building." Arguably, these actions of outside experts may further delimit the scope within which difference in the world operates, since they overlook, or worse perpetuate, structural forces of domination that impinge on communities, forces that would require a reordering of the global economic structure in order to address them.

INDETERMINATE DISASTERS

As I am sure the reader has noticed, I have structured each chapter of this book to analyze the Simbo tsunami through different analytical lenses. This approach is inspired by the anthropology of disasters, which urges not only a diachronic analysis beyond the triggering biophysical perturbation but also a reflexive stance centered on the question pithily captured by disaster scholar Roberto Barrios: "For whom does a disaster reveal what?"[40] Barrios's question hints at a useful distinction between an ontology of simple complexity and one of emergent complexity and indeterminacy.[41] Simple complexity posits that phenomena are closed and that an absolute distinction between the phenomena under question and the surrounding world is identifiable. From this external position the relevant variables and relationships can be known and modeled exhaustively and with precision. The goal, then, is to provide increasingly detailed knowledge and to fill in the gaps of what is not yet known. The assumption is that the more knowledge we have, the better we can understand.

My argument here is that gains in understanding about disasters might be better achieved if we approach them from an *ontology of indeterminacy*. From this standpoint, it is presupposed that disasters are complex phenomena (or what ecologists refer to as complex adaptive systems) of whose dynamics we can never fully attain a totalizing grasp. Unlike more simple systems, there is no external position outside of the phenomena by which to authoritatively frame its components or judge its performance. In this sense, an account inevitably, although only partially, composes the object of analysis rather than transparently revealing and representing some previously hidden code. With emergent complexity the problem is less about attaining the best-suited frame since the notion of single transcendent principle or single framing is rejected as inadequate. Instead, it signals a reflexive and polyvocal register expressed by the question: "What does a particular framing do?"

Here I diverge from the now popular "multiple-world thesis" in anthropology that assumes that different lifeworlds are incommensurate realities.[42] As noted by Michael Cepak, anthropologists who seek to illuminate the radical and incommensurable alterity of other lifeworlds tend to flatten the complexity of ethnographic encounters in their quest to highlight differences.[43] In contrast, my approach is an attempt to bring into view different facets of the tsunami disaster in each chapter, not to reify them as eternally stable objects but to experimentally deploy different framings and assess how they may advance our understanding or usurp injustices or forces of domination.

If we assume that calamities such as the one that occurred on Simbo will always overflow the boundaries in which we attempt to describe them, it is also important to resist the idea that disasters are inexorably chaotic phenomena and that interpretations are impossible. This stance would quickly lead to the solipsism of extreme "anything goes" relativism. Those involved in disasters and those who study them most certainly succeed in stabilizing and organizing their collective experiences and accounts, yet they always must be maintained and nurtured as new ideas, concepts, entities, or actors emerge. At the same time, the themes of each chapter were not selected haphazardly. They address either important questions derived from the scholarly literature as experts attempt to improve their concepts and understanding through theoretical work (e.g., How do historical circumstances precondition disasters?) or key questions proposed by my Simbo interlocutors (e.g., Why do experts think our land is vulnerable?) in their attempts to impose order and organization on their experience of the tsunami and the recovery process.

With an ontology of indeterminacy as a guiding principle, the goal is to turn Barrios's question "For whom does a disaster reveal what?" from a liability or obstacle into a catalyst for generating different meanings and outcomes. Rather than judging these accounts from some transcendent principle or committing, a priori, to the dominance of any single contextualization, my intention is to bring into view new aspects that might have been missed. Although some may construe this approach as "comprehensive," it most certainly is not exhaustive or complete, for there are always more stories to be told about a disaster and more details to be brought into view. Any account, however comprehensive, is limited and partial. Rather than steering toward closure to Barrios's question, the idea here is to increase our capacity to be sensitive to possibilities of how it and other questions may be answered. In a world where climate uncertainties proliferate and new entities such as plastic-munching biota or SARS viruses burst onto the scene, we must be humble about our capacity to grasp emerging novelty and extraordinary events. My goal, then, is stated quite explicitly in the title of the book: it is to produce new modes of *sensing disasters* so that we can unsettle established forms of perceiving and knowing and sensitize ourselves to catastrophe in new ways.

RESEARCHING AND LEARNING

As has happened to many anthropologists who have studied disasters, the 2007 earthquake and tsunami abruptly entered my life and took over my research program.[44] Prior to the calamity, I had visited the Solomon Islands seven times, first as a graduate student and then as a postdoctoral researcher, conducting field research in Roviana Lagoon, a region that lies on the southwest coast of New Georgia Island, some 60 kilometers east of Simbo. I had been carrying out exciting research exploring marine ecological knowledge and the human ecology of fishing. In 2005 I secured a postdoctoral position funded through Packard Foundation that involved establishing a network of marine protected areas (MPAs) across Roviana Lagoon and helping form a conservation organization to manage the network.[45] Throughout this period of research, I never could have imagined that someday I would write a book about a tsunami.

For most of my Roviana research I based myself in Baraulu, a village of about nine hundred people located about 15 kilometers east of Munda. Over the years I had developed deep bonds with a number of people in the village and with members of the Roviana Conservation Foundation, the organization that managed the MPA network. One person I had grown very fond of was Tomi Roe. He and his delightful spouse Alenaru were the owners of a leaf house I rented during my first few visits to Baraulu. Tomi was a reserved, soft-spoken man with high cheekbones and an insatiable appetite for betel nut. He was also easy to spot from a distance because he loved to wear bucket hats with downward-sloping brims. When I asked about his fashion statement he told me that donning hats was common among his kin on Simbo, his birthplace and what he still considered his home. Over the many nights chatting with him I learned that he had married Alenaru when he was in his twenties and moved to Baraulu, her natal village, soon after. Tomi thought of himself as an intellectual of sorts and, unlike most villagers, he was an avid reader. He established his literati status by discussing with me the plots of nearly all of the John Grisham novels. Every evening he would stay awake late with his heavy-rimmed glasses perched on his nose and read under the warm light of a kerosene lamp. Each year before I departed to the United States from Roviana he would request that I bring him on my next visit new, best-selling novels, so I would make sure to fill any remaining space in my luggage with paperbacks.

Over the years we developed a close bond, spending many hours "talking story" on his veranda about our lives, and he often mentioned Simbo. He painted a bucolic picture of his home island, describing how it was blessed with many attractions, including an active volcano named Ove where locals and sometimes tourists would picnic and cook food in steam-spewing holes that had been dug into the side of the volcano. The steam, as I would confirm later, imparted a wonderful sulfur flavor to the cooked fish or vegetables. With eyes sparkling he told me about the island's soothing and therapeutic hot springs, one of which was found in the lagoon on his part of the island. He bragged how the fishing was much better than at Roviana, especially on the underwater reefs to the south of the island that were named "woman" and "man" reef. Beaming, he would proclaim: "Your arm gets sore from all the huge fish you catch on Simbo!" Having returned to the island only rarely and not able to afford the long boat trip, he invited me numerous times to travel with him to Simbo and offered to serve as my guide. I was tempted, but it was a long boat trip, the fuel costs were exorbitant, and my crammed research agenda in Roviana left little time to take lengthy side trips.

With friends like Tomi in many parts of the lagoon, my heart sank when emails sent by fellow researchers and colleagues flooded into my inbox the day of the 2007 tsunami. My immediate response was to write an email message to Joanna Pina, the manager of Roviana Conservation Foundation's small office in Munda, sending my blessings and asking about the tsunami. At that time the internet was unreliable in the Western Province, but I thought she might still have access and be able to respond. Her reply to me and my wife gave me some relief, but like so many survivor accounts of disaster that I documented, was chilling:

> Hello Matthew and Eden, Yes, there was a big earthquake and also tsunami hit Western Province and Choiseul Province. We were all scared and ran up to the hills because the water rised up. . . . My family and I ran up to the hills and spent two nights, and now we just came down. There are total of 25 people who died in the tsunami and earthquake, but some are still missing, especially in Ranongga, Simbo, Choiseul. All my eating utensils were all broken and fell down, I am very sorry.

Then in her follow-up a few days later:

> Yesterday night there was another big earthquake, we are still in the bush, the water still rised up, while I am writing this email the ground is shaking now[.] Please, please pray for us, I am going to shut this office, and run back to my family and we going up to the hills now.

As more information began to trickle out of the Solomons about the tsunami, Simbo made the international news as one of the hardest-hit islands that had suffered fatalities. "Tsunami Wiped Out Entire Island Village" read a headline from the *Denver Post*.[46] Within a few days I was relieved to learn from Joanna that none of Tomi's close relatives had been harmed. He was from a village on the southern part of the island called Nusa Simbo, which sits on the edge of a protected lagoon. Wanting to help and support the relief effort I, along with the students and other researchers who had worked on the Roviana project, began to activate our professional and personal networks and seek out ways to send humanitarian aid to the Solomons. At the same time, we all wanted to know how the tsunami had affected our Solomon Islander friends and their families, how the recovery process was playing out, and if we could be of some assistance.

In our effort to learn more about the tsunami, I helped assemble an interdisciplinary team of researchers with experience in the Western Province. This included marine scientists Simon Albert from the University of Queensland and Ben Halpern from the University of California, Santa Barbara, as well as a Japanese medical anthropologist from Kyoto University, Takuro Furusawa. We wrote a successful National Science Foundation (NSF) proposal that was funded by their Human and Social Dynamics Program to conduct a four-year study of the tsunami's social and ecological effects and the recovery process across several islands, including Simbo. Many of our Roviana friends had suggested that we work on Simbo since it was one of the hardest-hit islands and so many of the Roviana people like Tomi had close ties with the island. As I discuss in more detail later, Roviana and Simbo were allies prior to European contact, and there was much intermarriage, entwining the two groups through kinship bonds.

In preparation for the NSF-funded fieldwork, I sent word to Tomi asking if he would be my guide and accompany me to Simbo for my first visit to the island in 2008. He graciously accepted and was excited to return to his island and introduce me to his family and the island's leaders. He would eventually accompany me during my first two visits (in 2008 and 2009) to Simbo and helped ingratiate me with the Simbo community and gain their trust. I kept in touch with him up until 2018, when sadly he succumbed to cancer.

Tomi was a brilliant host. Not only did he have close kinship ties with the leaders of the main clan in Nusa Simbo village, but he also was widely respected. Quick-witted, Tomi helped explain the goals of my research project to Simbo's political and traditional leaders, and I was graciously accepted around the island. Or at least I thought I was.

As Indigenous anthropologists such as Kim TallBear have made patently clear, in many Indigenous communities "research" and the researchers who carry it out are considered instruments of injustice and imperialism.[47] In most of the Solomons this deep-seated cynicism toward the presence of Western researchers is almost nonexistent, probably because relatively little research has been conducted in the Solomons Islands and the colonial experience has been relatively less impactful than in settler-colonized settings such as Hawaii, Australia, and New Zealand. Simbo, for its part, has hosted more researchers over the years than most islands in the western Solomons. Since the early twentieth century at least three researchers—Arthur Maurice Hocart, Christine Dureau, and Ross Sinclair—have spent extended amounts of time on the island, yet I have never experienced the resistance to my presence that was articulated in the terms described by TallBear. Indeed, I would like to acknowledge the prior researchers' success in conducting research that has been judged by Simboans as ethical and worthwhile. Christine Dureau in particular continues to be fondly remembered for her kindness, although many Simboans would like her to return so they can become reacquainted with her and her daughter, who lived on Simbo with Christine during the research in the early 1990s.

Despite the lack of deep cynicism toward research on Simbo, researchers should never assume they occupy some neutral, apolitical space where they can satisfy all the various and cross-cutting interests of any community. Elenore Smith Bowen taught us long ago in her brilliant novel *Return to Laughter* that not only can researchers not make friends with an entire community, only with individuals, but our relationships with interlocutors can be wielded for their social or political utility.[48] As relatively powerful outsiders, our presence is an opportunity for individuals or groups to leverage it to their advantage.

As noted previously, land disputes are a central dimension of Simbo placemaking activities. And as an ethnographer I did not stand outside of these practices; rather I was entangled in them. This is exactly what occurred during my first extended stay on Simbo in 2009. Unknown to me, my presence was drawn into a bitter, decade long power struggle within the traditional leadership of Nusa Simbo over several plots of land. I went to great lengths during my initial visit in 2008 and during the first weeks of my field visit in 2009 to meet and discuss my research with traditional leaders and government representatives across the island as well as to hold community meetings. This was in addition to gaining permission from the provincial government of the Western Province and securing a research permit through the Ministry of Education of the Solomon Islands government, the agency that processed official research permits.

In the community meetings I fielded many of the critical questions faced by researchers: Who is funding you? Are you earning money from your research? How will we benefit from it? I answered these questions the best I could, explaining how I would advocate on the island's behalf to secure the disaster relief funds that had been promised to them by the central government and that I would bring as many benefits as I could to their island. There was little hostility toward me and the research team, my answers seemed to be accepted, and there appeared to be agreement about granting me permission to conduct the research.

After nearly a week of securing what I thought was permission to conduct research, a bright white envelope was handed to me by a young man as I sat at a table on the bottom floor of Centenary Hall, the building where our team (I, Simon Albert, and two SDSU MA students, Douglas LaRose and Luke Campanella) was lodged during our visit in 2009. It had "Professor Mathew Lauer" printed on the front, and inside was a letter carefully handwritten by a man named Lawrence. It read: "As the Chief of Nusa Simbo, Vela Viru Tribe . . . I am issuing against your delegation under my power a notice of legal order that all your intent program and plan to be carried out in Nusa Simbo customary land will be stopped at once and I ask your team to vacate Nusa Simbo land and leave immediately." Confused and worried about annoying this leader, I presented the letter to the Nusa Simbo chief who had granted me permission to conduct work in his district. As he read the letter he chuckled dismissively and stated: "He thinks he is a chief, but he has no followers. Ignore the letter! I have given you permission and I am the true caretaker of Nusa Simbo land."

Upon further consultation with several other interlocutors about how to manage Lawrence's objection to my research, their advice was to visit Lawrence's house and formally ask his permission to conduct the research. This seemed like a more sensible course of action than ignoring him. So the next day I anxiously walked across the island from Lengana, wading through the shallow water between Nusa Simbo and the main island, to introduce myself to Lawrence and his family. It was a stressful moment. As an anthropologist I had never been so bluntly accused of misconduct. Even though I had been reassured that Lawrence had little influence and

authority, I could not help thinking about how he could damage the legitimacy of the entire project. Needless to say, I was deeply relieved when
I arrived at Lawrence's house and he greeted me with a pleasant smile.
As I shook his hand and introduced myself, he showed no tension or dis-
comfort whatsoever. We then "storied" about the goals of the project, and
I asked his permission to conduct research on Nusa Simbo land. After a
short pause punctuated by a common Simbo gesture of sharply snorting
through his nose, he proceeded to eloquently and carefully praise the project and the possible benefits it might bring to the island. He then granted
me "official" access to carry out the research.

Later in my consultations with the chiefs of the other districts I learned
that Lawrence and Goldie had been engaged in a long-term power struggle
over land in Nusa Simbo. The acceptance of my presence on Simbo was
an opportunity for the Simbo chiefs to exert their authority. I learned that
Tomi, my gracious host, had close kin ties to Goldie and that they intentionally avoided discussing Lawrence with me to undermine his authority
and bolster Goldie's. The controversy I had with Lawrence is just one example of the acrimonious land disputes that plague Simbo social life as
well as the inherently political nature of securing permission for anthropological research. Despite these difficulties, Lawrence and I would go on
to develop a cordial relationship even though I had much closer relations
with Goldie's kin group.

In total I have spent nearly eighteen months on Simbo. I made visits
spanning twelve years (my most recent visit was in 2019), and I formed
deep bonds with many people, especially two men who would become my
closest collaborators and friends, Nickson Sione and Gideon Tuke. Nickson, born in 1971 and son of the headmaster of Simbo's secondary school,
was Simbo's email station operator for the now defunct UNDP-sponsored
People First Network (PFnet). PFnet was a network of rural email stations
that used solar-powered high-frequency radios with modems. It was op-
erational on Simbo until the building of a solar-powered cell phone tower
in 2012 that provides phone and data service, albeit erratically. Because of
Nickson's association with PFnet, I was introduced to him almost immediately upon my arrival on Simbo. He was known on the island as well-versed
in tsunami disaster and recovery due to his training from PFnet and was
one of a tiny handful of people on Simbo who had formally learned about

tsunamis prior to the Simbo disaster. It has been an absolute delight to learn from Nickson over the years, and he has graciously incorporated me into his family and wider kin networks of Lengana and Masuru villages. I was deeply touched when he named his youngest daughter and son after my wife and father.

Gideon Tuke, who was born in Meqe village in 1959, also played a prominent role in the disaster recovery as the chair of the committee that managed the humanitarian aid. For most of my field trips I rented his small guesthouse in Meqe, where we spent countless hours discussing life in the United States and on Simbo. Extremely intelligent and articulate, Gideon received a scholarship to complete two years of seminary school at Eden Theological Seminary in St. Louis, Missouri, from 2003 to 2005. During his stay in the United States he experienced profound culture shock, and it gave him a unique perspective on Simbo life. We were able to bond quickly, as he would tell stories of adapting to the strange American ways. I am truly grateful for being able to meet and build friendships with Tomi, Gideon, Nickson, and many others in Roviana and Simbo.

Building on nearly sixteen months of prior field research in Roviana Lagoon, this book is based primarily on fieldwork conducted during two three-month visits in 2008 and 2009 with Tomi, as well as subsequent visits in June–August 2010, May–July 2011, May–July 2012, January 2014, June 2015, and January 2019. During the first visits I, along with several master's students from San Diego State University and local Simbo collaborators, helped conduct household surveys in which 18 percent of households on Simbo were interviewed on a variety of topics including demographics, adaptations to the tsunami, migration, remittances, time allocation, livelihoods, household income, fishing and agricultural practices, food consumption, and household living standards. We then conducted several follow-up surveys in 2010, 2011, 2012, and 2014, all focusing on the 2007 tsunami experience. In the two villages hardest hit by the tsunami, Tapurai and Riquru, I interviewed members of nearly every household and conducted numerous focus group interviews. I asked a range of questions about historic settlement patterns; customary tenure regimes; and the dynamics of community response, resettlement, and recovery. Ethnographic interviews on Simbo, but also on Ghizo (especially the Gilbertese village of Titiana), Honiara, and Munda, were, of course, critical. I interviewed dozens of chiefs, community leaders, politicians, aid workers, pastors, NGO staff, youth groups, women's groups, and government functionaries and experts. In addition, I interviewed several geoscientists who conducted the first assessments of the tsunami just weeks after the disaster. Most recently, in 2015 and 2019 I participated in an archaeological project in which I collaborated with Todd Braje and the wonderful staff of the Solomon Islands National Museum. One of our key collaborators from the museum, Grinta Ale'eke, was not only a meticulous archaeologist but also a brilliant cultural anthropologist. She was able to quickly build rapport with Simboans and made many keen observations about Simbo and Solomon Islander life. Her perceptive insights were grounded in her experience growing up as a villager in Kia, a community on the western tip of Santa Isabel. That region was a key target of Simbo headhunters prior to European pacification, and many captives were taken from there and brought to Simbo. Indeed, a number of Simboans trace their lineages back to villagers in Kia. These historical and genealogical relations provided Grinta the opportunity to build close relationships with many Simboans.

Much of this book was written during a sabbatical I was granted by San Diego State University. Unfortunately, my sabbatical coincided with the 2020 pandemic lockdowns. My plan was to visit Simbo before finishing the manuscript so that I could review drafts of it with my close collaborators. The Solomon Islands government, however, closed its borders to international tourism in March 2020, and at the time of writing this book, travel still remains closed to foreigners unless they undergo a fourteen-day, self-funded quarantine. I was lucky, however, in that Gideon Tuke, one of my closest Simbo friends, was working and living in Gizo, where he had somewhat reliable internet access. This enabled me to regularly discuss many of the topics through Facebook Messenger or Skype calls to gain his insights and feedback.

1 The Rise of Indigenous Ecological Knowledge

PAQA: We never experienced anything like this before. Waves like the one that swept our village clean have never happened here. We don't even have a word for tsunami, I first heard that word several days after the tsunami while we lived in the bush and some Japanese came and told us about the waves.

ML: So how did you know to run?

PAQA: I don't know. I just had a feeling. Something was not right. I ran for my life!

What a remarkable human achievement. The fact that only nine people died on Simbo during the 2007 tsunami is nothing less than astounding considering that the three-story-high wave arrived within three minutes of the earthquake. Moreover, the Simbo people's response to the tsunami stands in stark contrast to the thousands who died in the 2004 Indian Ocean tsunami, one of the most devastating tsunamis on record, which caused destruction around the Indian Ocean basin. Similar to Paqa, many people who experienced the Indian Ocean tsunami were unfamiliar with the phenomenon and learned only after the disaster that tsunami waves were even possible. A survivor of the Indian Ocean tsunami, for example, told anthropologist Michelle Gamburd that when he first heard the word "tsunami" three days after the event, "It was Greek to me."[1] Yet nearly everyone on Simbo survived, while four hundred thousand are thought to have perished in the Indian Ocean catastrophe.[2]

At the time of the Indian Ocean earthquake and tsunami, I was finishing up graduate studies at the University of California Santa Barbara, and

I was fascinated by the news reports and video clips being disseminated on the internet. I had read about tsunamis, but the Indian Ocean tsunami was the first major tsunami extensively captured on film, much of it by amateur photographers using newly available digital cameras. I learned later that my experience was common, and in the wake of the Indian Ocean disaster, knowledge about tsunamis spread rapidly to the wider public.[3] Prior to that time the vast majority of the world's population was unaware that earthquakes could cause oceanic waves, let alone that these waves could destroy coastal communities.

I can vividly recall watching videos in my cramped campus office. The scenes in Banda Ache, Indonesia, were horrific. Deadly torrents of debris-laden water raged through the streets, destroying everything and everyone in their path. Some videos showed the tsunami waves themselves forming far out at sea, appearing as a frothy white line across the horizon. In others there was noticeable "drawback," a phenomenon in which the ocean recedes as the wave energy offshore pulls water away from shore, like a quickly ebbing tide, exposing the intertidal zone and in many cases stranding fish. In other cases, there were less obvious signs, such as currents or a slowly rising incoming tide.

Much of this amateur footage was later compiled in a fascinating documentary, *Tsunami: Caught on Camera*.[4] The film presents a minute-by-minute account of the catastrophe, narrated by the photographers and other survivors who were there. It provides firsthand accounts of how people reacted as the tsunami formed offshore. A consistent theme in the film is how unaware many people were of the impending disaster. A hotel manager from Khao Lak stated: "As the water withdrew, people were drawn to it because it looks so strange. There was a sense of calm, there was no sense of panic whatsoever. You could see, forming out left to right a beautiful crest on the horizon, it looked quite lovely. We were spellbound, everyone one was looking at it. But at that time there was no way to know how big the wave was."[5]

In another case on Khao Lak, German tourist Stefan Kühn provided a chilling account of how he could not pull himself away from filming the wave building along the horizon; he was fascinated by it. You can hear him asking his partner in German, "What is it? What is it?" without any hint of fear in his voice. As it becomes more apparent that the wall of whitewater is approaching, his wife asks: "What if the wave hits the beach?" Even after the wave inundated a fishing boat moored out in the bay, Stefan continued to ask: "What is it?" It was not until someone near him blurted out "tsunami!" that he and his family fled.

In another horrific scene a woman in red shorts is seen sitting on the beach as a wall of frothy water charges toward her with frightening speed. Solemnly succumbing to her fate, she stands up calmly, methodically turns toward shore, and walks slowly as the wave completely engulfs her from behind.

It is apparent from the videos and numerous written accounts that both expatriate tourists and local people were completely oblivious to the approaching danger. A video from Koh Phi Phi Island, for example, shows a white tourist curiously observing the water drawback a few meters from the beach. Also in the scene are numerous Thai outriggers and wooden long tail boats moored to the beach with long ropes. As the water recedes and then rises, the Thai crews show no panic and, like the tourists, they seem unfazed by the water's strange behavior.

There were, however, several documented but not filmed cases during the Indian Ocean tsunami in which Indigenous peoples reacted similarly to Simboans and fled to safety before the wave crushed the coastline. In one well-publicized case, the coastal communities of Simeulue Island, located just west of mainland Sumatra, suffered only seven deaths during the tsunami despite their proximity to the earthquake epicenter and being hit within minutes by a 10-meter wave.[6] Just after the earthquake, eighty-five thousand villagers fled to the hills behind their coastal villages and escaped unharmed.

Another high-profile Indigenous group that survived mostly unharmed were the seafaring Moken people, more widely known as Sea Gypsies, who inhabit islands in the Andaman Sea and along the west coast of Thailand.[7] Other reports documented the survival of remote Ong, Jarawa, and Sentinelese hunter-gatherer groups on the Andaman and Nicobar Islands, India.[8] In an iconic image of survival in face of the tsunami, an Indian Coast Guard crew photographed a Sentinelese man, standing below the aircraft on dying coral reefs that had been abruptly raised above sea level by the earthquake, pointing his bow and arrow at the helicopter hovering overhead.[9]

Simbo's response to flee the tsunami, like that of those of other Indigenous peoples, is a fascinating example of the potentiality of other lifeworlds. Indeed, the Simeulue were formally recognized by the international community for their achievement and awarded the United Nations Sasakawa Award for Disaster Reduction. But what is equally interesting is how interpretations, both in the academic literature and among the wider public, are offered rather unproblematically. For the Simeulue, their response was attributed to "island folklore" and the local concept of *smong*, which was thought to be the Simeulue word for tsunami.[10] The popular press also reported that knowledge about tsunamis was embedded in traditional Simeulue lullabies, myths, and poems.[11] On the Moken, one newspaper article commented that they "did not have expensive advanced technology to warn them about the killer waves. They survived merely because of their close relationships with and observation of nature and because they heeded their ancient wisdom and even superstition."[12] It was reported that the Moken have a legend called Laboon, "the wave that eats people," that is "recited around campfires" and depicts seven deadly waves that appear after the water recedes.[13]

I heard similar explanations when I discussed the Simbo response with scientists, professionals, colleagues, friends, and family. In my discussions, many expressed great admiration for the survival skills of Simboans, but it did not come as a surprise to them. It is as if we expect Indigenous peoples like Solomon Islanders to know how to respond to a tsunami and that moderns like ourselves lack the capacity. Take an English professor at my university. When I discussed the Simbo case with her she responded matter-of-factly that she had read about how Indigenous peoples, particularly Pacific Islanders, have myths and oral histories about past events like earthquakes and tsunamis. She explained that her husband is well read in Hawaiian history and that Hawaiians have detailed oral histories that specify responses to these biophysical phenomena. To her, there was an obvious and rather straightforward explanation. The Simbo people, like Indigenous peoples around the world, maintained integrational transmitted oral history, and it informed their response as the tsunami approached. With this knowledge lodged in their memory, they simply followed the script and escaped to the hills.

In fact, my English professor friend's thesis was precisely the story described by the first two academic papers written about Simbo's response to the tsunami. Two geoscientists, who made separate visits to Simbo just weeks after the event to collect field data, wrote articles describing an "ancestral knowledge induced evacuation" and how "indigenous knowledge" saved lives.[14] The authors defined Indigenous knowledge as "a deep-rooted understanding of place [that] is integrated into the community's practice, culture, and cosmologies."[15]

I interviewed Brian McAdoo and Hermann Fritz about their field trips to Simbo, and they both recounted learning from local people in Gizo, the provincial capital, how Solomon Islanders knew stories told to them by their grannies about past tsunamis.[16] However, when I asked for details about any stories, they responded that they were never recounted specific myths, legends, or stories but rather were simply told by survivors about the stories.

These examples illustrate a widely held view that the response of Indigenous peoples such as Simbo Islanders is explainable through the registers of "Indigenousness" and "placed-based knowledge," two concepts that have come to be expressed in the academic literature as "Indigenous ecological knowledge." As mentioned in the introduction, Indigenous ecological knowledge studies have become so prevalent in the literature that the concept has acquired its own abbreviation and is commonly referred to as IEK.

In the popular press and scientific writings, interpretations of Indigenous responses to tsunamis and other environmental hazards tend to make a critical presupposition that Indigenous knowledge is embedded in oral history or "ancient wisdom" that is passed down through the generations. For many it is self-evident that Indigenous peoples are able to respond to disasters by drawing from a corpus of stock knowledge to organize themselves and their communities. The underlying assumption is that an adequate response is grounded in a formal corpus of abstract knowledge or mental models about previous events that has developed over many generations. Indeed, many analyses of Indigenous coping strategies focus on traditional myths or oral traditions about disaster response.[17] From this perspective, effective Indigenous disaster responses are activities guided primarily by a discrete body of local knowledge or a compendium of information about previous events that has accumulated over many generations.

For many survivors, like Paqa, the Tapurai woman quoted earlier, the tsunami was a novel phenomenon that they had never experienced or learned about from their elders. If intergenerationally translated knowledge was lacking, then how did Simboans know to run?

RUN TO THE HILLS

I had these conceptualizations of Indigenous response in mind when I first began to conduct research on Simbo, and my running hypotheses were that their intimate knowledge of the marine environment and their oral history about previous tsunamis were the primary factors that enabled a successful response. Indeed, the writings of A. M. Hocart, a British anthropologist who conducted several months of research on Simbo in 1908, contained tantalizing evidence that tsunamis had been concretized in Simbo mythology: "At the present day the god of Momara lives underground and causes earthquakes; when he leaves Eddystone [Simbo] at Pa Na Kelekele or returns, there is a tidal wave and a booming sound."[18]

Yet when I began to learn more about Simbo's experience with the tsunami the ancient wisdom hypothesis was clearly inadequate. I conducted sixty-five interviews with people in the two villages hit hardest by the tsunami, Riquru and Tapurai, and in those conversations fifteen people (23% of total) said they had heard stories about waves after earthquakes, but in no case did the survivors expect the massive waves that crushed their villages. Even more, when I asked if they had heard of Momara, I only received blank stares. Some had heard of the *tomate* (spirit being), but no one remembered it being associated with tsunamis.

Indeed, immediately after the earthquake, the responses were varied. The shock was so extreme and prolonged that many fled their houses to open space. In Tapurai, several people who lived closest to the ocean walked down to the shore, while others stood stunned in their houses. Several eyewitnesses from Tapurai noted that the children were the first to start running for high ground behind the village. Many villagers, in fact, were surprised by the children's reaction (see the prologue) to the quake. As one man explained: "When the earthquake hit, all the children ran to high ground. They didn't wait. The teacher didn't tell them to run, they all just ran like crazy. From fear they knew to run."

The church building, located about 15 meters above sea level and about 50 meters from the shoreline, was where most people escaped. At its highest point, seawater reached just below the church's floor. Over a dozen people, mainly men, did not reach the church and were caught by the mass of rushing, foaming water that swept into the village site from the east. Stunned villagers watched from the church as the waves swept nearly all the houses from their stilts, crushing and destroying many of them against the steep hills behind the community. Other houses floated, partially intact, out to sea. Several victims were visible as they were tossed and tumbled amid the debris and sand-laden water. Others were swept out to sea, stripped of their clothing, and clung to logs or other large, floating debris.

Of those who indicated that their grandparents had told them stories about waves after earthquakes, no one could provide a specific myth or story. One possible exception was a man from nearby Roviana Lagoon who recounted a story to me about a sinking island, a common motif among Pacific Island peoples:[19]

> Kololuka is behind Rendova and Tetepare. From Kololuka you can see Simbo.... People lived on Kololuka a long, long time ago. The spirits told the people to move out from this place. The spirits said you all should move because the island was going to sink.... The news that the island would sink and a tsunami would come spread across the island. The tsunami that hit last year [2007] was not the first tsunami. Before there were other tsunamis. The ancestors didn't call it tsunami, they called it *sage kolo* (rising water). It was perhaps 100 years ago when a tsunami hit Roviana Lagoon. The ancestors mentioned the tsunamis. The tsunami that hit Roviana Lagoon was the same that hit Kololuka. First the tsunami hit Kololuka then it hit Buravusu, the third place it hit was Roviana. This most recent tsunami is the fourth one. Tsunamis are not new. They have come before.

On Simbo my consultants had never heard the Roviana man's stories of Kololuka. Moreover, I was told repeatedly that there was no specific word in Simbo for tsunami.[20] Today, the word sunami, introduced by Western scientists who flocked to the region just weeks after the event, has entered the Simbo and Roviana vernacular and is regularly employed when referring to the event.

When I continued to inquire about oral history, one sixty-year-old man responded in this way:

Before there were many small earthquakes, but never a big earthquake like this. This is the biggest one anyone had ever felt, not even the old people had felt one like this. . . . Some old people would say, "If there's an earthquake, you shouldn't go down to the shore because the sea will rise up." Some old people talked about this. There was an understanding the sea could rise, but not this much. We don't have a word in Simbo for tsunami. We didn't expect this to happen.

Thus, oral history appears to have been at least partially an ingredient that contributed to the successful response of the Simbo people, yet most survivors were not convinced that stories about past tsunamis led to the successful evacuation. Importantly, a small handful of people had learned about tsunamis prior to the 2007 event. Eleven percent of my interview respondents mentioned learning about tsunamis through written materials or radio programs. These respondents were clear, however, that very few of the Simbo people had been exposed to these sources of information. Of the seven survivors who had learned about tsunamis from the radio or print media, in all cases they picked up this information while they worked or studied in Honiara or Gizo. In the history of Simbo, the Solomon Islands government had never conducted tsunami awareness workshops or distributed printed material about tsunami risks.

Moreover, the survivors found the oral history hypothesis wholly inadequate to explain the miraculous reaction of children, one of the most discussed themes in my interviews with the survivors. Parents were startled to find their own sons and daughters had run to high ground and were waiting for them behind the village. Except for a small child who was in the arms of his mother, not one child died during the disaster.

HISTORY

Contrasts always facilitate informative analytical descriptions, and in the western Solomons there was a widely known and discussed case of a tsunami response that stood in stark contrast to Simbo. It was the experience of Titiana, a community located on the south coast of Ghizo Island (see map 2). It, like Simbo, was hit hard by the 2007 tsunami, with wave heights reaching 6 meters.[21] Yet the outcome was much more lethal.

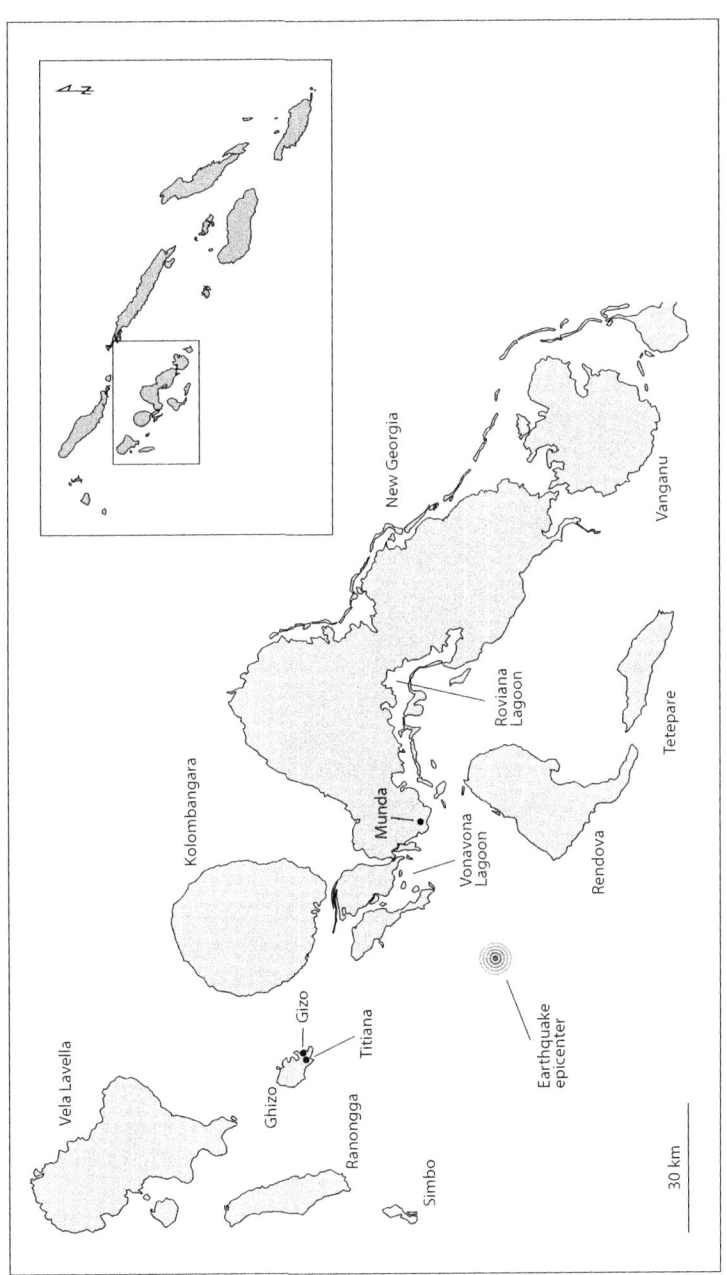

Map 2. Ghizo and other islands of the New Georgia Group.

Nearly three times as many people were swept away by the tsunami in a village that is just a third larger than Tapurai. Sadly, over half who died were children under the age of ten.[22]

This horrific outcome was widely discussed on Simbo, and many of my interlocutors theorized that the higher rates of mortality in Titiana highlighted that the community was non-Melanesian and "lacked history." Many pointed out that Titiana is comprised of immigrants from Kiribati who were brought by the British protectorate government in the 1960s.[23] They were granted coastal areas on the south coast of Ghizo to establish communities, land that had been acquired from the government in the early twentieth century when Gizo Town became the regional capital. These immigrants self-identify and are known by Melanesia Solomon Islanders as "Gilbertese," the British colonial term for I-Kiribati. Many on Simbo described how Gilbertese children, in contrast to Simbo children, were seen walking out into the exposed reefs as the water receded just before the tsunami. As one Simbo woman told me, "The Gilbertese aren't from here, this isn't their land, they don't have history like us, they didn't know to run away."

When Simboans refer to their "history," they are referring to the ways in which historical processes entangle with the present. Tongan scholar Hufanga 'Okusitino Māhina pithily described this temporality thus: "People are thought to walk forward into the past and walk backward into the future, both taking place in the present, where the past and future are constantly mediated in the ever-transforming present."[24] Bougainville scholar Regis Tove Stella notes that, "for Papua New Guineans, land and place are subject to the control of the past."[25]

I learned more about the Titiana case and how Solomon Islanders theorized the tsunami response when I ran into an old friend, Mathew, from Roviana Lagoon while shopping in a small store in Gizo Town. Mathew was married to a Gilbertese woman from Titiana and was living in the community when the tsunami struck. Mathew expressed shock that the Gilbertese were not fearful after the earthquake when the water started to move in strange ways. He described his experience in Titiana this way:

> It was a fine day with no wind and as the water dropped away many Gilbertese walked out to get fish or were just curious about the water receding

from the reefs. I started hollering out that people should run for high ground. I really didn't know what was happening I just knew there was danger. I never had been taught about tsunamis in school. I didn't know what a tsunami was. . . . I "sensed" the danger that day (*Mulongo arau pa rane asa*). The Gilbertese didn't "sense" (*mulongo*) that something was wrong.

ML: What is mulongo?

Some people are able to mulongo and others do not. When something is wrong in the world or out of place something is wrong with you. We Melanesians eat from the sea, we eat fish. It's a part of us. When something is wrong you mulongo it. This is different from *ginigilana* which is the ability to learn something. It's close to mulongo but it refers to learning something, not something you just have inside of you. Mulongo "stays in one's body", it is a power or talent that some people have. Dogs and other animals have mulongo too. It's not just in humans. It's a gift.

Learning about the concept of mulongo, which I gloss as "sense, feel, anticipate," challenged, or at least evaded, the interpretations and expectations of outsiders, including my own assumptions, about effective disaster response. As I discuss in more detail in the next chapter, mulongo and related concepts in Simbo such as *gila* ("mark," "sign," or "indication") forced me to reflect on how I and many scientists and laypeople alike were so quick and confident in our explanations of disaster response. They urged me to ask: What is the history of "Indigenous knowledge" as a concept, and how does it so tenaciously enroll the imagination of western scientists and the wider public alike?

ANTHROPOLOGICAL IEK

The widespread contemporary notion that Indigenous peoples have knowledge of their surroundings that may in some ways be superior to the knowledge of those in modern industrial or postindustrial societies is a near complete reversal of Western intellectual thought. Nineteenth-century anthropologists such as E. B. Tyler and James Frazer, as well as other social scientists, described Indigenous modes of thought as irrational, magical, and unscientific. This view was based on highly influential evolutionary models of social development, a framework that envisioned Indigenous peoples as "primitives" or "savages" who were intellectually inferior, tradition bound, and unchanging relative to Western Europeans, who had adopted rational thought and scientific methods.[26] This was particularly the case when these early anthropologists interpreted Indigenous philosophies about the workings of nature, in which in many cases animals, rocks, and other nonhuman entities were attributed animated souls. Tyler systematically described how the "belief in spiritual beings" was ubiquitous across the nonmodern world and theorized that it was a primitive substratum upon which more advanced societies built more rational and empirically verifiable systems of thought.[27] For Tyler, the reality of animated trees and spirits could not be scientifically verified, and thus he surmised that these beliefs were illusions of Indigenous peoples who erroneously attributed agency where there was none.

Émile Durkheim, for his part, famously reinterpreted the religions and ritual practices of non-Western people, specifically the totemism of Aboriginal Australians, as unifying symbols of society that underpin and reinforce a "collective consciousness."[28] His reimagined functional (supposedly) role of religion, however, remained grounded in the idea that social life among non-Western peoples "must be explained, not by the conception of it created by those who participated in it but by profound causes which escape awareness."[29]

Even the path-breaking anthropologist Bronislaw Malinowski, who conducted long-term fieldwork rather than producing an armchair account, relied on racist evolutionary models of Indigenous peoples when he theorized about their "magical" thinking.[30] However, there was a growing recognition that at least some aspects of Indigenous thought were empirically verifiable and hence "rational." In Malinowski's landmark work in the Trobriand Islands he stated that "the success in their agriculture depends . . . upon their extensive knowledge of the classes of the soil, of the various cultivated plants, and of the mutual adaptation of these two factors."[31] He also wrote in some detail about marine-focused knowledge and how Trobrianders were "skilled and industrious" fishers who used a variety of gears and exploited many different habitats and species.[32] Although Malinowski clearly had a deep appreciation for Trobriand environmental knowledge that was legible to him, this did not undermine his evolutionary perspective that Indigenous lifeways and thought more generally were inferior.

It was not until the 1950s that some of the first systematic anthropological investigations of local environmental knowledge acknowledged
and fully embraced its sophistication. Most notable was Harold Conklin's
work carried out in the 1950s among the Hanunóo, a group of swidden
farmers from Mindoro, Philippines.[33] In painstakingly meticulous detail,
Conklin documented Hanunóo botanical and agricultural knowledge, recording 1,625 native plant taxa recognized by the Hanunóo—more than
were known at that time to Western science. His work demonstrated the
encyclopedic depth at which island peoples understood the resource types,
soils, ecological processes, seasons, meteorological features, and fauna of
their local environments and gave rise to a body of literature that recorded
and analyzed folk classification systems, much of which was carried out in
Melanesia.[34] In Papua New Guinea, for example, Ralph Bulmer and his
Indigenous New Guinea collaborators assembled a comprehensive folk taxonomy, one of only a handful ever fully completed.[35] These early studies in
anthropology raised the profile of IEK among social and natural scientists
and helped establish that it is organized systematically and richly detailed.

The first systematic research to focus on marine ecological knowledge
was conducted not by a social scientist but by a fisheries biologist, Robert
Johannes. Based on long-term fieldwork in Palau, Johannes documented
the vast and detailed knowledge of Palauan fishers who described to him
current patterns, fish reproductive behavior, fish aggregation sites, moon
phases, tidal influences on fish behavior, gear types, seasonal variations of
both lagoon and pelagic fishes, and the influence of introduced eye goggles
on knowledge about fish.[36] Like Conklin's breakthrough studies of terrestrial flora and fauna, Johannes documented Palauan knowledge of more
than fifty species of food fish, which included details about their lunar
periodicity and the location of the spawning sites. This finding doubled
the number of species known at that time by Western biologists for the
entire world.[37]

The vast majority of IEK research, however, has relied on persistent
and specific conceptualizations of "Indigenous" and "knowledge." The "Indigenousness" of IEK is particularly controversial and disputed among
many social scientists. This is despite the fact that the term "Indigenous"
is now used in a wide array of contexts and has proved to be a potent and
effective signifier.[38] By organizing under the banner of Indigenousness,

many marginalized and disempowered people around the world have positioned themselves politically and effectively demanded rights.[39]

Although I wholeheartedly support the struggles of politically disenfranchised groups, the notion of Indigenous as conceptualized by some supporters of IEK studies has inherent limitations. A number of critiques relate the rise of IEK to what Kent Redford dubbed the "ecologically noble savage," an ecologically tinged version of a long-standing European imaginary that romanticizes Indigenous modes of existence.[40] This primitivist ideal, expressed most widely by Jean-Jacques Rousseau, was the dream that Indigenous peoples lived closer and according to nature, free of the complexity and other burdens of modern European life. The updated environmentalist version of this ideal, most ubiquitously cast upon native North and South Americans, depicts their lifeworlds as less ecologically destructive, despite scholars and native leaders themselves calling attention to the problems of generically painting Indigenous peoples and their relations with nature as equivocal to those of Western environmentalists.[41]

Ironically, the contrastive framework that positively evaluates and defines "Indigenous" as qualitatively different and distinct from the "modern" relies, in part, on a framework developed by nineteenth-century evolutionary social scientists that advocates of Indigenous peoples seek to overturn. In reaction to these disparaging contrasts, many twentieth-century anthropologists have been preoccupied with dissolving the persistent and troublesome primitive versus modern distinction. New and less obviously offensive terms such as "traditional," "face-to-face," "small-scale," and "Indigenous" have been invented but have not extinguished the lingering evolutionary assumptions about human progress. An unintended consequence of employing terms such as "Indigenous" is that they obscure and conceal inequities and neocolonialism rather than explicitly expose them.[42]

In efforts to avoid the "Indigenous" label, advocates of Indigenous knowledge have been favorably disposed toward the term "local ecological knowledge." But this invokes another long-standing and problematic assumption about nonindustrial societies: their spatial isolation. The uncritical adoption of the term "local" is remarkable considering that anthropologists such as Eric Wolf taught us long ago that non-Western societies are just as interconnected with wider processes as any others. Emphasis on "the local" is also colored by specific conceptions of the "community."

Influenced by Tonnie's formulation of gemeinschaft (community) and ge-
sellschaft (society), many scholars assume that "communities" are not only
confined within limited horizons but also small in spatial extent, homoge-
neous, undifferentiated, and more inclined to be egalitarian. The quaint,
warm "little community" continues to capture our imagination despite
vast evidence that communities have always been and continue to be inter-
nally differentiated and bound in relations with external actors.[43] Peoples'
lives and communities across the planet are now, more than ever, shaped
by mixtures of contemporary and "traditional" cultural practices, identities, and knowledges.[44] In Johannes's aforementioned studies of Palauan
fishing, he noted that the introduction of diving goggles at the turn of the
twentieth century caused a "revolution in the study of underwater life" and
fishers gained a heightened understanding of fish behavior, yet Johannes
continued to frame their knowledge as "traditional."[45] Hybridity like the
new Palauan knowledge about fish is the norm, and current conceptions of
Indigenous or local knowledge are ill equipped to accommodate it.

CARTESIAN LEGACIES

For many authors, not only is "Indigenous" a problematic yet effective
term, prevailing definitions of "knowledge" also rest on specific rather than
universal epistemological and ontological assumptions. Most Indigenous
knowledge studies rely on a theory of knowledge that stresses the articulated, cognitive, formal, or abstract aspects of knowing and understanding. They start from the premise that Indigenous knowledge is a corpus
of intergenerationally transmissible instructions or rules that are distinct
from day-to-day activities. A widely cited definition of Indigenous knowledge developed by Fikret Berkes, for example, reflects this conceptual
predisposition. He defined Indigenous knowledge as a "cumulative body
of knowledge and beliefs, handed down through generations by cultural
transmission, about the relationship of living beings (including humans)
with one another and with their environment."[46]

The conceptual roots of this understanding of Indigenous knowledge
can be traced back to several centuries' worth of Western thought and science that has divided human subjects into two mutually exclusive parts:

mind and body. Thanks primarily to Descartes, Western science has been built around the idea that our minds stand apart, disengaged from the physical world. It is the detached observer who, through conceptual categories, can sort our experiences based on socially approved schemas. Meanwhile, our bodies are fully immersed in the physical environment, divorced from the omnipresent and watchful mind. And this relationship between mind and body is clearly not symmetric. The body has consistently been portrayed in Western thought as needing the mind to regulate emotions and feelings that are generated through somatic sensory stimuli.

Current understandings of Indigenous knowledge have also been shaped by influential views in ethnoscience, known more generally as cognitive anthropology.[47] Early pioneers in this field, such as Harold Conklin, are credited with first drawing attention to Indigenous knowledge and establishing it as a worthy topic of research. But ethnoscientists approached their subject with Cartesian assumptions about the relationship between mind and body. The central premise of cognitive anthropology is that cognition consists of stable conceptual schemas that are imposed on a chaotic world by the mind. In other words, humans have "cultural models" lodged in their minds, which give meaning to experience and direct human emotions and action.[48] Ethnobiologists and ethnoscientists set out to understand the organizing principles of these cultural models and developed rigorous methods to document Indigenous biological classificatory systems that had developed from people's relationships with their local environments. This perspective continues to guide many Indigenous knowledge studies.

With its explicit focus on knowledge as the variable and culturally contingent domain to be documented, much of the Indigenous ecological literature presupposes that the biophysical realm is a stable, self-evident domain of reality that is ontologically distinct from cultural domains. Take the famous etic and emic distinction expounded by ethnoscientists to demarcate particular layers of reality under study. These concepts were derived from the suffixes of "phonetics" and "phonemics," linguistic terms that refer, in the former, to the universal acoustic phenomena that underpin all linguistic sounds and their notations, and in the latter, to the specific languages and associated syntax, grammar, and so forth spoken by cultural groupings. By analogy, the ethnoscientist's approach involved documenting how culturally specific perceptions, categorizations, and taxonomies (emics) were applied to the etic elements, those universal characteristics of physical reality that could be apprehended by the researcher through observation. These conceptual resources enabled researchers to presume they could identify physical aspects of the world independently without any contamination from their own cultural "biases." Thus Blumer could state categorically that cassowaries are birds construed metaphorically as quasi-humans, but certainly not actually quasi-humans, even though that was how his Karam interlocutors of the Papua New Guinea Highlands described them.[49]

ASYMMETRIC VALIDATION

I most certainly celebrate the explosion of interest among the wider scientific community in IEK as a viable knowledge base worthy of study, but there continues to be much debate about how to characterize knowledge production in nonscientific contexts and how scientific and nonexpert or Indigenous knowledge should relate.[50] Like the examples cited previously, the predominant model is infused with scientism, wherein scientific knowledge is deployed as the neutral arbiter by which to judge the validity of all other accounts. Johannes, for example, qualified nearly all the knowledge he collected among Palauan fishers by citing scientific studies. As he stated: "There are many examples of marine animals with habits that once seemed fantastic but are now well documented. . . . [I]intense skepticism greets accounts of strange phenomena until they have been confirmed by one or more reputable scientists. . . . Skepticism is essential to science. For every improbable story that turns out to be true there are many that are not, and it is the job of the scientists to sort one type from the other."[51]

This strategy to bolster the legitimacy through scientific validation of IEK has been central to many Indigenous knowledge studies and Indigenous advocates for decades. Yet the sociology of science literature highlights the problems of assuming that science, even when science practitioners avoid overt marginalization of nonexpert knowledge, can serve as a benchmark to judge validity because it, like all knowledge systems, imposes subtle yet critical epistemic commitments and normative concepts.[52] Moreover, other scholars have made it abundantly clear that the relationship between science and Indigenous or non-Western knowledge has been exceedingly asymmetric.[53] Modern technoscientific knowledge has a dubious history of validating racist, sexist, and exploitative treatment of marginalized groups within Western society itself and the global South more generally.[54] In more recent incarnations, scientism has formed the basis of development schemes and conservation initiatives in which expert knowledge takes precedence over local adaptations and practices even when they are ostensibly "participatory" and local knowledge is respected and valued.[55] In this body of research, science and expert knowledge are understood not as neutral forces for good but rather as hegemonic forces, tied to postcolonial power and in many cases to oppression of the marginalized.[56]

Acknowledging that science does not have a universal and unrivaled claim to truth is the first step toward a more inclusive conceptualization of IEK. But disavowing scientism is not equivalent to disregarding scientific knowledge and objectivity. Instead, I suggest, scientific knowledge production should be approached like any other form of learning about the world that has the potential to generate durable objective knowledge. This, however, does not preclude the possibility that nonexperts and Indigenous peoples assemble the world in radically different ways that are beyond the bounds of peer-reviewed science.

CONCLUSION

I opened this chapter with a quote from Paqa, one of the many survivors who fled the massive tsunami and lived to tell her story. Yet she, like many on Simbo, did not have an explanation of why she behaved the way she did. Nevertheless, many scientists, including myself, as well as the informed broader public in the developed world, were quick to provide what is assumed to be a self-evident explanation. Why are we so self-assured we know? This chapter has attempted to trace the roots of modernist conceptions of IEK that enable so many of us to feel confident that we understand disaster responses even if they occur among people in far-flung places such as Simbo.

As we have seen, our understandings of Simboans' responses are built on a long intellectual tradition that has a particular shape involving specific commitments to what we consider to be "Indigenous" and "knowledge." And yet what the Simbo people were telling me escaped these analytics. "We don't have any myths about tsunamis, we've never had tsunamis here. Why do you think we should?" I heard this and similar responses when I would ask about the veracity of stories written down by Hocart that discussed Momara, a spirit being that was thought to cause tsunamis.

My lack of understanding of the Simbo response was rendered even more apparent when I learned about mulongo and the role it might have played in the Simboans' response. It was at this point in my field research that I had an experience like that of anthropologist Anna Tsing. In her early fieldwork Tsing marveled at the rain forests covering the Meratus Mountains of Borneo as would a naturalist: for its spectacular biodiversity. And yet her Indonesian interlocutors talked about their forests differently. They were a space where "individuals and households traced their histories: House posts resprouted into trees. Forest trees grew back from old swiddens."[57] For Tsing, her misunderstanding led to an epiphany that forest landscapes could be social rather than natural.

I underwent a productive misunderstanding when I was compelled by my interlocutors to try to grasp disaster through different lenses, which challenged my ascriptions and encouraged reflection about the assumptions and commitments upon which "Indigenous ecological knowledge" was built. Importantly the Simbo people's response to the disaster provoked a concrete behavior witnessed and participated in by many, and thus there was an object that my interlocutors and I could contemplate deeply and discuss where our interpretations converged and where they diverged.

If IEK was not a sufficient analytic to make sense of Simbo's astonishing disaster response, what possibilities beyond its confines did Simboan interpretations bring into view? It is to these topics I turn in the next chapter.

2 Ocean Knowing

We Melanesians eat from the sea, we eat fish. It's a part of us.

—Tsunami survivor

The central role the ocean plays in the lives of Simboans is hard to over-state. As soon as young Simbo children can walk, they venture to the shoreline to play (see figure 4). Even earlier than that they begin devel-oping an intimate familiarity with the feel and flow of the ocean in their mothers' wombs as they travel through the calm lagoon waters in a dug-out canoe or bounce, sometimes ferociously, during the three-hour open ocean journey to Gizo. By an early age, children learn to swim without any direct instruction or supervision from adults. I was told that young chil-dren learn to swim simply by imitating older ones. When you approach a village by boat, you will inevitably see a pack of youngsters, usually sepa-rated into gendered groups, swimming and frolicking along the water's edge, body surfing small breakers with planks or pieces of flotsam, play-ing with toy boats, catching tiny fish with a simple hook and line, or just tinkering with the dugout canoes pulled up on shore. A lively and popular pastime is "water music," in which children produce different sounds in rhythmic patterns by slapping and splashing the water with their hands. Lullabies are also known for incorporating the sensorial experience of water, as this one recorded by Solomon Islands scholar Milton Galokale Keremama on nearby Choiseul island does:

Figure 4. A boy playing along the shoreline near Meqe with a small toy boat he made from soft wood. (Photo by author.)

Paddle and go in our small canoe
Quickly put up the sail because the wind is blowing
Paddle krung krung krung krung
Paddle krung krung krung krung[1]

In addition to canoeing, the other principal activity by which the Simbo people build their familiarity with the ocean is fishing. In fact, my interlocutors would identify themselves as *tinoni ababa* (fishing people) rather than *tinoni ivere* (sea people). And these skills are acquired very early in life. Frequently you will see boys or girls of four or five years of age paddling small dugout canoes (*mola*) near shore. On one occasion I noticed a young girl, maybe nine years old, paddling a canoe alone,

Figure 5. Young Simbo children handline fishing some 100 meters from shore. The rugged west coast of Ranongga Island lies in the background. (Photo by author.)

50 meters or so offshore, and I asked several of my consultants about the danger of drowning (see figure 5). I was astonished that they could not remember a single incident when a child had died by drowning. It should be noted that just balancing a Simbo dugout canoe takes a lot of agility and practice. Indeed, there is a specific technique to boarding the narrow and unstable dugouts. First you place one foot in the middle of the canoe while balancing on the other foot, which is in ankle-deep water. Then you place your hands behind you on the gunwales and quickly swing your second leg out in front of you and into the canoe as you sit down. My first failed attempts at this incited belly-busting laughter from the children watching nearby. Even more difficult than mounting a canoe in shallow water is pulling yourself up into a canoe floating in deep water. After many years of trying, I have never been able to master it. Paddling also requires excellent balance, agility, and core strength, particularly in bumpy, open ocean. This is especially the case when there is more than one person in the canoe or when the canoe is loaded with cargo. Just a

small shift in balance by a passenger or the bobbling caused by a boat wake can easily lead to capsizing.

Adult canoes are generally 2- to 4-meter-long dugouts. Most canoes are now purchased from craftsmen on other islands such as Ranongga and Kolombangara because of a lack of appropriate timber on Simbo. Simbo villages typically have numerous dugouts lying just above the high tide line on the coast. Canoes are generally owned by a household, although they can be loaned to others for a small fee or, if used for fishing, a small portion of the catch. When the tsunami struck, canoes were one of the key local resources lost by every village, and dozens of canoes were promised as part of the disaster aid, but Simboans had to wait nearly two years before they received them.

Like canoeing, the Simbo people also start fishing very early in life, and seafood remains central to their diet. The shorelines near villages seem to always have groups of small children fishing from shore. They frequently perch on fallen trees, wharfs, jetties, or rocks to fish, or they take dugout canoes and fish farther out into the lagoon. They never, however, venture past the reef into open ocean. Most villages are adjacent to protected lagoons, and these become playgrounds for children to explore. As they grow older, women, like children, will rarely leave the safety of the lagoon, while teenage boys will begin to accompany their fathers or other family members into the reef passes or other more exposed fishing grounds.

The fishing gear of young children is invariably a small hook tied to light monofilament, wrapped around a small stick or old plastic bottle. They bait their hooks with scraps of manioc, sweet potato, pieces of fish, hermit crabs, mollusk meat, or different kinds of insects and simply hand cast their lines from shore. Even very young children three or four years old will catch fish this way. The lagoon is filled with small fish species that take bait, and you frequently see a group of children huddled around a small fire roasting their catch.

Gleaning for small crustaceans, sand crabs, mollusks, or chitons is also common. In the past there was a healthy mud clam (*Polymesoda* spp.) fishery in the mangroves near Riquru, but it appears to have been overfished, and the clams are no longer present. By the age of ten or twelve, children are familiar with most of the prominent food fishes and organisms, different fishing gear and techniques, baits, and habitat types of the fringing

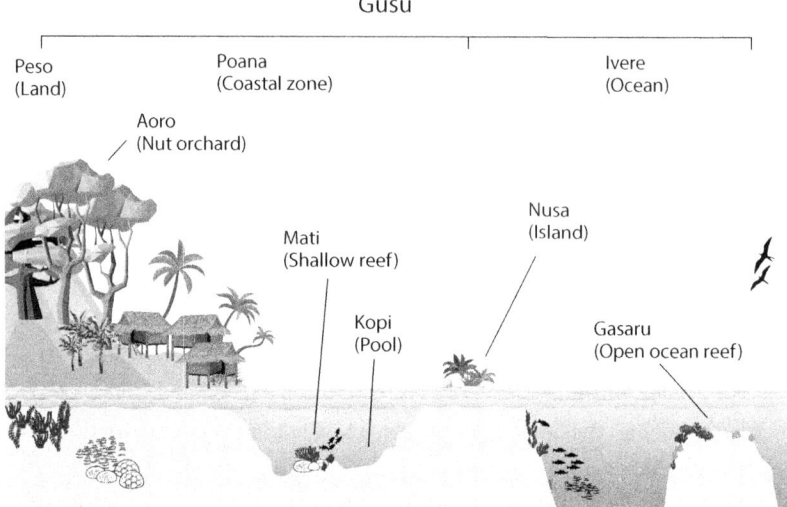

Figure 6. Schematic of a gusu (land/sea district) with major habitats.

reef and inner lagoons. As they grow older, young girls will focus their efforts on handline fishing the inner lagoon habitats and gleaning the intertidal zones of the barrier islands and fringing reefs.

One index of the skilled marine-focused practices on Simbo is the rich linguistic repertoire employed by adults to describe the various marine habitats around the island, all of which are contained within a gusu, which I gloss as "place" (see figure 6).[2] My consultants identified thirteen marine habitat types—*gasaru* (open ocean reef), *mati* (fringing and lagoon reef), *taqelese* (reef drop-off), *bobole* (coral rubble), *koquna* (bay), *ngangagasa* (sand flat), *evevu* (sea grass), *nusa* (island), *kopi* (pool inside reef), *lamana* (deep sea), *pepetu* (mangrove), *kobosona* (reef pass), and *kekelena* (point)—as well as dozens of major fishing grounds.[3] Most adults can easily name thirty to forty fish species, while those who are recognized as highly competent fishers, usually men, can identify double that. Within the lagoon the most common fishing method employed by women and men is *ipipa* (bait and hook), in which a hook is attached to lightweight monofilament line, usually coiled around a stick, and tossed out into the water. Free-dive spearfishing (*subu*) is also practiced within the lagoon and on the outer reefs (gasaru), but it is rare due to the stigma associated with the method.[4] It is thought that spearfishing spooks the fish from biting the baits of line fishers. Netting (*vaqara*) is also practiced inside the lagoon with large nylon nets, but the high cost of nets limits many households from engaging in this activity.

To assess fishing practices, I recruited thirteen fishers from different parts of the island to participate in a yearlong study in which they documented their catch. The group documented 492 fishing outings on which they caught 8,272 fish weighing 7,800 kilograms. This dataset showed that on average, protected lagoon habitats are fished most, but in terms of yield outer reef drops and open ocean reefs are most important. The most caught fish were *bebera* (striped surgeonfish, *Acanthurus lineatus*) and *podala* (big-eye bream, *Monotaxis grandoculis*), while the pelagic fish *babalu* (rainbow runner, *Elagatis bipinnulata*), *isu* (skipjack tuna, *Katsuwonus pelamis*), and *tangiri* (Spanish mackerel, *Scomberomorus commerson*) were the top fish caught by weight. Simbo lacks extensive shallow lagoon reef ecosystems like those in Marovo and Roviana Lagoons, where fishing in the protected waters of the lagoon provides a large proportion of the households' seafood needs.[5] On Simbo most fishers must also venture beyond the lagoon into unprotected, open water.

It is widely recognized that two submerged reefs south of the island are the most productive and cosmologically significant fishing grounds on Simbo. The first reef is 3 kilometers from the southern tip of Simbo and is called *gasaru rereki* (woman reef). The other, *gasaru marane* (man reef), is another 3 kilometers farther south. Both of these spectacular reefs are circular shaped, and their edges drop nearly vertically into deep water. They are an ideal habitat for a range of reef food fish species, including travelies (Carangidae), surgeonfish (Acanthuridae), snappers (Lutjanidae), and groupers (Serranidae). The biggest attraction, however, is the abundant pelagic species that frequently school along the edges of the reefs. All the major pelagic species are caught, including large schools of chevron barracuda (*Sphyraena qenie*), skipjack tuna (*Katsuwonus pelamis*), yellowfin tuna (*Thunnus albacares*), albacore tuna (*Thunnus alalunga*), and mahi mahi (*Coryphaena hippurus*). The reefs are also notorious for sharks, especially oceanic sharks such as oceanic white tips (*Carcharhinus longimanus*) and bronze whalers (*Carcharhinus brachyurus*). Sharks present a constant nuisance, as they attack fish that are being hauled in, in many cases cutting the fishing line and taking the tackle, bait, and fish all at once. Trolling (*karumae*) is a popular technique employed around these deep-water reefs, especially for those few who own or have access to outboard motors.

One of the more popular fishing techniques for pelagic fish on these outer reefs is pazu patu. This method involves attaching a baited hook (usually flying fish [*Exocoetidae*]) to a palm-sized stone by wrapping it with a narrow strip of palm frond and then tying it off with a special knot that can be pulled loose. I have watched many times as fishers from Nusa Simbo negotiate the passage to open ocean in canoes weighed down heavily by rocks with their gunwales precariously just clearing the water. After paddling over an hour to reach the outer reefs, the fishers first assess the direction of the current. They usually position themselves 50 meters or so from the reef on the up-current side where water flows toward the reef and draws phytoplankton from deep water that attracts small bait fish. The stone and baited hook are then dropped into deep water and let sink to a depth where fish are thought to be located. When the baited hook has reached the desired depth, the fishing line is given a sharp upward yank that releases the stone from the knot, leaving the baited hook to float in the water column.

Fishers also described several new techniques that have been adopted during their lifetimes. One is an adaptation of pazu patu called *kura*. Unlike pazu patu, in which the baited hook is taken to depth by the stone so that it floats in the water column, in kura fishing the stone is dropped to depth and released so that the line can be hauled in steadily, pulling the baited hook upward toward the surface in a form of vertical trolling.

Safely fishing these outer reefs in dugout canoes is precarious and requires a keen sensitivity and familiarity with currents, winds, and swells, all of which can suddenly shift direction or strength, making the return trip to Simbo treacherous. The nearer reef is shallow enough that during large swells waves break across it, causing a major hazard for fishers. For safety, fishers almost always travel in groups of three to four and carry sails, usually constructed by sewing together old rice sacks, to aid their paddling. Unless the ocean is utterly placid, which is rare, fishing in groups poses challenges because if the canoes spread apart too much, they can easily lose sight of each other behind the rolling ocean swells. Raising the sail in

Figure 7. A Simbo man fishing the important reefs known as gasaru marane (man reef) and gasaru rereki (woman reef), which jut up from the deep ocean several kilometers off the southern shore of Simbo. Note in the background the distinct profile of Simbo's two hills. This unique profile and the island's exposed position on the southwestern edge of the New Georgia Group enabled European explorers and whalers to easily identify the island. (Photo by author.)

a canoe significantly increases its visibility and is done for that purpose if fishers become separated. During my numerous fishing trips to these outer reefs in the relative safety of an outboard motor–powered boat I have been astonished to find a group of two or three fishers in their seemingly minuscule canoes disappearing from sight in the troughs of open ocean swells.

The agility, strength, and stamina required to sit inside a canoe and paddle in open ocean for six or seven hours are simply astounding (see figure 7). With only a small water bottle, a few coils of fishing line, a paddle, a few extra hooks, a knife, a stick to club fish, and a packet of crackers,

Simbo fishers are a stark contrast to the high-tech wizardry of recreational fishers in the United States and elsewhere. I have attempted to follow fishers in my own dugout canoe, and even though I am quite physically fit I could not endure squatting inside the canoe for more than twenty minutes without my legs falling asleep, not to mention the brutal tropical sun. When I followed fishers in an outboard boat I learned that turning off the motor and floating with them was a fundamentally different sensorial experience than when the engine was rumbling. The feel and sounds of the ocean in addition to sight are critical to successful fishing and navigating.

As noted previously, to reach the deep-water reefs fishers from the village of Nusa Simbo on the southern half of the island must navigate a treacherous passage that connects the narrow lagoon to open ocean. There is a narrow channel on the west side of the passage where canoes can paddle through without being clobbered by breaking waves. Fishers must carefully time the sets so as not to meet a wave that closes out the entire passage. On the return, fishers will typically surf their canoes back through the passage to the calm water of the lagoon. In heavy seas the passage becomes a froth of breaking waves and currents, inhibiting any movement in or out. In that case fishers must make the lengthy paddle around to Narovo Bay, leave their canoes, and walk back to Nusa Simbo. Despite these challenges, fishing is highly productive on Simbo, and seafood is always available, a condition that some have described as "subsistence affluence."[6]

NOTICING

In addition to the intimate familiarity Simboans have with the waters and marine habitats of their island, one of the more pertinent questions germane to the tsunami response is the extent to which Simboans detect different kinds of changes to their local marine environments. This was one of the key research questions of earlier work my colleagues and I carried out in Roviana Lagoon.[7] When attempting to assess environmental change, however, we run into the sticky problem of validation and the relationship between Western scientific knowledge and IEK. As discussed in chapter 1, much IEK research implicitly or explicitly privileges scientific knowledge production as the "baseline" against which IEK is compared and validated.

Indeed, this was the primary method by which pioneering IEK researchers such as Robert Johannes drew attention to marine Indigenous knowledge and were able to convince Western scientists that it was a valid body of knowledge.[8]

I conducted a number of studies to explore the overlap between the IEK of Roviana fishers about changes to their local environment and changes detectable through marine science methods. We conducted three different studies, one of which assessed changes to the lagoon benthos caused by the 2007 tsunami. Our research group had conducted marine benthos surveys in several different areas of the lagoon in 2006, prior to the tsunami, as part of a marine resource management initiative.[9] The impact of the earthquake and tsunami on the western end of the Roviana region, an area known as Vonavona Lagoon, was significant since the mouth of the lagoon faced the epicenter of the earthquake. Protected by the barrier islands, no villagers died in Vonavona, although it was a life-changing event that has had lasting impacts, including extensive coastal flooding, changes to the local ecology, and major property damage, not to mention much human suffering and psychological distress.

Our Roviana consultants described how the lagoon water first receded from the shoreline then returned as several 1-meter-high pulses or waves, impacting coastal areas. The tsunami waves swept into the lagoon, flooding many areas and causing violent currents and major movements of rubbish- and silt-laden water. A long, narrow island called Rokama, near the entrance of the lagoon, was permanently cut in half by the tsunami. The landmass containing the lagoon sank 0.51 meter, which left many low-lying areas permanently flooded.[10] The coastal areas of Parara Island suffered much saltwater intrusion, killing large swaths of mangrove.

After the tsunami, in July 2008 and in May 2010 our research group conducted follow-up dive surveys in the same sampling locations as in 2006 to document any benthic changes. The 253-hectare study area was an inner lagoon reef system that extends off the southeastern edge of Repi Island. We repeated the same sampling procedure for the three marine surveys. This involved selecting underwater site locations by creating a grid using GIS software that generated points every 60 meters, for a total of 982 sampling points across the study area. Using the GPS receiver, I and two trained, local research divers navigated by boat to each predetermined

Figure 8. Participatory mapping workshop in Kinamara village, Vonavona Lagoon, in which villagers were asked to draw on an aerial photograph of their lagoon the benthic habitats that had changed due to the 2007 tsunami. (Photo by author.)

field point location and documented the underwater habitats. At each site we lowered a 1-mx 1-PVC frame onto the seabed and recorded the dominant substrate and dominant benthic habitat categories within the sample unit. The three surveys provided assessment of the benthos prior to and twice after the tsunami that we could then compare to villagers' knowledge of any changes.

To document local knowledge, we employed a participatory image-interpretation technique (see figure 8) we had developed to map habitats across the entire lagoon area.[11] For the Vonavona study we asked a group of ten fishers, both men and women, from three villages adjacent to the study area to visually assess an enlarged aerial photo of the reef system. Specifically, we asked our consultants to identify the biotic and abiotic marine substrates and draw boundaries around them directly on the laminated, enlarged photos. The same group of fishers from each village were chosen to carry out the exercise before the tsunami and two times afterward.

Through these methods we found that these Roviana fishers detected similar changes to the benthos as those we had documented through the marine science surveys. There was good agreement in detecting a major increase in sand and silt and a decline in seagrass following the tsunami in 2008. Then when comparing the results of 2008 with 2010, fishers' assessments and marine science surveys were in high agreement that seagrass increased and sand and silt declined as the benthos recovered from the effects of the tsunami. From this we concluded that fishers appear to be quite sensitive to the abrupt shifts in local marine habitats.

In one way or another these research findings all suggest that Roviana villagers, and we can assume Simbo villagers, too, monitor and detect the changes—slow, incremental, and rapid—in similar ways as marine science. Our studies make a strong case that Roviana villagers, and by extension the people of Simbo, are actively tuned into their surrounding marine environments and detect environmental changes. Can we, however, conclude from these studies that an intimate understanding of a local environment led to Simbo's successful tsunami response?

There are some indications from the 2004 Indian Ocean tsunami that in-depth environmental knowledge may not be enough. In an interview with several Moken people who were at sea during the tsunami, for example, they described how they escaped to safer, deeper water before the tsunami hit. But other Burmese fishers who were near them did not flee and were killed. "'How come they knew something was wrong, and the Burmese fishermen did not?' Simon asked the Moken man. 'They weren't Burmese businessmen; they were fishermen. They should know the sea, too.' 'They were collecting squid, they were not looking at anything. They saw nothing, they looked at nothing. They don't know how to look,' said the Moken man. 'Suddenly, everything rose up, their boats were thrown up in the air. The violence was unbelievable.'"[12]

Another notable case is the Gilbertese villagers and their response in Titiana, mentioned in chapter 1. Many Gilbertese failed to flee the tsunami, and Titiana children were seen walking out onto the reefs to collect stranded reef fish just before the waves took their lives. Yet the Gilbertese are known throughout the western Solomons as expert fishers and a people who depend more than Melanesians on the sea for their livelihood. Indeed, if you visit the Gizo market, the stalls of fresh fish are dominated by Gilbertese selling everything from herbivorous surgeonfish taken by speargun, to small, netted parrotfish, to huge yellowfin tuna trolled far offshore around government-installed fish-aggregating devices. The Gilbertese are also known as expert navigators and boat captains, and they travel far from their villages on Ghizo Island to fish the waters of the surrounding islands. Occasionally they are even reported by the Simbo people to the Gizo authorities for spearfishing and trolling Simbo's reefs without permission.

ANTICIPATING

For both Burmese fishers and the Gilbertese, in-depth ocean knowledge alone failed to generate the response we witnessed in Simbo. Sensing the strange movements of the ocean was a vital element of the Simbo response, but Simboans also interpreted those strange movements as a sign of danger. What were the other ingredients that produced this interpretation? As a starting point, I followed the lead of my Roviana friend who was living in Titiana during the tsunami disaster and suggested that he and other Melanesians had mulongo, or what he and others described as the capacity or sense to anticipate or sense future events.

When I began to inquire systematically about mulongo I learned that the same term is found in several languages on the surrounding islands, including Marovo, Roviana, and Zabana (language of the far western tip of Santa Isabel). In the first edition of J. H. L. Waterhouse's Roviana dictionary it is defined as "an omen, as the cry of *kuarape* (*nycticorax caledonicus* or night heron) and other birds."[13] The expanded 1949 edition of the dictionary added the verb form *va mulongia* (in Simbo *va mulongo*), "have a presentiment, perceive, expect." As I inquired about mulongo on Simbo, references to birds and other animals were a common theme. It was expressed to me that animals in addition to humans have the capacity to va mulongo occurrences.

The Simbo language is semantically rich when describing the conceptual field involving "sensing." For example, the Simbo word *vagigilai* describes the feeling one has when a person senses that another person is looking at them from behind. The root of vagigilai is *gila*, which my interlocutors glossed in English as "mark," "sign," "indication." Another related word, *ukukana*, was mentioned in my interviews; it is the word to describe fleeing to the safety of a bush cave before enemies approach. As I describe in more detail in chapter 3, Simboans engaged in interisland headhunting prior to the arrival of Europeans and were constantly on the lookout for attacking enemies. As it was told to me, warriors could mulongo enemies as they approached and would ukukana (flee to the safety of caves) before the attack. Here Simboans associated mulongo with not just a capacity to sense but a capacity to sense *something dangerous*. Some tsunami survivors suggested that this practice to flee enemies indirectly informed the response to flee the incoming tsunami waves.

Here it is appropriate to note a unanimous observation of my interlocutors: no animals died from the Simbo tsunami. Survivors noted that not one dog, cat, pig, or chicken perished, and that these animals fled to safe ground before the earthquake, a phenomenon widely reported during earthquakes and tsunamis.[14] Many people described the restless behavior of the island's animals before the earthquake as a gila or sign that something was not right even though most did not recognize it at the time. One of my collaborators described it this way:

> At Tapurai just an hour before the tsunami struck dogs, birds, and roosters all made their own sounds which is unusual that they do so all at the same time. Not everybody realized that this was a sign or *vinagigila* that gave some sense that something was happening.

In another case, a large pig owned by the chief in Masuru burst through its wooden seaside pen and fled to the hills. The chief was surprised by the pig's behavior and the effort needed to escape its pen, and he did not realize until after the earthquake that the pig was sensing (va mulongo) its arrival. Rather sheepishly the chief admitted that he did not va mulongo the pig's behavior but only later heeded the warnings of his kin to flee after the earthquake. Another dramatic example of a pig sensing the tsunami occurred in Tapurai. A sow was corralled with her half-dozen small piglets in the middle of the village, but she and all her piglets escaped from the pen and fled to high ground before the wave struck.

Animals of all sorts express their mulongo through odd or unusual calls, movements, or other out of the ordinary behaviors. Birds will call out at odd times, and other animals, such as sharks, crocodiles, or butterflies, will act strangely. Here is how one man from Lengana described his experience of mulongo:

> I was about nine years old at the time and I remember it well. It was a windy day and I was sitting in the patio of my grandma and grandpa's house with some other kin. Then a butterfly appeared and flew towards my grandma and circled her head. It was odd because it was so windy that normally butterflies aren't flying about so much. Then my Grandma asked the butterfly "Eehhh, what do you want, did something not right happen?" The butterfly then flew away. It soon returned and circled her head again. The butterfly wanted my grandma to follow it. So she followed it down the path and it took her to Harold's house in Bulolo [a village 0.5 kilometer away]. Just as she arrived to his house, she heard her kin cry out. Her brother had just passed away.

Examples involving the death of kin were a common theme. Children also va mulongo. One experience recounted to me by Grinta, my research collaborator who grew up in Kia on Santa Isabel, involved the death of her uncle. She had traveled to her uncle's house in Honiara in anticipation of his death. He was elderly and had been suffering from cancer. It was late at night, and many of the adults were seated on the floor around their dying uncle, who was lying prone on a mat in front of them. The young children were in another room sleeping. Without any apparent reason or prompting from the adults, the children unexpectedly woke up and entered the room of the dying uncle. Just after the children entered, the man sighed his last breath and died. Grinta explained that everyone attributed the children's behavior to mulongo. The children had anticipated their uncles' death and entered the room to be in his presence when he passed.

Although mulongo tended to be associated with dangerous or untoward events like death, that was not always the case. For example, nonhumans may signal to humans a positive future occurrence such as the surprise arrival of close kin who have been away from the island for many months. Food was also mentioned as a domain in which mulongo operates. If, for example, someone makes an unexpected visit to a friend or relative, and that person is preparing the visitor's favorite meal, the coincidence would be interpreted as a case in which the visitor had "anticipated" the meal.

Importantly, mulongo was described as a skill that is variable among both humans and nonhumans. Some people, like the grandmother described earlier, were known to be more sensitive to animal signs and better adept at interpreting them, while others were completely inept. I could not obtain a detailed description of why the skill was variable among people other than that some "have it in their blood" and others do not.

INTERRELATINGS

As we have seen, the Simbo concept of mulongo suggests that nonhumans have capacities for action and communication similar to those of humans. Rather than emphasizing and presupposing that nonhumans lack traits that distinguish them from humans (e.g., consciousness, free will, sociality, intentionality), the Simbo people presuppose interspecific interrelatings.[15] They have closeness to or "being-with" certain nonhuman "companion species."[16] As just mentioned, Simboans conceive of insects and other nonhumans, especially animals and birds, as having the capacity to perceive future events and the ability to communicate with humans. Moreover, larger animals such as sharks, crocodiles, and common food fishes are treated as sentient beings that smell, listen, and respond to humans and understand human language.

Male fishers who target large pelagic fish such as skipjack tuna, trevally, kingfish, yellowfin tuna, and rainbow runner talk or shout out to their prey while fishing. Usually this takes the form of insults and "talking down," as they might do to another man whose aggression they want to arouse. Rather than placating the fish in a mode of mutually beneficial and reciprocal exchange, as is practiced when ancestor spirits are addressed at shrines, a fisher's intention is to arouse the fish's greed and provoke it into asocial behavior. The insults follow a particular discursive pattern in which the fisher sarcastically questions if the fish has any deformities such as missing teeth or injured eyes.[17] The fisher's language is linked to notions of respect (*pinamanga*), where direct references to the head and face of elders, high-status individuals, or between opposite-sex siblings (*lulunu*) is considered deeply insulting and vulgar. To avoid direct descriptions, an idiom of euphemisms or "respect phrases" (*vateungu*) is employed to describe human body parts. Turns of phrase such as "front of face" would be used to refer to the mouth, "sight" (*dodoma*) would be used to refer to the eyes, or "stones" for the teeth. A chief might be asked, "How is your sight?" rather than "How are your eyes?" Today these discursive strategies have waned considerably, and although touching the head of another person of high status remains a social impropriety, euphemisms now reflect Western conceptions of the body, in which anatomy associated with sex is described indirectly.

When I asked how the fish could hear their insults, I was told they had the capacity to "listen" or "sense" the fisher speaking to them. This human-nonhuman mode of communication is a manifestation of the pre-Christian cosmology, in which spirits associated with food fishes and garden crops were propitiated at specific shrines (*tabuna*). In the past *iso* (skipjack tuna, *Katsuwonus pelamis*) in particular were of such great importance that ritual and technical effort focused on them was exceeded only by head-hunting and canoe making. A. M. Hocart's remark that "bonito [tuna] fishing is constantly mentioned in the tales, and is a common topic of conversation, and the sight of seabirds hovering over a shoal always creates excitement and shouts all-round the bay" is as accurate today as it was in 1908 during his visit.[18]

For my male Simbo interlocutors, tuna fishing continues to be one of the most exciting activities. I regularly fish with my Simboan friends and have gained the same sense of thrill and excitement when venturing offshore in search of a tuna school. During pre-Christian times tuna fishing (*valusa*) was distinguished from regular fishing (*ababa*). Although tuna continue to be regularly fished in the waters around Simbo, they no longer valusa, since that term refers to a specific fishing technique and ritual practices. Most Simbo fishers can still describe the technical details of valusa, but knowledge of its ritualistic aspects is almost nonexistent.

Contemporary Simbo fishers catch tuna by trolling homemade lures or bait behind dugout canoes (mola). A single fisher paddles his own canoe, and if the distant reefs to the south of the island are targeted, groups of canoes will travel and fish together. The fisher's gear typically includes several sticks or plastic spools with nylon line wrapped around them, lures or hooks, a stout club to kill the fish, and a knife. They use their bare hands to haul in the line and land the fish. The lure or baited hook is dragged along the surface 5 meters or so behind the canoe while the fisher paddles vigorously to maintain a trolling speed. He usually secures the line by wrapping it a few times around his foot, and it is with his foot that he sets the hook when a fish strikes. He then, with astonishing agility, grabs the line and hauls it in as quickly as possible to evade sharks, who are a constant nuisance and frequently cut a fisher's line.

In the past, valusa fishing involved a crew of at least three men who paddled planked-constructed canoes (*geto*), the same high-prow vessels that carried warriors on headhunting raids. Instead of handlining, sections of thin bamboo were used as fishing poles. Lines made from a fibrous vine were attached to the bamboo poles and baited with a lure (*gaile*) whose body was constructed from clam shell and its hook from hawksbill tortoiseshell. If a school was sighted the fishers would rush toward it, turn the canoe around so that the stern faced the rising fish, and toss the short line into the feeding school. As one fisher held the pole another would use a special bamboo bailer to throw water out over the school, which helps camouflage the lure.

Prior to Christianity, tuna was the only species of animal that had shrines, called *inaru*, built specifically for their propitiation. Other shrines were dedicated to harvests and reef fishing, but these sites of propitiation were not indexed to any specific plant or fish species. The tuna shrines, like the harvest and fishing shrines, were similar in appearance to ancestor shrines and built from heaps of stones adorned with upright stela, but they lacked the skull repositories. Tuna shrines were almost always located on the coast, and chiefs and other prominent men in each of Simbo's four districts owned and maintained their own shrines. Although the owner of the shrine had individualized recitations or activities that they would perform prior to a tuna fishing outing, the intent was always the same: to ensure a bountiful catch by channeling the efficaciousness of the tuna spirit that inhabited the shrine. Typically, the owner visited the shrine the day before a fishing outing to manipulate its stones and make verbal requests that the spirit accompany the fishers. Upon returning from the fishing outing, one of the fish would be brought to the shrine and burned along with canarium nut puddings (*iamu*) to feed the shrine's spirit. A young boy who wished to begin tuna fishing had to pay shell money to the owner of a shrine and was required to provide some of his catch to the owner so that it could be burned as an offering at the inaru.

What is notable about the inaru spirit beings is their parallels with the ancestor beings propitiated at ancestor shrines. Like human spirit beings, these nonhuman spirit beings had to be continually maintained through specific practices so as to harness their cosmic vitality that was necessary for life to continue. In other words, tuna spirit beings were assigned similar qualities and capacities as human spirit beings, an indication that humans and nonhumans were of similar ontological status.

More explicit equivalences between human and tuna were drawn when Hocart asked about the consequences of omitting offerings at inaru. He was told: "The tuna would not bite: 'he savvy all same man (*he knows like a man*).'"[19] One quality of this "knows like a man" is a tuna's capacity to listen and understand human language. Like contemporary Simbo fishers, tuna were addressed verbally to encourage the fish to bite. Each inaru shrine had a specific fishing call (*vavagita*) associated with it, and a fisher who was initiated at that shrine learned the call from the shrine's owner and would shout it out when the first tuna struck the lure.

It is unclear from Hocart's texts if these pre-Christian fishing calls were analogous with the contemporary Simbo idiom of "insulting the fish," but the parallels between pre-Christian vavagita and contemporary pelagic fishing practices are notable.

Interestingly, these modes of communication are not applied to lagoon fish, now or in the past. My interlocutors told me it was not necessary nor efficacious to insult reef fish. Prior to Christianity, however, there were shrines dedicated to lagoon fishing where, like the inaru, burnt offerings from the catch were made to the shrine's spirit beings. According to Hocart's interlocutors, several of these lagoon fishing shrines were inhabited by a being known as *kesoko*. Contemporary Simbo people still are aware of this being and describe it as an amalgam of fish, human, and sea bird, although the arcane knowledge to channel its efficaciousness was lost during Christianization.

Although tuna appears to be the only fish that has the ability to hear and understand human beings, all fish can smell people. Today and in the past, there is a particular odor called *bosi* that fish abhor. Some people, usually men who have an aversion for women, carry this smell on their bodies, causing them to fail at fishing. There are treatments, however, that usually involve cleansing the person of this rank odor by wiping their body with certain leaves or plants such as *qoli*, a sweet-smelling liana that grows near the shoreline.

Not only are tuna capable of hearing and understanding human language; they also are thought to have emotions. Fish are frequently described as being scared or angry. When a fish is landed it is treated gently and killed swiftly without outward signs of jubilation. In the past there appear to have been specific practices focused on calming the fish after they were caught. Hocart described a case in which a fisher attempted to "feed' a fish he accidently dropped into the bottom of the canoe while landing it by rubbing a piece of betel nut, a luxury and highly prized food item, inside the fish's mouth and telling it, "Eat, thou bonito, be not angry."[20] This was done to placate the fish's anger. Hocart was told angering a fresh caught fish would cause the other fish in the school to stop biting.

Birds also played a critical role, technically and cosmologically, in tuna fishing. When schools of tuna fish begin feeding, they force the baitfish to the surface, where birds such as *elekai* (black-napped terns, *Sterna sumatrana*) and, when the fish are larger, *belama* or frigate birds (*Fregata minor*), dive into the water to pick them off. Thus, birds are an indicator of the presence of a tuna school and fishers today, as in the past, scan the horizon in search of diving birds. Sometimes birds will travel high above the water following a school, and fishers will use them as guides to navigate. In pre-Christian Simbo, fishers spoke to birds with the intent of bringing the fish to the surface so that the fishers could catch the tuna and the birds could feast on the baitfish. In my experience, contemporary fishers no longer verbally engage with birds to enhance their catch, but knowledge of their behavior remains critical to successful tuna fishing.

Ocean birds are also known to give signals in times of stress. In one spectacular example that was talked about on Simbo, a heavily loaded boat, in the blustery *peja* season from January through March, was attempting to make the crossing from Ghizo to the west coast of Ranongga. The long dugout canoe had a tiny fifteen-horsepower motor and was heavily loaded with approximately twenty-five people, including a small baby under one year old. As is typical of this season, a storm formed quickly, creating intense wind and rain, and in this case the boat capsized in the seething, tightly bunched swells. Struggling in the water, the group lost hold of the dugout canoe and were treading water in the open ocean. Through the roaring wind and rain a man heard the unusual cry of a white tern, which, the story goes, was a sign that something was floating in the water nearby. Responding to the call, the man swam in the direction of the sound and found a floating log. He shouted to the rest of the group, and they all were able to drape their arms over the log or partially sit on top of it and ride out the storm. This was late in the evening, however, and the group had to float in the open ocean all night until the next morning when a search party located them. They were wet and hungry, but alive. Miraculously, the small baby survived by being placed inside a plastic bucket and held securely on top of the log.

NOT-ALWAYS-PLEASANT NONHUMANS

Relations between humans and nonhumans, however, are not always amicable. The most feared and dangerous nonhumans are sharks (*bagea*) and crocodiles (*eoro*); they figured prominently in pre-European Simbo cosmology and continue to be the foci of much discursive and material attention today. Many different species of sharks inhabit the waters around Simbo, but it is the large oceanic species such as bronze whalers and oceanic white tips that garner the most attention due to their aggressiveness. Saltwater crocodiles (*Crocodylus porosus*) also inhabit the lagoons, especially the brackish lake (Kosiri) at the base of Ove and the mangrove areas of Riquru. Reaching 8 meters in length and swift swimmers, these aggressive creatures are by far the most feared animals on Simbo.

Contemporary Simbo people identify sharks as the totemic species of Ove, while Karivara is associated with the crocodile. Surprisingly, Hocart's interlocutors only mentioned the crocodile briefly as the "sacred animal of Karivara," and they were prohibited from eating it, but there are no further details about their interactions with these beings.[21] Today the people of Simbo avoid eating crocodile and shark not for explicit cosmological reasons but because the meat of these creatures is deemed "sour" and unpleasant. The other two districts, Narovo and Nusa Simbo, have ancestral relations with the sea eel (*Muraenidae*) and the osprey (*Pandion haliaetus*) respectively.

My Simbo interlocutors described how these nonhuman beings were hewn from the same ancestral essence as human ancestors. Each district on

Simbo has a distinct creation story wherein the ancestors, human and non-human, of the district emerged from specific locales in the landscape. These totemic beings were referred to as *tamasa* (gods) but also tomate (spirit) or in Pijin as a kastom shark, eel, and the like. "Kastom" is a common Solomon Island Pijin term that might be glossed as "traditional" but more specifically refers to an idealized reconstruction of past events, genealogies, or other aspects of the pre-Christian cosmology deemed important. I was told that prior to the arrival of Europeans, these tomate would guide war canoes during headhunting expeditions or give warnings if enemies approached. If intruders were detected, the totem would arrive at the seaside and call out to the men to prepare for battle and encourage the others to take shelter in the district's fortress (*bara*). Requests were also made to the totems to travel to other districts of Simbo or other islands to kill enemies or eat the catch and damage the fishing gear while the enemies fished.

It is appropriate to mention that the Simbo people's relationship with these beings is distinct from Australian totemism, in which in many cases each totemic group of humans and nonhumans were thought to share physical and moral characteristics.[22] Among the Nungar of southwest Australia, for example, a moiety is called "the watcher," which is not only the name of a crow (*Corvus coronoides*) but also a term that denotes similar behavior of the birds and the humans.

On Simbo, the people from a specific district are not thought to share specific behavioral or moral attributes of the totem species, but rather share an ancestral essence with the species that enables, but does not guarantee, a special and mutually beneficial relationship. People would build relationships with a particular individual totem animal rather than the species in general. For this reason, each of the totems was designated by a specific place-name. Ove's shark's place was Kelamamasa, a passage between Patui and the main island; Karivara's crocodile was of *pa pesi*, a section of coastline inside the lagoon; Narovo's eel *pa koqu* was from the bay of Narovo; and Nusa Simbo's osprey was from Kololuka, a place-name for a prominent set of rocks near the south coast of Nusa Simbo island. The specific individual beings were fed human foods and could be summoned by their caretakers, usually a chief or high-status member of the district. Just like tuna, certain sea birds, and ancestor spirit beings, these totem beings could understand human speech and provide signs that were interpretable by their caretakers.

Figure 9. Eel painted on the inside of a paile (hall) built by members of the Narovo clan (*bubutu*) in Masuru village. The eel is the clan's totem. (Photo by author.)

Today on Simbo these special human-animal relationships are no longer maintained. My elder consultants estimated that the last knowledgeable ones who had learned the specialized knowledge to interrelate with these beings passed away in the 1940s and 1950s.[23] Today, the totem animals of each district continue to figure prominently on the *paile* (hall) walls that have been constructed in response to the government's request to formalize traditional leadership and are celebrated and displayed with pride as evidence of Simbo's rich heritage (see figure 9).

Even though Simboans lack the incantations, charms, and capacity to speak with and understand the responses of sharks and crocodiles, there are known experts in the region. Indeed, just such a "kastom man" was recruited from Choiseul to kill several troublesome crocodiles around the island that arrived after the tsunami. One outcome of the tsunami and earthquake was a notable spike in the crocodile population on Simbo. According to several accounts, crocodiles were seen swimming across the channel from Ranongga toward Simbo for several months after the 2007 tsunami. The local theory was that the Ranongga crocodiles had lost their habitats when the coastline lifted several meters during the earthquake. According to geologists who measured the uplift, the southern half of Ranongga rose nearly 3 meters, raising large sections of the coastline and coral reef out of the water.[24] In search of new habitat, the crocodiles crossed the channel and made their homes in Simbo's lagoons and estuaries. This resulted in an increase in crocodile incidents. In most cases, the reptiles would just encroach on canoes, showing little fear of people. Lethal crocodile attacks are thought to only occur when the slain person or their family committed a hidden wrongdoing, such as engaging in an incestuous relationship or adultery. Indeed, the causes of most untoward deaths are explained by Simboans in this manner.

In 2009 there was a near-death incident involving a crocodile that spurred community action. Qetson, one of the most experienced and highly regarded fishers from Meqe, was night-diving behind the barrier reef on the west side of the island when a crocodile he estimated to be 4 meters long bit his forearm just as he was lifting a lobster out of the water to place it in his dugout canoe. This same crocodile had been identified as one of the new arrivals and was seen prowling near several fishers on previous occasions. Qetson described in gory detail how he heard his arm crack "like a stick" when the animal clamped down its powerful jaws on his arm. It then pulled him underwater and started rolling. This method of drowning its prey is well-known crocodile behavior among Simboans, and Qetson knew that if he could hold his breath long enough the crocodile would eventually tire and would surface to take a breath. In an astonishing physical and mental feat, Qetson was able to hold his breath as the animal furiously rotated its body underwater with his arm in its massive jaws. He described that he was giving up hope but then he felt the speed of the crocodile's spinning slow. He recognized that the reptile was tiring and would soon surface for air. Just as predicted, the crocodile stopped spinning, surfaced, and opened its mouth just enough for Qetson to pull his arm from the beast's jaws and climb into his canoe. He learned later that his forearm suffered multiple fractures and he was eventually flown to Honiara for surgery. When Qetson finished his mesmerizing story, he held up his arm and knocked it with the knuckles of his other hand and stated to me with a glint in his eyes: "It's practically all steel now!"

This near-death incident occurred in one of the most important and popular fishing areas on the west side of the island, where villagers from Lengana, Masuru, and Meqe frequently harvest seafood. Fearing more attacks, local leaders sought out a kastom man from Choiseul, renowned for his power to interact and communicate with sharks. My Simbo consultants described how the man had a highly tuned sense (mulongo) to smell crocodiles from any distance. To hunt down the crocodiles he was taken to known crocodile locales such as Ove lake and the Riquru estuary, and he quietly paddled his canoe while sniffing the air. When he detected an animal, he would paddle toward its location, speaking gently to calm it. He used only a large spear as his weapon, and it required that he approach the crocodile within just a meter or two. Once within range he thrust the spear powerfully just behind the head where there is known to be a soft spot that is penetrable. Using this technique he killed four animals on Simbo. When I asked why the kastom man was needed, my interlocutors responded that not only would someone without the proper skill have difficulty locating the elusive animals, but other, more docile crocodiles on the island would become enraged and start attacking people.

Although Simbo lacks specialists like the man from Choiseul who have the skills and knowledge needed to maintain amicable relations with crocodiles and sharks, Simboans are still capable of reading the signs these beings present to humans when danger threatens. A common theme found in stories about fishing is that sharks, when they behave strangely or are overly aggressive, warn fishers to be cautious. Fishers will recount these experiences with a mixture of awe, bravado, and respect:

> One day a group of us encountered a school of balubalu (rainbow runner) who were vigorously feeding. We were sitting still in our canoes kura fishing (vertical trolling) and a rainbow runner jumped over my canoe's bow. Right behind, a shark jumped after it. It jumped clear over my canoe! I was scared. That does not happen often, it was a sign of danger. I coiled my line and paddled to a different location.

I had a similar experience in 2005 when I was fishing with Jimi, a Roviana man and close friend, near the island of Tobatuni off the coast of Roviana Lagoon. We were trolling for tuna and rainbow runner in my 20-foot fiberglass boat. Offshore handline fishing for pelagic species is thrilling, fast paced, and hectic. The schools move rapidly, requiring full-throttle pursuit across the bouncing waves. Once in a school, the boat is slowed to a trolling speed of a few knots; each fisher then throws their line into the water, and the driver steers the boat around the school with the intention to drag the lures in front of the moving school. The day I was fishing with Jimi, the fish were striking our lures almost immediately. Within fifteen minutes we had a dozen fish in our canoe, the freshly caught ones still flapping their bodies around in the bow where we threw them after removing the hook. The boat's gunwales sit just six inches above the waterline, so if the sea is rough and the wind is blowing, as it was on this day, you invariably get soaked. As we excitedly caught fish after fish, I was stunned when a 10-foot shark, probably a bronze whaler, dashed just below the surface in an attempt to swallow the fish I was lifting up and into the boat. It missed the fish but was just inches below me in the water. Noticing the shark's behavior, Jimi stated bluntly: "We're leaving." Without hesitating he pulled in his line and waited for me to do the same. Although we could almost certainly have caught more fish, he was resolute that we needed to stop fishing and leave. Several hours later as we enjoyed our meal of balubalu, I inquired about the incident, and Jimi said that that the shark was telling us to leave and that if we continued fishing something awful would have transpired.

When sharks or crocodiles show aggressive behavior, people will occasionally address them verbally, requesting that they leave fishers alone. In many cases fishers will also employ verbal requests prophylactically to avoid shark attacks. In one memorable case, again in Roviana Lagoon, my wife and I went to surf the passage near Baraulu. We had asked one of my close interlocutors to take us in a canoe to the passage where he would drop us in the water and then he would fish as we surfed. As we jumped in the water with our boards my wife commented that she was apprehensive and frightened by the sharks (sharks are abundant in the passages). The Roviana man responded, "You don't need to worry, I'll ask the sharks to leave you in peace." He then spoke to the sharks briefly, asking their permission for us to surf the passage. When he finished he turned to us and said, "It's safe now."

ORIGINS AND SHRINES

These relationships with marine animals are enmeshed with and complemented by many ocean-focused kastom stories and myths detailing the origins of the seascape itself. Similar to land areas discussed in chapters 3 and 4, submerged physical features around the island are imbued with names and histories. Prominent marine features on Simbo such as the barrier island on the west coast, the rocky pinnacle (Patuai) near Ove volcano, and especially the two open ocean reefs to the south of the island have widely known origin stories. Indeed, I was told the following kastom story about these two reefs just as a group of us prepared our lines to go fish them during my first visit to Simbo in 2008:

> A God-woman (tomasa) called the old woman of Matidingi (*goele pa* Matidingi) had two children: a girl (rereko) and a boy (marane). The goele had the power to change into a lizard (*rako*). One day the woman left the village and her two children cried. She had turned into a lizard. The two children went down from Matidingi to Nguzuna point at the southern tip of Simbo to find their mother. The girl dove into the water and swam looking for her. When she ran out of breath and had to come up for air, she had transformed into a reef we call girl reef (gasaru rereko). Then the boy jumped in and he went farther than his sister. When he was tired, he came up and became a boy reef (gasaru marane).

In addition to these histories and stories, there are a number of ocean-focused shrines that are still thought to be imbued with metaphysical power. One prominent example is a shrine called *patu bou* or "rogue wave stone," located up from the lagoon in Karivara. It consists of four upright stones leaning outward, each a meter in length and set in a square pattern. When they are manipulated they have the power to influence waves that break in the southern passage of Nusa Simbo's lagoon. In pre-Christian times the shrine was used to bring large waves and render the passage impassable by invading headhunters. Today several elders of Karivara are the shrine's owners, and they will visit it during extended periods of rough seas and move the stones in a particular manner to calm the ocean so that fishers can reach the open ocean or make trips to Gizo. I was also told of a case in which some mischievous boys pulled the stones from the shrine and carried them down to the seashore of the lagoon. This caused rough seas for many days. When the owners of the shrine discovered that the stones had been removed from the shrine, they brought them back, and the seas calmed down.

LOCAL KNOWLEDGE RECONSIDERED

Inspired by those tsunami survivors who discussed their response in terms of "ocean knowing," we started this chapter with an exploration of how Simboans become familiar with the many entities that inhabit the coastal waters. Yet their familiarity with and complex grasp of their ocean is only a partial explanation for their successful response. Other communities in the region such as the Gilbertese, who live on the nearby island of Ghizo, have vast experience fishing and boating the local waters, but they tragically did not respond like many on Simbo did. The Gilbertese did not sense the impending danger. In fact, Gilbertese were seen collecting fish that had been stranded on the reefs in front of their village as the ocean pulled back just before the tsunami. A Roviana man who was living in the Gilbertese village of Titiana when the tsunami struck was the first person to mention to me the concept of mulongo and how he had sensed the impending danger and fled before the wave struck the village.

But we must not lose sight of the fact that mulongo was one interpretation among several that Simbo survivors employed to make sense of their response to the disaster. There was no single IEK-grounded response, but rather a mélange of different responses. Oral history as well as nonlocal sources of tsunami knowledge and improvisation were all mentioned. To register this heterogeneity and multiply the possibilities for exploring concepts like mulongo and IEK more generally, it may be more productive to envision the knowledge underpinning the disaster response as a *situated practice*. A number of scholars have forwarded concepts around practice, such as situated strategies, "metis," performative knowledge, "motley" knowledge, and situated learning, all of which seek to expand our capacity to register knowledge-making conditions.[25]

Mulongo, in particular, helped me identify a prominent dimension of conventional understandings of IEK, its "cognitive" commitment. As a number of scholars have pointed out, modernist conceptions of knowledge assume that learning processes are "contained in the mind of the learner," separated from the lived-in world.[26] Instead, mulongo pointed to what I and other scholars have described as a "practice-oriented" view of knowledge that stresses the emergent, relational, embodied, and contextual dimensions of knowledge that are "constituted by a past, but changing, history of practices."[27] While cognitive models suggest that knowledge consists of intellectual processes (i.e., cognitive schema) that are necessary preliminaries to guide action, the practice perspective acknowledges the possibility of cognitive knowledge but also opens space for registering modes of action and being that may not become codified, intergenerational transmitted myths or oral history or remain unrecognized by Western science.

Portraying IEK as situated practices also implies a particular spatiality to knowledge production and presumes that knowledges are produced somewhere—in a canoe on a lagoon or in a scientific lab—and hence "local" since they are generated in practical activities and everyday experiences.[28] Practice theorists make clear that their vision of knowledge as embodied, situational knowing is not some sort of *pensee sauvage* found only in small-scale societies. Rather, it is an alternative approach to all forms of knowledge making that is as relevant in contemporary industrialized society as in any other. Jean Lave's work among grocery shoppers, for example, has shown how the differences between classroom arithmetic tasks and parallel problems carried out when people are shopping for groceries are incorrectly contrasted as different modes of thought.[29] From a practice perspective all knowledges are local and contextualized. Thus, the notion that arithmetic knowledge and scientific knowledge are exemplars of rational mental activity is considered a manifestation of modernist assumptions rather than of distinct, universally identifiable modes of thought.[30] If anything, this challenges scientism, which presumes that rational, scientific thought has privileged access to the world and is purified of subjectivities, values, or commitments.

A practice approach assumes the stance that scientific knowledge should also be treated as a form of practice wherein the practitioner and hence the knowledge produced are not free from the peculiarities of place, time, ongoing activity, and multiple interpretations. This resonates with science and technology studies scholars, who have long abandoned the separation of science from the world.[31] An important implication of treating both scientific and Indigenous local knowledge as emerging from situated practices is that it places all forms of knowing and knowledge making on an equal playing field. This shifts the analysis from attempting to discern if a mode of thought is more rational than the other, to describing the instruments, concepts, humans, discourses, and nonhumans that are associated and mobilized.[32]

The strength of the conventional IEK concept is derived from its capacity to circulate in and contribute to the enormous network of institutions, universities, labs, and interest groups involved in scientific and bureaucratic enterprises. But in so doing this enormous and powerful assemblage only accepts entities and concepts that have enabled its spectacular growth and durability. Spirit beings, human-animal communication, kastom sharks, ancestral power, rogue wave stones, and other components discussed by Simboans as possible elements contributing to their response to the tsunami are granted room, but only on limited terms. These aspects of the response are either cherished as cultural curiosities by those who romanticize Indigenous ways of being or rejected as cultural gobbledygook by ardent realists.

Rather than universal science on the one hand and localized Indigenous knowledge on the other, these first two chapters have attempted to follow the concepts, conditions, and entities that enabled the existence and production of Simboan local knowledge. Conceptualizing knowledge as a product of situated practices enables a comparison not by using the measures of one to assess the other or by assuming one is universal and the other is parochial, but by unearthing the various elements involved in their composition, which in some dimensions might intersect but in others might diverge.

A question remains, however: Why was there so little intergenerationally transmitted knowledge about tsunamis? It was a surprise to me and to experts and laypersons alike that the inhabitants of an island with a three-thousand- if not thirty-thousand-year history of habitation did not have the knowledge about past tsunamis. Simbo is a region of high seismic activity, yet the myths and other forms of knowledge described elsewhere were lacking on Simbo. Why was that the case? To begin to investigate this question, we have to expand our inquiry beyond the tsunami and the immediate response to a longer temporal horizon and explore the fascinating history of Simbo.

3   Ancestors, Steel, and Inland Living

My first glimpse of Tapurai, the village of fifty households wiped clean by the 2007 tsunami, was from a small outboard powered fiba (fiberglass boat) during a preliminary visit to Simbo in June 2008. I spent just over a week during this first visit to establish relations with the local leadership and ask permission to return a year later to conduct research on the impact of the tsunami. Having already carried out a number of research projects in Roviana Lagoon, I was accompanied by Tomi, a close associate from Roviana who was from Simbo and had married a Roviana woman. As part of my visit I intended to survey the Tapurai site and visit a few of the Tapurai families now living in the relocated village. I was told that walking from Nusa Simbo to Tapurai would take several hours, half of which was on a rough, muddy trail. Encouraged by Tomi and Jimi, who did not want to make the long walk, we instead boated around the island to Tapurai with several community leaders as our guides.

As the old Tapurai village site came into view from the boat, I was struck by the idyllic setting. A ribbon of white sand beach contrasted pleasantly with a verdant green background, belying the horrific scene that had occurred just a year earlier. Directly behind the beach was a flat plain, now partly overgrown with low brush. Behind the nearly flat coastal area, approximately 80 meters from the beach, the hillside jutted up steeply, and in some areas there appeared to be abandoned, overgrown garden areas. A few coconut palms peeked through the larger trees that forested the rest of the hillsides. On a small rise, nestled up next to the hill was the only structure still standing, a white structure with a small porch, a corrugated tin roof, and large openings where wood louvers would normally be hung. It was the now abandoned United Church, which had served as a safe refuge for fleeing villagers because it was perched just high enough to avoid the deadly waves.

Along the beach stood a number of huge *buni* trees (*Calophyllum inophyllum*) that cast their cool shadows over the sand. A few of them had fallen after the tsunami and were dead, lying perpendicular to the beach with their leafless crowns reaching out and touching the ocean, their trunks suspended a meter or so above the sand. The tangled jumble of the trees' massive root systems splayed out symmetrically. These fallen trees were the only obvious reminders that powerful waves had swept through the former village.

A colorful fringing reef named locally as three segments—Nobata, Tapurai, and Toi—graced the crystal-clear waters in front of the site. The bottom profile declined gradually before dropping off steeply into deep water. The shallow water provided an ideal depth for large *Porites* corals. A single canoe was anchored here, and next to it a diver's head could be seen bobbing along on the surface. With a kick of his fins he disappeared under the surface. As we navigated through the coral heads to the beach, Tapurai's vulnerability to a tsunami was obvious to me. Except for the narrow fringing reef, it lacked any protection from the open ocean.

But as I would learn in my discussions with Tapurai's survivors, there had never been a hint of fear that the site was vulnerable. In fact, many lauded the beachside site as an excellent locale for a village. For starters, its location on the northern tip of the island meant that it was a shorter and less expensive boat trip to Gizo, the provincial capital and center of commerce in the region. Moreover, many former residents of the village commented that the village's immediate access to the seaside facilitated loading or unloading cargo. For an island now engaged in the cash economy and somewhat dependent on extra-local goods and services, coastal access is critical. The main drawback of the site, I was told, was its lack of a protected harbor. During peja, a season usually from January through March, strong northwestern winds battered Tapurai, making boat landings challenging. But the notion that the unsheltered beach site would ever be susceptible to huge waves was almost nonexistent on Simbo. Except for a handful of people who had read or heard about tsunamis inflicting other parts of the world, huge tsunami waves had been completely unknown to the Simbo people. As we learned in chapter 1, I was told repeatedly that the tsunami was novel and beyond the horizon of their knowledge. On an island that has been inhabited for thousands of years, why did the Simbo people lack substantial intergenerationally transmitted knowledge such as myths or stories about large waves after earthquakes? Moreover, why establish villages on sites vulnerable to tsunamis?

It is the task of this chapter to elucidate the historical processes that prefigured the tsunami catastrophe and led not only to the lack of intergenerational knowledge but also to the settlement history. Indeed, unearthing the history of socio-environmental relations prior to a disaster was one of the critical breaks from earlier hazards research that focused analytical attention narrowly on the "extreme event" and the response.[1] Disaster anthropology has taught us that a tsunami or other biophysical perturbation is not the starting point of calamity; it is somewhere in the middle of a long trajectory that precedes the triggering event and continues many years and decades afterward.

Anthony Oliver-Smith's observation that the 1970 Peruvian earthquake, one of the most destructive disasters in the Western Hemisphere, was an "event which in certain respects began almost hundred years ago" has many parallels to Simbo.[2] We will learn in this chapter how toward the end of the nineteenth century Simbo's settlement patterns underwent radical change when the island was drawn into the global economic system and colonized by the British. Prior to that time Simbo's inhabitants lived up from the immediate coastline either on ridges, steep hillsides, or even the mountaintops inside the volcanic craters. Both local narratives and oral history about the recent advent of coastal villages corroborate the writings of European chroniclers, anthropologists, and archaeologists who described a widespread shift in residence patterns that occurred in much of the western Solomons. Harold Scheffler, for example, indicated that until about 1905 the inhabitants of Choiseul (northwest Solomons) "dwelled inland, dispersed in small hamlets on the numerous ridges."[3] He considered this the "traditional" settlement pattern of the western Solomons.

In addition to illuminating the processes that drew the Simbo people to vulnerable coastal sites, this chapter also explores why a society that depends on the ocean for subsistence would dwell so far from the coast. In so doing, it is necessary to address one of the core issues that lies at the center of the processes of displacement and recovery that occurred in the wake of the tsunami: *place*. On Simbo, and across much of Island Melanesia, places are experienced in ways that confound modernist assumptions about the relations between humans and the nonhuman world.[4] And as we will see in this chapter, the identity, movements, and effects of these entities that inhabited the island and participated in composing the Simbo world prior to the onslaught of colonialism were central in motivating their inland mode of living. Moreover, the shifts in place that occurred with European contact, colonization, conversion to Christianity, and growing entanglements with global capitalism have traceable effects on the recovery and relocation processes.

Of course, describing Simbo's past invariably involves reconstruction. Although many elders and even younger people on Simbo are familiar with what they refer to as their kastom, their idealized reconstruction of Simbo pre-Christian customs or traditions, most Simbo people have only a faint understanding about outsider accounts of their island's history, even though the island has a one of the richest historic records in the western Solomons. Simbo was one of the first islands to have sustained contact with Europeans, and there are numerous ships' logs, traders' accounts, and colonial reports describing island life during the contact period.

The Simbo people have the most familiarity with the work of two British anthropologists who visited the island in 1908, A. M. Hocart and W. H. R. Rivers.[5] Rivers and Hocart resided nearly four months on Simbo, documenting with meticulous detail many aspects of life and interactions with local people, which Hocart published in a series of articles and nearly one thousand pages of unpublished field notes and manuscripts.[6] Their work stands out as an early example of modern ethnographic fieldwork, and through their accounts, we gain a unique view of Simbo's past practices and cosmology in the early twentieth century, before the arrival of

Christian missionaries. Today, local people tend to remember "Hoka," the local vernacular term for Hocart, for the genealogies he recorded, information that serves as evidence for adjudicating contemporary land disputes and composing place on Simbo.

VENERATING ANCESTORS, GENERATING LIFE

As I began to discuss Simbo's history and the reasons their ancestors lived away from the coast, one of Simbo's more flamboyant elders responded with a memorable yet graphic gesture to illustrate headhunting: he flattened his hand into an imaginary knife blade, made a chopping motion to his neck, kinked his head to the side, and stuck his pink, betel-nut-stained tongue out of the corner of his mouth. For people who typically move and gesture with a deep gentleness and soft, supple grace, the violence of the gesture has stuck with me. For the Simbo people, headhunting continues to be both fascinating and horrifying. Most people today have only a faint understanding of headhunting practices; thus, I was quickly directed to elders, usually chiefs (*bangara*), whose grandparents had told them stories of pre-Christian life. These interviews inevitably led to broader discussions about the cosmology of the pre-Christian world, of which headhunting was just one expression.

As it was described to me, headhunting was instigated by chiefs who competed among each other or sometimes collaborated to mount raids (*kana*) and acquire enemy heads.[7] Enemy skulls, especially those of enemy chiefs, were the primary marker of a Simbo chief's political status and military might. Skulls were also needed to inaugurate new chiefs and new war canoes (geto) or canoe houses (paile) and to free the widows of chiefs from social confinement. More broadly, the skulls indexed chiefly *mana*, a widely known concept found across Oceania that describes a state of being powerful or efficacious.[8] To fully grasp the logic of headhunting, however, we must first describe the central characteristics of the pre-Christian Simbo world and especially its key social practice: ancestor veneration.

In the Simbo pre-Christian world ancestors, spirits, animals, plants, landscapes, seascapes, and human beings were not assigned to different orders of reality where living human beings stood apart from the physical,

Figure 10. Remnants of ancestor skulls on an old shrine in Narovo district. In 1908 A. M. Hocart described this site as one of the finest collections of skull houses on Simbo. His interlocutors referred to it as Pa Na Ghundu. Today only a few partial skulls remain. (Photo by author.)

biological, and spiritual; rather they were entwined, codependent, and on an equal ontological footing. To sustain this human and nonhuman collective, all the worldly activities important to humans, such as food production, fishing, warfare, and protection from disease and dangerous animals, were predicated on the living being able to elicit and channel the mana of potent human ancestor spirit beings known as tomate. Tomate were the lived efficacy of a person distilled into a nonmaterial agency, and their potency was proportional to an individual's worldly achievements. It is important to note that the Simbo language does not distinguish between a deceased ancestor and what we would define as "spirit" or "spirit being"; both are encompassed by the term "tomate." This elision is critical, for it indicates that at death, a person's worldly mana did not cease to exist but rather could continue to influence the world.

The dwelling place of beneficent tomate were skull repositories (tabuna) (see figures 10 and 11). These shrines dotted the landscape and contained

Figure 11. An old crumbling ancestor shrine in Karivara district. The spaces around shrines are imbued with ancestral mana (power); when approached, the ancestors are verbally addressed and asked for permission to visit the site. (Photo by author.)

the skulls and important worldly possessions of the deceased and served as the focal points of ancestor veneration activities. Although they varied in size and design, they usually were circular platforms built from coral rubble a few meters wide and a meter or so high. On top was an open-fronted, lean-to style stone structure with walls and roof built from stone slabs. The skulls and other items would be placed inside, visible from the front. High-status individuals were built more elaborate repositories, sometimes of thatch and wood, on stilts, and by the turn of the twentieth century, topped with corrugated metal roofing.[9] Other shrines were much larger than this, sometimes 10 meters in width, and had a more elaborate architecture of faced stone slabs, tightly spaced and placed on edge.

Shrines of men and especially male chiefs would include their warrior paraphernalia such as stone or metal axe heads, spear points, and after European contact, firearms.[10] These important worldly possessions were not just inert objects to wage war but agents themselves, which when wielded effectively participated in a warrior's mana. Before being placed in the shrine the shell valuables or other items were broken into pieces, denying others the possibility of benefiting from their efficaciousness and ensuring the repository would encapsulate the residual efficacy of the dead. Rather than passive reminders of wealth or inert human bones, the valuables and skulls were visible and present indices of the ancestor's power. In this sense, the skull repositories were unlike burial sites in the modern Western world where people go to worship symbolic tokens and evoke memories of ancestors; instead, they were vital spaces where the living would engage in ontologically necessary activities to sustain life. A key propitiation activity that took place at the shrines was the feeding of offerings to the tomate. Special starch puddings, pork meat, or fish were burned in a hearth located at the base of the shrine. The burning converted the foodstuffs into a form, smoke, that was consumable by the tomate.

Upon the death of a person, however, their tomate did not automatically come to reside in a skull shrine. It was the business of that person's living kin to safely guide the tomate to their new place of dwelling so that relations with the ancestor could occur. A living person was constituted through a tomate, a soul-shadow (*malaunga*), and their body (*tinina*). Death was thought to release the tomate, but unless it was guided to a shrine it would be disoriented and placeless, free to roam the world untethered, aimlessly killing or causing sickness among the living. Guiding the tomate to their skull shrine was achieved through a funerary practice known as the "Days of the Dead" (*lodu*). This ritual began at death when the person's soul-shadow and spirit would exit the body via the mouth and perch in the roof ridge of the deceased person's dwelling. The corpse was then dressed in finery, including arm rings, tapa, beads, and sweet-smelling leaves; carried into the bush; placed upright; and left to rot facing west, the direction of Sonto Island, which was thought to be the home of souls. After depositing the corpse in the forest, a ceremony took place at which the soul of the dead was called from its hiding place in the rafters and caught in a special shell ring (*ovala*). After four days, the skull of the deceased was twisted off the rotted corpse, cleaned in salt water, and left to bleach in the sun for several weeks. Then, on the eighteenth day, the skull and the soul-containing ring were placed in the skull house along with the deceased's important worldly possessions. Finally, on the thirty-sixth day, ceremonies were held inviting the ghosts from Sonto to carry away the deceased soul to the afterworld, leaving behind the tomate, safely housed and confined to the skull house where it could be propitiated. These funerary rights underscore how there was a mutual dependence between the living and the dead—the living needed their ancestors' ancestral endowment to sustain the world, while the dead depended on the living to reach the afterworld and not be condemned to an amoral and asocial existence terrorizing their living kin.

MADEGUGUSU

Critical to our understanding of headhunting and ancestor worship are Simbo notions of "place." According to local narratives, Simbo has, since time immemorial, existed as four autochthonous yet interdependent land/sea units or districts known as gusu, with the names Karivara, Ove, Simbo, and Narovo (see map 3). In fact, the name employed today and in the past by the Simbo people when referring to their island is Madegugusu, literally "four places." These districts are demarcated by prominent points, mountains, and in the case of the Simbo gusu, the small island and its surrounding reefs constitute the district.

This primordial partitioning of the island is evidenced most clearly by the fact that there is not a common mythological history describing the origin of its inhabitants, nor is there a creation story of the entire world. Instead, leaders of cognately organized descent groups (bubutu), or what I gloss as "clans" from each gusu, recount specific mythological narratives that chronicle the genesis of the human and nonhuman ancestral beings to which today's descendants owe their specific existence. The narratives have a similar form, known as a toponymy, in that they describe how ancestral beings arose from holes or rocks near the highest point in the gusu and through time began to progressively spread down from the mountainsides across the territory, creating gardens, entombing their dead, planting nut trees, and building ancestor shrines. In this way the territories were given form and character, and at the same time the truly human ancestors fused their group's agency into the terrain. These spatially explicit narratives are found in similar form across the Austronesian world, and the knowledge of the places, people, and other beings involved

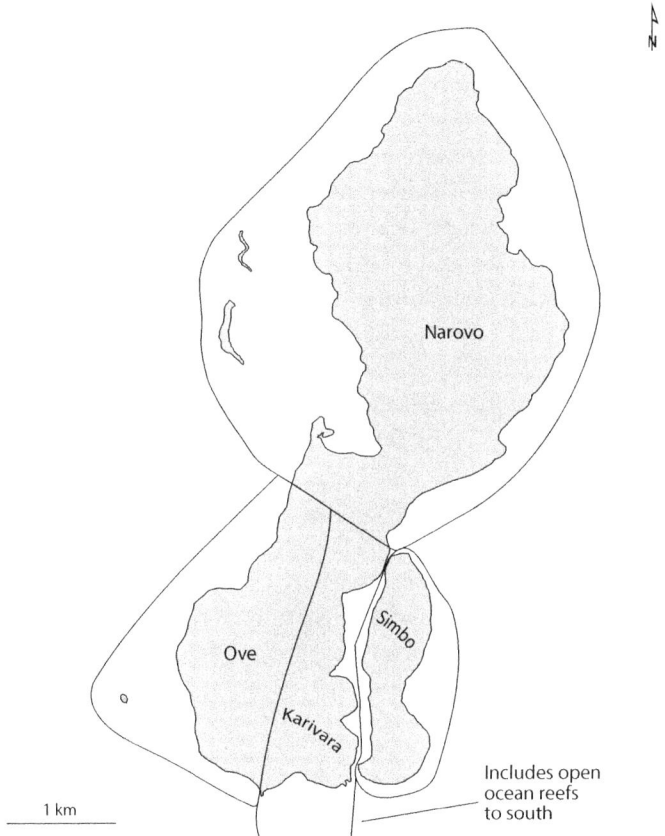

Map 3. The boundaries of Simbo's four gusu (districts). Simboans call
their island Madegugusu, or "four districts."

in these movements through space form the basis of each group's claim to
authority to manage and access resources within the districts.[11]

Each district formed a unique collective with a distinct identity that
was maintained and reproduced through their own specific practices to
propitiate their ancestors; their own district-specific accents; their unique
healing, fishing, and garden rituals; and their special relationship with a
specific totem animal. Marriages were regulated by leaders and endogamy
was preferred, although intradistrict marriage was also present. Indeed,

the districts did not exist in isolation from one another, and there was frequent exchange of objects, magical charms, and healing practices. At times relations between districts would sour, resulting in violent conflicts. Hocart, for example, described how a war almost broke out between Simbo and Narovo when a man from the former district was killed by someone from the latter.[12] These interdistrict conflicts appear not to have involved the taking of heads. That was reserved for extra-island raids. District strife was characterized by Hocart as motivated by revenge, usually precipitated by adultery or murder rather than the taking of heads.

The Simbo world I am describing aligns with Michael Scott's notion of "poly-ontology," whereby the original state of the world was a plurality of distinct nature-culture collectives.[13] In contrast to modernist dualistic thinking that objectivizes the discontinuity between contingent cultural or supernatural phenomena (e.g., politics, cosmologies, identities, languages, rituals, spirit beings) and universally natural phenomena (e.g., animals, land, fish, rocks, trees) on the other, on Simbo humans and nonhumans were experienced as having both a shared yet unique materiality and subjectivity hewn from and brought into existence by the original ancestral human and nonhuman beings of each district.

INLAND HOMELANDS

This brings us back to headhunting and the critical necessity to live inland and avoid being killed and beheaded by enemies. If the head of one's own kin was taken away, it denied the living the ability to induce their own ancestors' tomate to participate in making worldly activities efficacious. Without a skull to place in a shrine the most potent material index of the deceased person's mana would be lacking and the containment of their tomate would be uncertain. Without a safe dwelling place the tomate would roam freely, and possibly wreak havoc by causing death, illness, and misfortune. Sometimes substitute heads were made from stone or wood and placed in shrines in attempts to propitiate the tomate, but these were rarely as effective.[14] Thus, the threat of attack and the loss of a kin's head undermined a community's ability to sustain the relationships with the ancestors upon which all life depended.

Considering these factors, the occupation of inaccessible inland areas or high, coastal sites was a critical strategy of self-defense. Living up from the coastline in defensible locales obviously would have decreased Simbo's vulnerability to attack. In addition, there was an important material benefit connected with successful warfare other than the demonstration of mana mentioned earlier: demographic enrichment through the taking of captives.[15] During raids it was common to take enemies captive rather than kill them, and this was especially the case for children and youth. In fact, captives were the preferred choice for the important position of priest (*iama*). Priests were responsible for building and consecrating new skull houses for chiefs and carrying out their mortuary practices, such as cleaning skulls and disposing of bodies.[16] These activities were considered to be particularly risky, and foreign captives were thought to be less susceptible to these malign forces that could cause illness or death. In addition to priests, captives served as lieutenants (*bagu*), or in the case of women, female servants (*ukuka bangara*). Although foreign born, captives could marry, earn wealth, and even inherit land. Children and prepubescent youth were also frequently captured to be brought back and adopted or, on occasion, sacrificed prior to headhunting expeditions. Simbo, like most preindustrial populations, most certainly had high infant mortality and relatively low population growth rates, thus the importation of people to boost the local labor pool was probably significant. Indeed, the importance of captives on Simbo is evidenced today by the fact that descendants of one of the major landholding lineages trace their genealogy back to captives taken from Santa Isabel.[17]

Despite these possible benefits associated with warfare, living inland obviously involved enormous trade-offs. Fear of attack would have attenuated fishing activities, and living hundreds of meters above the coast on steep slopes would have increased workloads significantly. Several of my consultants also noted the threat landslides posed to these hillside settlements. In fact, a near vertical section on the north flank of Patu Kio mountain gave way during the 2007 earthquake, covering old habitation sites on the slope.

Another critical vulnerability created by inland living is the potential dulling of intergenerationally transmitted knowledge that could accumulate about past tsunami events. Inland settlements, insofar as they are safely above the vulnerable coasts, would not have experienced the trauma and destruction that is generally thought to be necessary for the emergence of myths or other codified oral history.[18] It is important to note that there is some debate among archaeologists about the antiquity of headhunting in the western Solomons, although the balance of evidence suggests that it may have arisen in the sixteenth and seventeenth centuries. Archaeological work conducted on New Georgia shows that a shift in shrine architecture occurred sometime in the sixteenth and seventeenth centuries that was concurrent with political consolidation in the region.[19] These pre-sixteenth-century shrines are found inland and have been documented on New Georgia, Rendova, and Tetepare. They consist of raised platforms faced with basalt slabs. Importantly, they lack human crania, shell valuables, and hearths, an indication that these shrines may have predated the emergence of headhunting.

Although inland living may have emerged as a settlement pattern less than five hundred years ago on Simbo, the fact that the Simbo language lacks a word for tsunami suggests that large destructive waves were rare.[20] Indeed, geologists estimate that destructive tsunamis are quite rare in the region, occurring roughly every five hundred years.[21] In Hocart's 1908 accounts he employed the word "tsunami" in a reference to an important God or mythical figure (tamasa) called Momara, who lived underground and caused earthquakes.[22] According to Hocart's interlocutor, when Momara traveled, his departure from Simbo was said to create a large wave accompanied by a roaring sound. Hocart did state, however, that knowledge of Momara was not widespread and that there was disagreement about the stories associated with the tomate. As I discussed in chapter 1, during my interviews with tsunami survivors many indicated that earthquakes sometimes produced waves, but that the size and force of the 2007 tsunami was unexpected. Moreover, in no case did someone provide a myth or other narrative told to them about waves associated with earthquakes. Like much of the pre-Christian cosmology, the stories of Momara's deeds have been lost in the mists of time.

Compared to tsunamis, knowledge about earthquakes is widespread. Not only is there a specific word in Simbo, "nunu," for earthquakes, there are specific strategies employed when an earthquake strikes, the most common of which is to sit still during the quake so as not to lose balance and risk falling. Children are warned about getting a <u>round head</u> (dizzy) during earthquakes and are instructed to sit quietly as the ground shakes. Moreover, many Simboans associate the cause of earthquakes and volcanic eruptions with a well-known tomate called Ratovo.

STRANGER DANGER?

The headhunting and warfare I have described might suggest that the pre-Christian Simbo world was dominated by enmity and hostility, but this is only half the story. Amicability among both districts and other islands was central to Simbo's existence. For example, in order to mount large raids against distant islands, the four districts on Simbo would frequently join forces. This intradistrict cooperation highlights the permeability of the gusu. Rather than an immutable collective, practices and material items were exchanged and borrowed, and eventually amalgamated into the landscape of the respective district. Gusu were composites of local and extralocal relations and entities were imbued into the landscape over time.

Amicable relations were not restricted to districts on Simbo but extended to the surrounding islands. Indeed, ethnohistoric and archaeological accounts indicate that Simbo was enmeshed in a network of trade in which objects, people, and practices from across the New Georgia Group and beyond were exchanged.[23] Hocart described numerous magical charms, myths, building practices, and even skull house designs that were adopted from other islands such as Vella Lavella, Kolombangara (known as Nduke in Simbo), and Choiseul (known as Lauru in Simbo).

As among Oceanic peoples more generally, a diversity of practices was valued and cultivated through translocal relationships and "engaging with strangers."[24] Clearly not an inward-looking society, Simbo was dynamic and openly receptive to some foreign social practices and innovative artifacts and technologies. The ocean surrounding Simbo was certainly a protective barrier against attacks, but was also a conduit to reach other islands, learn new ideas, and adopt or purchase efficacious practices. As eloquently noted by Tongan anthropologist Epeli Hau'Ofa, Oceania is a "sea of islands" rather than "islands in a far sea."[25]

For this reason, it might not have been that shocking for people of Simbo to peer out across the horizon sometime in the eighteenth century and see a European sailing ship. Statements recorded by A. M. Hocart suggest that during Simboans' initial interactions with Europeans they had little trouble incorporating these new arrivals into their world. Although wary, Simboans were quick to grasp the significance of iron and the benefits of building relationships with the people who could provide it. That Europeans arrived on ships is still evident today in the local vernacular. Any white person who visits Simbo will inevitably be identified as *tionivaka* (*tinoni* [person] *vaka* [sailing ship]), or "ship people."

Although European ships probably passed through the area earlier, the first unambiguous description of Simbo by Europeans was made by John Shortland in 1788. Shortland stumbled upon the western Solomons while en route from Port Jackson (Sydney) to Great Britain.[26] He set sail under the command of four ships, but just four days into the voyage they battled inclement weather and the *Alexander*, which Shortland captained, and another, the *Friendship*, lost contact with the other two. Off course and lost, the two ships sighted the Russell Islands and later a larger island Shortland named "New Georgia." Then, on August 5, Shortland noted in his logs two "remarkable hills," which he called the Two Brothers. These were Simbo's two southern hills, Matidingi and Patu Kio, which have near equal elevation and distinct cone-shaped profiles.

The morning after sighting the Two Brothers, Shortland approached what he erroneously thought were the steep cliffs of a point jutting out from a large island. To the north and west of Simbo lie the larger and more imposing land masses of Ranongga, Vella Lavella, Kolombangara, New Georgia, and Rendova. When approached from the south, as Shortland did, these islands could appear as a single impenetrable landmass, and he did not attempt to navigate through them. As Shortland closed in on what he thought was a point, which he later named Cape Satisfaction, he and his sailors noted a shape just to the southwest that they thought was a ship under sail. Only after coming within just a few miles of Simbo did they discover that the ship was in fact an imposing rock pinnacle jutting up from the ocean. This rock, known to Simboans as Patuai, was named Eddystone after similarly shaped rocks off the southern coast of England. For the next 120 years Europeans referred to the entire island of Simbo by that name.

An entry in Shortland's logbook dated August 6, 1788, indicates that the people of Simbo were already aware of iron and were familiar enough with Europeans to offer needed trade goods such as citrus:

Canoes were seen with Indians in them, who came close up to the ship without any visible apprehension. Ropes were thrown to them over the stern, of which they took hold, and suffered the ship to tow them along; in this situation they willingly exchanged a kind of rings which they wore on their arms, small rings of bone, and beads of their own manufacture, for nails, beads, and other trifles, giving however a manifest preference to whatever was made of iron. Gimlets were most acceptable, but they were also pleased with nails, and pieces of iron hoops. . . . At the same time they appeared extremely desirous that our people should anchor on the coast, and go ashore with them; and, by way of enticement, held up the rind of an orange or lemon, the feathers of tame fowls, and other things, signifying that they might be procured on shore.[27]

After Shortland's brief encounter with Simbo, maps of the region became available to ships' captains and enabled more European vessels to pass through the area with confidence about their location.

Evidence from ships' logs and other written accounts show that Simbo, with its distinctive geographic position relative to the major islands of New Georgia, Rendova, and Kolombangara, was visited quite regularly in the early nineteenth century by vessels shipping cargo between Australia and China. Jackson found documentation indicating that at least seven trading vessels contacted Simbo's inhabitants.[28] Although the islands of New Georgia were increasingly gaining a reputation among Europeans as a region filled with bloodthirsty and ruthless headhunters, Simbo appears to have been seeking out and cultivating amicable relationships with the passing European vessels. Many of the documented interactions involved people from Simbo boarding ships to engage in trade. In some cases, ships' captains were intimidated by the arrival of daunting, high-prow, fifty-man war canoes (geto), and would fire at them to ward off what they thought was an attack.

TORTOISESHELL AND TOMAHAWKS

Early documented interactions foreshadowed the shifting interests of Europeans. In addition to trading for Simbo breadfruit and coconuts, European ships received from the Simbo people mother-of-pearl, spears, arrows and most significantly, sea turtle shell jewelry. Known as "tortoiseshell" by Europeans and *kapu* in Simbo, the shell of the hawksbill sea turtle (*Eretmochelys imbricata*) would become one of the most important trade items in the western Solomons.

The harvesting of sea turtles for their meat, eggs, and shells has been a practice in the Pacific for eons. Archaeological evidence from the region indicates that as islanders colonized the Pacific, the sea turtle was one of their main targets, with sea turtle remains dominating early middens and in some cases its abundance exceeding all other vertebrates.[29] Because of their large size, green sea turtles (*Chelonia mydas*) were and continue to be the species Simboans target. Hawksbill, although smaller, is also hunted for the keratinous scutes of its carapace, which is harder and more durable than that of the green sea turtle. Hawksbill shell is fashioned into rings and other jewelry. Occasionally you will see polished turtle shells hanging as adornments on the walls of Simbo houses.

The most common method to fish turtles is by spearing them in the front flipper, attaching a float to the line, and waiting for them to tire out. Turtles are commonly spearfished at night in shallow seagrass beds where they rest. When awakened they attempt to escape through the shallows toward deeper water, stirring up a trail of sparkling bioluminescence that aids pursuit. In general, turtles are rare on Simbo. The island's small reef and lagoon system and paucity of sandy beaches provide only limited habitat for turtle grazing or nesting. Turtles, like most sea beings discussed in chapter 2, such as sharks, crocodiles, eels, and fish, are not assigned a fundamentally different ontological status than humans, and Simboans relate to them as equals.[30]

European whalers and traders conceived of turtles in a fundamentally different manner: as objects to exploit and generate wealth. In Europe and Asia hawksbill shell has been fashioned into jewelry, ornamental pieces, and furniture inlays for several millennia. Early traders quickly realized that shell, prized by artisans for its decorative color pattern, workability, and pliable strength, could generate fat profits. Demand for the shell appears to have increased in the western Solomons in the 1820s. This was due primarily to the growing numbers of whalers, rather than just trading ships, who were plying the waters off the New Georgia Group. Whalers, in contrast to cruising naval explorers and cargo ships, resided for protracted periods and in some cases went ashore to trade for supplies or to seek out women. Violent conflict between whalers and locals was not uncommon across the New Georgia Group. On Simbo, however, relations appeared to be mostly amicable. In fact, it was one of the first islands where Europeans lived voluntarily. In 1839, a whaling captain reported in his log that a canoe approached his ship paddled by not just islanders but also a white castaway.[31]

Whalers, more than earlier vessels, carried significant amounts of hoop iron as well as tomahawks and were probably responsible for introducing most of the iron into the region. But it was the arrival of traders that propelled the demand for tortoiseshell. The shell of this turtle was much more profitable than any of the other trade items, and ships began plying the waters of New Georgia in search of it.

Indeed, it was tortoiseshell as well as bêche-de-mer that brought the British trader Andrew Cheyne to Simbo in 1844. He provided the most thorough description of the island during this period, and his account made abundantly clear that by the mid-nineteenth century the Simbo people and Europeans were deeply entangled.[32] Arriving aboard the trading ship *Naiad*, Captain Cheyne spent six weeks on Simbo. Upon his arrival he was greeted by canoes carrying three English castaways and two Simbo chiefs. The castaways had a good grasp of the Simbo language, suggesting they had spent a considerable amount of time among the Simbo people. Moreover, they did not request to be transported off the island, a sign that they were treated well.

Cheyne's boat was guided into a harbor on the east side of the island, which he described in glowing terms: "I discovered a snug little harbour on the N.W. side of the island, with a fine cove at the head of it, completely land-locked and secure from all winds, with sufficient water for a line of battle ships close to the shore, where a vessel could be moored to the trees, and lie as safe as in a dock."[33] This ideal access point became the epicenter of first European and later Chinese trading activity for the next century.

Intent on procuring bêche-de-mer and especially tortoiseshell, Cheyne was aghast to discover that islanders would no longer trade tortoiseshell for any item other than tomahawks (*manja*). The Simbo people readily traded bananas, coconuts, and other foodstuffs but not tortoiseshell. They had become astutely aware of its value to Europeans, and in response the Simbo people were seeking iron hatchet heads, an item that they considered of equal value and significance.

Unbeknownst to Cheyne, hatchets were beginning to be subsumed into existing Simbo categories of thought and action.[34] Rather than simply conferring material advantages in warfare and subsistence activities over stone and wood tools, as Hocart described, they were treated as entities with special properties:

> The so-called tomahawk is by the natives termed manja, like the aboriginal club it has displaced. It is made with Harrison's No. 2 iron blade set upon a handle 90 cm. long, with a section like that of a convex lens. It is broadest below the axe head, where it is curved with the convex side towards the blade. The extremity is pointed to be stuck in the earth, for the owner will never lay it down flat while he is squatting, but always keeps it planted head up, and when one of us used to lay his tomahawk down it was always set upright again. This is doubtless founded in caution, for it is sooner snatched into the right position; besides that, it is easier to keep in sight.[35]

As Hocart suggested, the efficacy of hatchets was derived from certain qualities that had to be attended and maintained through specific modes of treatment.[36] Similar to the spirits of people, dogs, other animals, and shell rings, hatchet spirits were thought to travel with a recently deceased person's spirit and reach the afterworld in Sonto, where Simbo souls resided. Hatchets, like shields, spears, and the clubs that hatchets replaced, also had a special relationship with their owner and were broken when a person died and placed beside them during funeral rituals.

Although it is striking how an object constructed from nonlocal material and produced by and bought from Europeans was seamlessly incorporated into Simbo cosmology, it is not that surprising. Hatchets displaced wooden war clubs, which along with other valuable items of war such as war shields were specialized trade items produced on other islands in the New Georgia Group. The Simbo people acquired these foreign items by exchanging two of their specialty items: canarium nuts and megapode eggs. Trading with Europeans and localizing them through specific practices was well within the scope of established praxis.[37]

Cheyne's account provided a glowing description of Simbo as a potentially lucrative European entrepôt in the New Georgia Group. He urged whalers and traders to seek pilots and interpreters on Simbo before venturing to other parts of the region.[38] This upbeat opinion of the island was due in part to one of the Simbo chiefs, Lobie, who was Cheyne's confidant and protector. Lobie stoked Cheyne's fears about other New Georgians, describing them as an untrustworthy and bloodthirsty lot who would attack any Europeans attempting to make contact and trade. McKinnon argued that Lobie exaggerated the treachery of New Georgians in an effort to establish monopolistic control over trade and enhance his power as a leader.[39] Indeed, by this time iron and especially hatchets were well known throughout the region, and surely some New Georgians would have been aware that it was more effective to trade with Europeans and acquire their iron rather than attack them. Thus, it is quite plausible that Lobie was creatively embellishing his descriptions of other New Georgians to solidify his position as an intermediary and monopolize control of European trade goods. Cheyne was convinced that the Simbo people would soon be demanding muskets and gunpowder rather than just iron and hatchets in return for their tortoiseshell.

From Cheyne's account we also are provided a window, although clearly colored by European assumptions about the region, into the scale of mid-nineteenth-century headhunting. Cheyne was taken to Nusa Simbo to visit a prominent chief who resided in that district, and he described a canoe house (paile) adorned on the inside with dozens of freshly prepared skulls, many of which had hatchet marks. He was told that the chief had led a headhunting expedition just a few days prior on which his men obtained ninety-three human heads, including women and children.

At the height of headhunting, toward the end of the nineteenth century, flotillas involving dozens of canoes paddled by hundreds of New Georgian warriors were raiding distant islands, a favorite being Santa Isabel. Santa Isabel is reached by passing through Manning Straits, an area that is home to what is known to be the largest hawksbill turtle rookery in the entire Pacific Ocean. The rookery is focused on the sand-fringed beaches of the Arnovan Islands, which lie halfway between Choiseul and Santa Isabel. These islands were used as stopovers during long-distance headhunting raids. Thus, Simbo headhunters would not only acquire enemy heads on Santa Isabel, they could also collect tortoiseshell, the key trading item sought by Europeans, enabling them to acquire ever more iron weapons.

Although there is debate about the inception of headhunting in the western Solomons, there is little doubt that it underwent a rapid increase in intensification during the eighteenth and nineteenth centuries as metal weapons entered the region, giving an advantage to some groups over others.[40] Cheyne's visit in 1844 seems to confirm that Simbo's half-century of active engagement with passing European ships had led to the island becoming the most cosmopolitan in the New Georgia Group and a ferocious protagonist in the regional headhunting complex. Simbo built alliances with Roviana, and together they rose to control the political economy of the western Solomons and were responsible for decimating many of the surrounding islands' populations, such as Tetepare and Ghizo, both of which were completely depopulated over the course of the eighteenth and nineteenth centuries.[41]

This period, however, would also turn out to be the zenith of Simbo power. Toward the latter half of the nineteenth century traders instead of whalers began to enter the region and copra rather than tortoiseshell emerged as the principal trade item. Without extensive land for coconut plantations, Simbo's ability to attract traders diminished, and the focus of European trade shifted to Roviana Lagoon.

EUROPEAN TRADERS, LAND, AND COPRA

During the latter half of the nineteenth century itinerant whalers who made short-term visits to the western Solomons began to be replaced by resident traders. Whaling was declining precipitously as Pacific whaling grounds were depleted and demand for whale oil was plummeting in Europe and America. Although castaways and deserters had been living on Simbo since the 1830s, permanent traders appear to have taken up residence on Simbo sometime in the 1890s.[42] By this time locally harvested marine resources such as tortoiseshell, mother-of-pearl, and bêche-de mer had been eclipsed by copra as the principal trade commodity. Coconut oil, the key product derived from copra, had experienced increased demand in Europe, as it was a critical ingredient in soap and other useful products such as explosives.

This shift to copra began to alter the relationships between Europeans and local people throughout the western Solomons. Copra required permanent investments and labor power to be profitable. Of course, coconuts have long been an important subsistence crop on Simbo as they are across Oceania. The leaves are woven into useful items such as women's skirts, sun visors, and food baskets and plates. The outer edge of a palm's trunk is a durable building material. The dried husks are an excellent fuel for burning. And the coconut meat and milk are as nutritious as they are delicious. Despite the importance of coconuts as a subsistence crop, copra was a new entity that brought shifts in coconut production since it demanded large plantations and labor in order to be profitable.

While relations with earlier whalers appeared to be amicable and mutually beneficial, the traders' demands on local people were greater and led to increased tensions and occasional violence. Most significantly, the traders needed land to build their permanent trading stations to collect copra. Indeed, Hocart's consultants expressed clear distaste for European traders. An old man told Hocart that tionivaka were mad (*tutura*) and unpopular for their lack of generosity and insatiable thirst for Simbo women.[43] These sentiments contrast with the accounts from earlier in the century when Europeans, such as Shortland, were avidly courted to visit Simbo and trade.

The first known trader to take up residence on Simbo was the Frenchman Jean Pratt, who established a trading station there in the 1890s.[44] For Pratt personal safety was a concern. He gave this advice to a German tourist who visited Simbo around 1897: "We went across in the boat of a lone French trader, who stressed to me never to disregard the following points in all the Solomon Islands: 1, always carry a revolver; 2, never allow a man to go behind me or to be surrounded by people; and 3, never insist on something if somebody has said 'no.'"[45]

Simbo chiefs were increasingly becoming more assertive with Europeans and apt to manipulate their relations with traders. While tensions with traders grew, local chiefs were simultaneously becoming more dependent on them. Simbo chiefs needed steel weapons and later firearms to maintain their intensifying headhunting raids. Luxury goods such as caps, clothing, pipes, and tobacco were also quickly emerging as status items needed by chiefs to motivate their warriors. Tobacco, although initially shunned, would become one of the most valuable trade items and in some cases became a form of currency.

Chiefs also were quick to take advantage of easy targets when they presented themselves. This was the case when two men from Simbo allegedly murdered a European trader named John Childe, who was attempting to establish a farm on Baqa Island (near Vella Lavella). The Simbo chief who led the lethal raid was building a canoe house and needed heads to inaugurate it.[46] This incident put Simbo in the headlines of the *Sydney Herald* when Jean Pratt's brother, Peter Edmond Pratt, published an article detailing the tense relations between islanders and Europeans. Pratt's article was part of his strategy to encourage the British Navy to assert more authority and be less lenient to Solomon islanders. Pratt was making the case that violence against European traders was growing, and although the Royal Navy was charged with protecting British traders and their interests, it sent vessels to the region only once a year; its influence was relatively modest.

Pratt's published, and possibly inflated, pleas for protection helped to instigate the British to send the HMS *Royalist* to Simbo in 1891 to avenge the murders of traders, including Childe's. The vessel shelled Narovo villages for several days, and the sailors severely flogged a Simbo man. The ship went on to wreak havoc in Roviana Lagoon, where eighty troops were deployed and destroyed hundreds of war cones, burned houses, and smashed skulls. Despite the devastation, the *Royalist* did not quell the violence, and traders continued to be targets. The violence in the western Solomons was, however, gaining increasing attention in Britain. Thus, one of the key outcomes of the traders' presence was growing intervention from British authorities, which eventually led to the establishment of the British protectorate in 1893 and ultimately pacification.

The rise of copra and European traders precipitated the decline of Simbo as a regional powerhouse. Simbo was less than ideal for large-scale copra production due to its small size and rough terrain. Roviana Lagoon, on the other hand, had numerous protected islands with abundant coast suitable for coconut plantations. It also was centrally located in the New Georgia Group and had a passage into the lagoon near Munda where vessels could find a protected anchorage. Although the Simbo people introduced Europeans to the Roviana area, chiefs there, like the famous leader Hingava, avidly pursued relationships with them and rose to dominate the region.[47]

What had once given Simbo an advantage, its relative remoteness from the rest of the New Georgia Group, had become a liability. Moreover, its small size, while possibly an attractive attribute for whalers, turned into a vulnerability that continues to persist today. Its relative lack of suitable land for cultivation of copra and extractable resources such as timber has led to common discourse on the island that Simbo is poor and lacks resources compared to other islands in the region.

Amid the growing tensions and waning influence of Simbo, its chiefs, like many across the western Solomons, "sold" land. The buyer was Jean Pratt, who in 1893 purchased 100 acres of land in Narovo known as Tubi for a trading station and coconut plantation.[48] The coming of permanent traders with commercial interests across the region marked the beginning of shifting relationships between the Simboans and their land as well as the balance of power between traders and the Simbo people. Selling land as if it was a commodity that could be freely exchanged was a foreign concept, and there most certainly were significant misconceptions by both Simboans and the traders about the nature of the transaction.

Nevertheless, Simbo's small size and rough terrain were less conducive to profitable copra production. As a result, Roviana Lagoon, an area with abundant coastline areas for copra plantations, gradually eclipsed Simbo and by 1900 was the hub of European activity in the western Solomons.

AN OUTLIER AT THE CENTER

By building a reputation as a friendly locale for Europeans and overplaying the ferocity and bloodthirstiness of the surrounding islands, Simbo successfully monopolized European goods during the early years of European contact. Moreover, the Simbo people readily incorporated foreign objects and practices, mobilizing them to their own advantage and against their adversaries. Simbo's outlying position relative to the other islands of the New Georgia Group also gave them a decisive advantage for attracting Europeans. Thus by the mid-nineteenth century the island was so successful in cooperating with passing European ships that it emerged as the preeminent entrepôt for the entire New Georgia Group. Through the sheer ingenuity of the Simbo people, they made their island the obligatory passage point for Europeans. Sitting at this node, the small island was able to control the flow of European goods across the region for the next fifty years, and as a result the island emerged as one of the most successful and aggressive centers of the headhunting complex.

Up until the twentieth century Simboans had managed the shifting material and social conditions without a fundamental reorientation of their lifeworld. Yet if we dig deeper there clearly were key transformative effects on the island. Their rapid adoption of steel weapons and tools turbocharged not only warfare in the region but also basic subsistence practices. The time-saving efficiency of bush knives (machetes) and other steel implements freed up labor that could be devoted to feasting and warfare rather than subsistence. By harnessing the available labor and the military advantages conferred by steel weapons, Simbo chiefs were able to expand and intensify their status. This expansion quite possibly enriched Simbo not only through the looting of foreign lands but also demographically through taking of captives, especially the young.

Importantly, these shifts were under the control of the Simbo people, or more specifically, powerful Simbo chiefs. Chiefs, in large measure, dictated the terms of engagement with Europeans and intensified autochthonous practices. As the example of steel hatchets suggests, European objects were readily incorporated into the cosmological system. Simbo chiefs were able to gain influence across the region like never before. The propitiation of ancestor spirits and the harnessing of ancestral mana went unabated while the threat of attack necessitated inland living. Thus the arrival of Europeans intensified autochthonous practices rather than radically altering them. Nevertheless, the island's ability to navigate early European influence, and the headhunting complex more generally, produced a critical vulnerability that came into play during the tsunami—the relative lack of intergenerational knowledge about the threat of tsunamis.

But the flow of objects was running in the other direction too, as traces of Simboans and their island began to circulate through Europe. While steel emerged as the critical materiality that was progressively spreading and simultaneously enabling Simboan spheres of influence to spread across the western Solomons, *paper* was the principal materiality going in the other direction, at least initially. The traces of Simbo that I tracked down to provide this account of Simbo's history were the same ones, or at least re-representations of the ones, that marked the beginning of Simbo's circulation through European colonial technoscientific networks of power. The meticulous documentation about Simbo written down in captains' logs and diaries and brought back to Europe enabled others in the expanding

European empires to contemplate aspects of Simbo from afar and in the comfort of their stately Victorian homes. Those first rather crude maps and snippets about Simboans enabled subsequent ships' captains to know something about Simbo before they arrived. An arriving European ship's captain, for example, could associate written accounts of Simbo's distinct profile with the actual profile that was visible off his ship's bow. As he cautiously navigated toward the Two Brothers, he could strengthen his assumption that this was indeed Simbo by noting the resemblance of the Eddystone rocks he had seen off the coast of England to the Eddystone pinnacles off the coast of Simbo. Rather than steel hatchets that were being exploited by Simboans to behead their victims on the surrounding islands, it was paper, pencil, sketches, and words that were being mobilized and with great effect by Europeans.

The early, crude maps and descriptions of Simboans would over time be refined by other European arrivals, who would add and accumulate new information about Simbo that would later entice not just explorers but also European whalers and traders seeking out riches. What initially was a symmetrical encounter between Europeans and Simboans was gradually tilting toward Europeans through their recurrent visits and their increasingly accurate charts and detailed descriptions of the natives, not to mention the collected Simbo artifacts now on display in European museums. By the middle of the nineteenth century, a European who entered Simbo's harbor for the first time quite possibly knew more about Simbo and its inhabitants than Simboans knew about Europeans. Europeans were beginning their "domination at a distance."[49] Yet the extension of colonial networks of power had not overrun the island. Only the 100 acres purchased by Jean Pratt, just 3 percent of Simbo's total land area, was legible to colonial authorities at the dawn of the twentieth century. Scaled down into a polygon neatly plotted in Cartesian coordinates, this piece of land could now be measured with a ruler and contemplated by colonial officials no matter if they were in Gizo, Honiara, or London. Colonists could not hold Simbo land itself, but they had invented ways to hold a form of it and hence secure it from a distance for their new European "owners" so that it could be calculated and capitalized. Luckily for Simboans this would be the only and last piece of their land to be mobilized at that fine scale. Colonial control of the island would remain at the coarse level of the island's outline, with a few additional but insufficient details about the local population.

Nevertheless, by the turn of the twentieth century, Simbo would become enmeshed decisively into European colonial networks. As discussed in the next chapter, the western Solomons was transformed from a frontier where islanders controlled the nature of their relations with Europeans to a colony imposed upon Simboans by the military might of the British empire. In response, Simboans would abandon ancestor veneration in favor of worshipping a new European God, and headhunting would give way to growing entanglement in the global economic system, elements of which would eventually be interwoven with the 2007 tsunami to produce the disaster.

4 New Villages, a New God, New Vulnerabilities

One of the first entries I jotted down in my field notes after formally launching my fieldwork in June 2009 reads: "People went after money in their houses. That is why they died. Lust for money." As you might expect, this was one of the most unsettling outcomes of the disaster.[1] I would come to learn that everyone who perished during the tsunami, except one small child, ignored the pleas of relatives and friends to flee to high ground. Some families related to me how they argued about what to do with their valuable belongings:

> My wife and I, we argued, I didn't know what to do. My wife said to me "Go inside the house and grab some of our belongings. Don't you want our things." I said "Ehhhhhhhhh. . . . No way, let's get out of here, we have to save our lives." If I would have run inside my house my small twin boys would have died. Who would have carried them to safety?

A dramatic and tragic scene described to me several times was the behavior of Luke, a man in his mid-forties who was killed by the tsunami. Luke was the owner of a small store in Tapurai. Most rural Solomon Islands villages have small shops with shelves stocked with desirable goods such as rice, canned fish and pork, cigarettes, fishing line and hooks, tea, and sugar. Typically, these stores are small, secure structures attached to the dwellings of the proprietors. Luke was the proprietor of the only store in Tapurai. His small shop and house were located on the water's edge so that he could easily carry goods purchased in Gizo to his store. Luke's nephew, who was with Luke just before he perished, described to me how his uncle ignored warnings to flee:

> When the earthquake shook Luke fell down. We both noticed the water starting to rise and people were running away. I said to him "Let's go, quick, the water is rising!" He didn't run away, he went inside his house. He sat down on a wooden trunk that had all of his money in it. His mind was inside the trunk. He didn't talk, he just sat there. He said to me he was dizzy from the earthquake and couldn't walk. I just ran away and left him there [sighs and drops his head]. We found his body tangled in the rubbish of his destroyed house.

The visiting bishop from United Church, one of just four in the entire country and highly respected, died in a similar way. He was seen fleeing, but he turned around and headed back to the house where he had stored his luggage. Four other victims were also last seen inside their houses searching for belongings. The victims at Riquru behaved similarly. One was a middle-aged adult male who also owned the only village shop. He, just like the victims in Tapurai, failed to heed the warnings of other villagers and ran back to his house to collect money and other valuables.

In contrast to the more speculative theorizations about the capacity of survivors to flee the tsunami, there was unanimous agreement among my interlocutors that victims were consumed by a specific condition known as bulo poata. As Luke's nephew put it:

> My uncle Luke he was bulo poata. If you lost a ten-cent coin, he'd get cross. He'd swear at you for wasting money. He had big gardens and sold the crops, he baked rolls and sold them, he marketed everything. He also collected shells on the reefs to sell to [Papua New Guinea].

A woman described this condition similarly when she told me: "If you see a man go fishing, and selling it in the market, go again fishing, and selling in the market, day after day, he is bulo poata." I was initially confused by the term because in the Simbo language "bulo" most commonly

Figure 12. A dugout canoe donated to Simbo after the tsunami with "bolo dola" painted on the side. This is a misspelling of bulo dola, which I gloss as "money crazy." (Photo by author.)

refers to a person's or animal's heart or to a drinking coconut.[2] I learned, however, that when qualifying a noun it has a connotation similar to "obsession" or "fixation" (as I gloss it), in which a person is compulsively preoccupied with a certain activity.[3] "Poata" is the Simbo word for money, referring to both traditional shell money and modern currency.[4] Thus, bulo poata describes a person who is destructively "in love with money" or "money crazy" (see figure 12). Other widely used synonyms for the condition include the hybridisms bulo dollar or bulo selen (selen and seleni are the Solomon Islands Pijin terms for "money," derived from "schilling").

In everyday usage, bulo poata is a stinging insult. It taunts those who obsessively pursue money above all else. As it was described to me, the term is rarely employed in formal settings like church sermons or community meetings. Rather, it is considered as a kind of slang that is reserved for informal exchanges when people joke with and poke fun at each other.

More broadly, bulo poata is a commentary on the anxieties the Simbo people have about the island's engagement with the cash economy and articulation with the global economy, a sentiment that is widespread across Melanesia and the Pacific as these societies grapple with the intensification of individualizing commodity and capitalist relations that run counter to modes of reciprocal interdependence that underpin social life.[5] Throughout much of the region, a "person" is understood not as a bounded individual but rather as what Marilyn Strathern famously described as a "dividual," a composite person made up of the social relationships in which they participate.[6] The rise of modern currency and capitalist relations, although they are positively valued by Simboans for the perceived benefits they have brought to Simbo, have led to a decline on the island of the extended networks of sharing and mutual assistance that are stereotypically Melanesian. Manifestations of these tensions emerged in the idiom with which Simboans conceptualized the fatal behavior of most of those who perished in the disaster.

In this chapter I trace the material and conceptual reconfigurations that have occurred on Simbo over the last century that inform these local interpretations of the victims' behavior. We will learn how over the course of the twentieth century Simbo underwent radical transformations as the British took formal control of the Solomons archipelago, ending headhunting and establishing a protectorate. One of the principal changes was the movement of villages down from the hillsides to more accessible coastal sites. If the 2007 tsunami had struck Simbo in 1900, there is little doubt that the outcomes would have been radically different. With villages high up on the mountain slopes out of harm's way, the waves would have washed over the uninhabited coastal areas with little effect. This spatial reorganization of the island involved not only the movement of communities to the coast but also the introduction of a new Christian God and a growing entanglement with capitalist systems of exchange and logics. These shifts generated a new repertoire of vulnerabilities, including the anxiety that now surrounds modern currency and the capitalist relations that have been imposed on the island.

More broadly, this chapter is about social-ecological change. Conceptualizations that assume change is an aberration rather than the norm have in large measure been abandoned in the social sciences. Marshall

Sahlins eloquently makes the case that one of anthropology's early errors was to dichotomize the world into traditional and modern societies, with the former encased in an assumed ahistorical world "without history" and the latter on a path toward progress.[7] Anthropologists and most social scientists more generally now assume that societies and their local ecologies are always undergoing change as people refashion their lives, institutions, and ecologies when confronted with new challenges and opportunities, a process provocatively described by Jerry Jack as "alchemy."[8] Indigenous peoples, rather than simply being victims of progress lying passively in the path of globalization, actively indigenize extra-local practices and "aim to take cultural responsibility for what has been done to them."[9] This shift from stasis to change has also pervaded the ecological sciences in its "new ecology" turn, in which the dynamics of ecological systems are now presumed to be nonlinear and emergent and to display multiple equilibrium points rather than being predictable systems characterized by homeostatic regulation, equilibrium, and stability.[10]

Indeed, in chapter 3 we learned how the Simbo people actively made and remade their island through their headhunting alliances, the borrowing of magical practices from other islands, and the absorption of European objects such as metal. It certainly was not a case of an Indigenous peoples being stuck in time. As we shall see in this chapter, even with a demonstrable increase in the pace of change, the Simbo people in large measure have maintained control over their island and their lives, reshaping certain practices and concepts, eliminating others, and adopting new ones. In the process of fashioning their lives, however, new vulnerabilities emerged for the island as old ones faded. Living on the coast was a response to the realities of the twentieth century, yet it had dire consequences during the 2007 tsunami for those who ignored their kin's pleas to flee to high ground.

PACIFICATION AND COLONIZATION

By end of the nineteenth century Simbo had already been eclipsed by Roviana Lagoon as the center of European trade, and the establishment of the British protectorate and expansion of state power would accelerate

Simbo's declining role in the political economy of the region, eventually leading to its current status as an impoverished backwater. It is important to note that colonization in the Solomon Islands was mild relative to other Pacific Island colonies such as Fiji or New Caledonia, where large settler-colonizer populations took up residence and significant colonial infrastructures were developed. The Solomons lacked large tracts of arable land and had little in the way of precious metals or other resources desired by the European powers. The relatively light hand of colonization provided space for the indigenization of European concepts and practices. Not only did the Simbo people maintain control over the entire island; they also embraced many of the newly introduced practices and concepts.

Without resources to exploit, the British were motivated more by their rivalries with other European powers and territorial control than by economic interests when they established the British Solomon Islands Protectorate in 1893. In fact, the British expected their new protectorate to finance itself, and the first resident commissioner, Charles Woodford, saw the development of large copra plantations as the only means by which to raise revenue for his administration. To do this, however, required security for both the labor force and the tracts of low-lying land that would be put into commercial production. For that, pacification was necessary, especially in the western Solomons, where headhunting, turbocharged by the influx of steel weapons, was chronic and widespread.

Although British warships had frequented the New Georgia Group to increase the security of European traders, shelling Simbo at least once, these occasional visits were inadequate. Islanders mounted headhunting raids at will and in general controlled the terms of their relationships with traders, who remained dependent on local chiefs for security.[11] Woodford chose centrally located Tulagi on the island of Savo as the British Solomon Islands Protectorate's administrative seat.[12] This capital, however, was much too distant from the New Georgia Group to effectively control the islands some 300 kilometers to the west. In recognition that a permanent colonial presence was necessary in the western Solomons, a government station was established on the island of Ghizo in 1899. Having been depopulated by headhunters, Ghizo Island was easily settled by colonial authorities, and this enabled them to exert their power throughout the New Georgia Group.

The first administrator assigned to the post on Ghizo was Arthur Mahaffy, and along with twenty policemen, he began to investigate headhunting raids, alleged crimes against Europeans, and the taking of captives. To do this he confiscated a large war canoe and hired police recruits from islands such as Santa Isabel, who had been the targets of New Georgia headhunting raids and relished avenging the deaths of their relatives and ancestors.

One of Mahaffy's early policing operations targeted Simbo, where he and his newly formed force carried out a destructive raid in May 1900. Their intention was to free several captives allegedly taken by a Simbo chief, Belenanga, who several years earlier had led a headhunting raid in Marovo Lagoon. Belenanga had been taken into custody, but repeated attempts to obtain the captives from Simbo were unsuccessful. Thus, Mahaffy sailed to Simbo, forced his way onto the island, and set up a provisional camp. He and his armed police force spent over a week destroying canoe houses, war canoes, gardens, and pigs. This was the first and only time the people of Simbo would suffer the direct brunt of colonial firepower on their own soil. According to colonial documents, Simbo capitulated and surrendered the captives. Mahaffy would go on to conduct similar operations throughout the New Georgia Group, and within a year he declared that Simbo, Roviana Lagoon, and Vella Lavella, the three main headhunting centers, were pacified and had "friendly" relations with the government.

The cessation of headhunting affected much more than just warfare; it overturned Simbo's political system and ended interisland alliances. As discussed in chapter 3, the focal point of a chief's political life was the acquisition of enemy heads, which were the primary way in which a chief's power or mana was measured. In a practical sense, headhunting raids were large-scale activities requiring the mobilization of a significant labor pool, not only to conduct the raid but also to build war canoes and canoe houses. To motivate commoners in their gusu, a chief held frequent feasts to propitiate the ancestors and distribute food and possibly shell valuables to followers. As one of A. M. Hocart's interlocutors described: "He (a chief) did a great deal: he made big feasts, built big houses, and many were his retainers; he had plenty of gardens and shell rings; his property was large, that was why he was a big chief."[13] With the cessation of headhunting, Simbo chiefs rapidly lost their influence. It was remarked to Hocart that "formerly the chiefs ordered their men to build canoes and go out together; that was before my time; now it is not done; the chiefs are dullards (tuturu) and like commoners (tinoni hoboro)."[14]

One of the critical effects of pacification was to throw into question ancestral mana.[15] A chief's mana was not generated only by him and his followers. A powerful chief was a concrete demonstration of a strong and positive link between the living and the dead and the efficaciousness of a district's ancestral endowment. Ancestral mana and the practices of ancestor veneration underpinned political power. Mahaffy's campaign, wherein he and his police force ransacked Simbo, was an affront not just to the chiefs but also to the ancestors themselves and the cosmological system more broadly. It was a demonstration, in the eyes of the Simbo people, that Europeans were more powerful than Simbo ancestors and were impervious to the illnesses and other maladies inflicted on the living by spirit beings that imbue the landscape. By decapitating the political system, the British demonstrated the relative weakness of Simbo ancestors and opened space for Christian missionaries' preaching about an all-powerful white man's God.

This blow to Simbo's political and cosmological system, however, did not lead to a full-scale collapse of Simbo cosmology and social life. The people of Simbo continued to maintain control over most of their land as well as the subsistence base. Moreover, the most important factor determining Simbo sociality, ancestor veneration, although challenged, continued, and the relations between the living and the dead remained central to social practices such as healing, successful fishing, and garden productivity.

On the heels of pacification, Christian missionaries quickly entered the region, providing a new, and in the eyes of the Simbo people, more powerful, spiritual framework in which they could reorient their lives.

CONVERSIONS

Although the Anglican Melanesia mission began to enter the central and eastern Solomons in the 1850s, warfare and the general lack of security in the New Georgia Group inhibited missionary expansion into the region until after the newly established protectorate government had brought headhunting under control. As the possibility of expanding into the western Solomons emerged, the United Methodist Church of Australia took steps to secure a mission in the New Georgia Group despite protests from the Anglicans, who claimed it was within their sphere of influence.[16] In 1901, just one year after the New Georgia Group was declared peaceful by the British protectorate authorities, the Methodist Church dispatched Rev. George Brown, a veteran missionary who earlier had established missions on New Britain in Papua New Guinea, to find a site on which to base operations. Simbo was in fact visited by Brown and initially considered for the new headquarters, but ultimately Roviana Lagoon was selected due to its larger population and also the presence of traders who advocated for the mission to the Roviana chiefs. Although local leaders such as the powerful Ingava never approved, a team of pioneers was sent in 1902 to Roviana to found the Methodist mission.

Under the leadership of the young and energetic minister John Francis Goldie, the missionary group, which included several Samoan and Fiji converts, began their operations on a small island owned by a trader.[17] Although there had been initial animosity, the mission was able to gain converts and eventually purchased more land near Munda.

In 1903 two new outposts were selected to expand mission influence in the region. One was planned for Bilua on the southern tip of Vella Lavella and the other on Simbo, which along with Roviana were the three locales that dominated the headhunting complex. Goldie, accompanied by two Munda chiefs and a Fijian teacher and his family, traveled to Simbo, landing in Tapurai. According to some accounts, Kave, the founder of Tapurai, requested that the missionaries establish the church in Tapurai, although my other consultants indicated that there was resistance. In one recorded account an old woman from Tapurai who was alive during the arrival of the missionaries described the situation this way: "The first time the missionaries came to Tapurai, a ship called the *Bondi* anchored in order that the passengers could disembark. . . . Then they all came down, the people of Tapurai, all the men, and they awaited them on the beach carrying their axes, shields, spears, and so on, and [the ship's people] prayed to 'cool' [calm] them before they disembarked."[18] This narrative is indicative of how Christianity's arrival was celebrated for its power to neutralize ancestral mana and provide protection against malicious forest spirits or attacks by crocodiles and sharks. However, this positive evaluation of Christianity was typically paired with descriptions of how the first missionaries failed in their attempts to convert the Simbo people. As my interlocutors explained, the missionaries were allowed to disembark and build a church, but the Fijian and later Samoan missionaries working at the station not only failed to convert Kave and his followers, they also abandoned Christianity and joined in the propitiation of Simbo ancestors. With a chuckle one man told me: "We converted the missionaries to worship our ancestor spirits!" Indeed, missionary documents corroborate local accounts, indicating that the Tapurai mission station was abandoned in 1909.[19] These first missionaries perished, but their graves survived the tsunami and can still be found near the old church of Tapurai. Not until 1912 was a new station founded, this time in Masuru, and there Christianity began to penetrate Simbo society to an appreciable depth.

Over the next several decades the island began to embrace the new cosmology, and it appears that by the 1930s Simbo was Christianized. The Christian cosmology and its promises of love, peace, and unity were attractive and contrasted sharply with the violent aspects of pre-European life. Today, the Simbo people emphasize and celebrate how Christianity has liberated them from their violent and discordant past. Indeed, the arrival of missionaries in 1903 remains one of the most salient historical moments in the lives of contemporary Simbo people.[20] Oral history describing the first Europeans has been altogether forgotten, while the arrival story of *lotu* (church, Christianity, Christian service) on the shores of the island is cherished and widely known. In 2003 large celebrations were held for the centenary, when the arrival of missionaries was reenacted with much fanfare and local pride.

However, not all aspects of pre-Christian life are rejected. The past is also understood as a time when people were less selfish and truly cared for one another through practices of mutual help. Today Simboans lament how life is tarnished by overly individualistic behavior, especially regarding land use. "Brothers will even dispute their brothers" is a common phrase heard around the island to describe the contemporary conditions. In the past, people were thought to have lived quietly, shared their garden produce and fish, and habitually engaged in mutual help. These affirmations of certain elements of pre-Christian life typically are referred to as kastom.[21]

Other aspects of the pre-Christian world are cloaked in ambiguity and ontological dissonance. One reason for Simbo's rapid adoption of Christianity was its promise to neutralize the powers of dangerous spirit beings while also providing a more encompassing envelope of security than those offered by the ancestors. Yet even though devotion to Christianity is unwavering, this has not extinguished the pre-Christian spirit world nor fully displaced pre-Christian modes of being. As we learned in chapter 2, nonhumans such as crocodiles, sharks, fish, birds, insects, and many other species are not treated as mere objects but as beings that demand respect and require specific modes of interaction. Moreover, other existents still animate Simbo's landscapes and seascapes, and ancestral power lingers. Old shrines, habitation sites, and other sacred sites that dot the island are approached with caution so as not to disturb the ancestral spirits, who may inflict the careless with illness or misfortune. However, for Christians explicit worship of these beings is considered sinful, and as a result much of the knowledge about how to act respectfully toward them and interpret their omens has been lost. Yet illnesses still afflict those who are disrespectful to old shrines. Thus, there is a certain level of caution and anxiety about the ontological status of ancestor and nonhuman spirit beings and about how best to both be a Christian and maintain amicable and constructive relations with these entities that inhabit the land and sea.

MOVEMENTS AND ORIGINS

The adoption of a Christian cosmology was not simply a change of heart; it also involved a change in landscape. New Christian villages were established on the "safe" ground of the coast away from the ancestral imbued shrine sites and habitation areas and organized around the new focal point of social life, the church. Indeed, even before Simbo adopted Christianity when Hocart visited in 1908, the Narovo people had already colonized the sandy, flat neck of land known today as Lengana, forming more nucleated settlements of clustered households. With the rise of copra, the enmeshing of Simbo in the global economy, and removal of the threat of attack, propelled the establishment of new villages on the coast. The abandonment of inland settlements was complete within a decade or two of when

Christianity had taken root and the British colonial administration was firmly established.

It was during this period that the two villages destroyed by the 2007 tsunami were founded on their vulnerable beachside locales. I chronicled the specific settlement history of Tapurai and Riquru and learned that the entire northern area of Narovo was never permanently inhabited until the end of the nineteenth century. The island's settlement history was told to me through narratives by the chiefs of the island's principal clans.[22] As mentioned in chapter 3, these histories take the form of spatially explicit narratives known as a toponymy and start with the mythical "origin place" or *vunagugusu*, of each clan, which is typically rocks or caves near the highest point within each of the respective gusu, where ancestral spirit beings emerged to eventually produce human beings, who then moved down the mountain slopes and established new settlements and entombed their dead in shrines. It is the names of these ancestral beings, their human offspring, and the names of the places of habitation that form the core kastom history that underpins a clan's legitimacy as the caretaker of the gusu land and sea areas. Importantly, there is no single comprehensive topogeny that encompasses the origins of all the gusu. Each gusu is conceived as an autochthonous unit, and it was through intermarriage that these original progenitors mixed with the clans of other districts.

I had the privilege to explore on foot the entire topogeny of one of the two Ove clans as told by Aseri, the father of my close friend and collaborator, Nickson.[23] My exploration of the Ove settlement was part of an archaeological research project I helped initiate in 2015.[24] I organized the project based on a request from Simbo's elders, who had expressed an interest in learning what archaeologists could tell them about their island's past. With Aseri as our guide, several archaeologists and I first visited the most recent pre-Christian village site of Vuluqao, located on a small hill between the ocean and Ove Lake. Each site of the topogeny is saturated with cosmological, historical, and political significance, and Aseri narrated many past events as we walked. Aseri was born in Vuluqao, and we visited his mother's grave. The grave was "modern" in that her body was placed in a wood casket, buried, and then topped with a cement cap and tombstone. Embedded in the tombstone were the indentations of shell money (poata). This village was occupied during the arrival of Methodist

Figure 13. A platform (korovona) upon which houses were built prior to the arrival of Christianity. Note the Christian grave in the center. I helped Grinta Ale'eke from the Solomon Islands National Museum clear the area during an archaeological survey we conducted in Karivara district in 2019. (Photo by author.)

missionaries in 1903, and hence Aseri's mother's grave reflected the Christian burial practices.

The old village was composed of a number of house platforms (*korovona*) (see figure 13). In most cases they were nearly undetectable due to heavy vegetation. After we cleared the area with machetes, the knee-high stone walls of the rectangular platforms became more visible. We then began an exhausting climb uphill, retracing, in reverse chronological order, the clan's ancestral habitation areas and shrine sites. We entered thick forest, meandering our way up the slope and recording several different settlement areas, dance circles (*kakabare*), shrines, and other sacred sites. As we entered these sites Aseri would first address his ancestors verbally, asking their permission to enter the space, and then he would proudly narrate stories about their activities.

After hours of hiking through thick forest and up steep terrain, we reached the summit of the 400-meter-high hill, which on the west face is called Watidingi, not to be confused with the east face, known as Matidingi. Near the summit of Watidingi we visited the origin place (vunagugusu) of Aseri's clan, a sacred stone known as *patu mateana*. There Aseri narrated his clan's origin story, where three angel-like spirit beings called *mateana* appeared and produced the first human ancestors. Near the summit we also identified a meter-high rock wall running some 50 meters long, the remains of a fortress (bara). Prior to pacification, fortresses were maintained by each of the four gusu near the highest point of the district. They served as refuges to which people would flee during enemy raids. From inside the fortress assailants were pelted with clamshells, stones, and other projectiles.[25]

As I learned the topogenies of each district it became apparent that the northern half of Narovo, nearly half of the entire island, is unique in that it is not referenced as a space of previous habitation or the site of clan origins. Although the entire northern half of the island is within the Narovo district, the topogenies of its two main clans, Vunagugusu and Katapana, as recounted to me, only discuss the crater and hillside of Patu Kio, where three mythical beings emerged from a hole near the summit and then villages were sequentially established down its steep slope.[26] Despite its lack of settlement history, the northern area of Narovo continues to this day to be universally recognized as contained within the Narovo district and under the guardianship of the Katapana and Vunagugusu clans.[27]

As for the origins of Tapurai and Riquru, they both were founded by non-Narovo chiefs around the end of the nineteenth century. Both oral history and Hocart's writings indicate that the founder of Tapurai was a prominent chief called Kave who migrated from Ove and is also credited with bringing Christianity to the island (see figure 14). Kave was an influential chief and one of Hocart's key interlocutors who, at the time of Hocart's work, had permanently taken up residence in Tapurai but maintained ties with his Ove kin. According to Hocart, Tapurai had "good houses and a good hall," although when I asked my consultants about house foundations in Tapurai they were not aware of any. Under the influence of missionaries the Simbo people stopped building their houses on rock foundations and adopted stilted, platform houses that stand, as most do today, a meter off the ground and typically have flooring constructed from roughly hewn timbers. The reason for Kave's migration from Ove to Tapurai was in part

Figure 14. A photograph of Kave, the founder of Tapurai, taken by A. M. Hocart in 1908. At the time of Hocart's fieldwork Kave had moved his clan from Ove to Tapurai. Today many of the descendants of Tapurai consider themselves "Ove People." (Photo credit: Museum of Archaeology and Anthropology, University of Cambridge, UK.)

the threat posed by the active Ove volcano. According to my interlocutors the Solomon Islands government also urged the Ove people to move away from the active volcano.

That Tapurai and Riquru were founded by migrants from other districts emerged as a key vulnerability for these communities during the relocation efforts after the tsunami. As discussed in more detail in the next chapter, these communities had less secure ties to the land, and disputes emerged over the relocation of the villages away from the beachside sites.

PERSISTENT EXISTENTS

When discussing and visiting these past settlement areas and sacred sites, it became clear that although the conversion to Christianity was a major blow to the pre-Christian conceptual order, it was not an instance of one cosmology fully displacing the other. Respect for ancestral power and relationships with invisible entities inhabiting the land and seascape were never fully extinguished and continue today to play an active role in contemporary Simbo life.

As I learned more about the pre-Christian cosmology with my Simbo interlocutors, I noticed that a derogatory missionary discourse dominated, and many vocally disavowed the efficacy of ancestral power or spirits. The pre-Christian era was described as a "time of darkness" when their "pagan" ancestors worshiped "devils." Despite these pejorative labels and formal denunciations, ancestral power and spirit beings frequently imposed themselves, as they do in other Pacific Christian societies.[28]

During my walk with Aseri and my many visits to old shrines and habitation sites around the island, I experienced firsthand how these locales continue to be inhabited by ancestor spirits, who indicate their presence through signs such as strange bird calls or other unusual noises or the sudden falling of tree limbs or tumbling of stones. My interlocutors expressed trepidation about visiting these sites unless they had strong ancestral ties to them, for without the proper ancestral links the visitor or the visitor's family will be punished for the transgression and succumb by illness or misfortune. The mountaintop birthplaces of the primordial ancestors are areas known to have a particularly potent ancestral presence. At the summit of Matidingi, the birthplace of the Karivara people, for example, there is a specific large stone called "jumping stone"; visitors are required to climb on top of it and jump off four times to show respect for and gain permission from the ancestor spirits lest they fall ill.

Foreigners are thought to be particularly vulnerable to the effects of ancestral power. For example, whenever I planned a visit to Ove volcano, my interlocutors would invariably suggest that a guide with strong ancestral ties accompany me so that the spirits would not be angered by my presence. The offensiveness of foreigners to ancestor spirits is widespread across the Solomon Islands. The Arosi people of Makira aptly described their ancestors' beings as employing a kind of "radar" emanating from sacred areas like shrines, detecting and punishing intruders, especially foreigners, as they deemed appropriate.[29] When I inquired about the possible effects of visiting Matidingi or Ove without a proper guide, I was told that I might slip and get injured as we climbed up the steep slopes or, worse, we would fall seriously ill afterward.

Today my Simbo interlocutors employ the generic term "tomate" or the Pijin word devol when describing most of these entities, although there are other terms that refer to specific supernatural phenomena, such as *resana* (certain kinds of rainstorms), *sea* (shooting stars or bright lights), and mateana (angel-like beings). Ancestor spirits are contrasted with the almighty and benevolent Christian God (tamasa). The two categories of spirit beings that continue to create the most fear among contemporary Simbo people are forest tomate. Forest tomate roam the areas outside of villages, usually at night and away from shrine sites protected by ancestral forces. These beings can cause illness and other maladies such as psychosis. One of the most dreaded forest existents, *rerege*, rushes around the forest splitting trees and knocking over bushes. If the being runs over a person, he or she will die instantly. A story recounted to Christine Dureau during her fieldwork describes in detail an interaction with this being:

> Last Tuesday was the Men's Fellowship, so Kera [and named others] joined lotu. They went, they participated and then they left to return home. They were few, only five. So they walked back (i.e., they did not use a canoe).
>
> All right, in the middle of their journey it was resana, a fine rain in sunshine, but they kept walking because they wanted to reach home quickly. But, in the middle of their journey, they heard the rerege. They FLED! . . . It's [the path is] steep, it's slippery and when it rains it['s] extremely muddy. So, they heard rerege and they fled! [begins laughing]. They fled because they were terrified, they wanted to run but it was a mire. They slipped, they fell, they fell in the mud, they truly fled to the village.
>
> Alright, when they arrived in the village I saw them. They had mud all over their bodies. Mud on their clothes, their legs and arms bespattered, mud in their hair [extended laughing description of their appearance].[30]

What is notable about this incident is that it occurred to a local United Church pastor who openly preached against the efficaciousness of spirit beings. These examples suggest that nearly a century after the islanders converted to Christianity and became entangled with capitalist logics, spirit beings coexisted with Christianity. This is likely due to the Methodist Church's focus on eliminating pre-Christian practices such as propitiation at ancestor shrines rather than on theology and beliefs.[31] Unlike other Solomon Islands missions such as Seventh-Day Adventists and Catholics, the Methodist mission did not go to great lengths to discredit ancestral power and its metaphysical effects.[32] Instead, the success of Christianity was underpinned by the notion that God and Christian practice were more powerful than the pre-Christian cosmology and would afford protection against malevolent entities.

MODERN TENSIONS

Concomitant with the rise of Christianity, in the early twentieth century Simbo became further marginalized in the regional political economy. In general, the Solomon Islands lacked exploitable natural resources, and therefore the overarching colonial interest in the Solomon Islands was financial self-sufficiency. To sustain the newly established protectorate, copra plantations run by European expatriates became the central economic development strategy. To expand copra production, uninhabited land was alienated across the Solomons since it was assumed to be "waste land" without any landowners.[33]

Simbo's small size and limited land suitable for cultivation meant that European interests were focused on larger islands such as Kolombangara, where nearly 75 percent of the land was brought under protectorate control. On Simbo the plot of land around the head of Narovo Bay that was purchased by Jean Pratt was eventually sold to another European trader, Fred Green. Green's trading station at Tubi, which was later leased to two Europeans, Collinson and Pybus, had both European and local goods for sale, and his coconut plantation was the largest on the island. The trading store served as the hub of commerce on the island and fueled the monetization of Simbo's economy.

The Great Depression of the 1930s, however, devastated many of the European traders across the Solomon Islands as the price of copra plunged. Unable to turn a profit, most traders like Green, who had been living in the protectorate for decades, sold off their landholdings and left the country. Green sold his Simbo plantation and trading station to the Methodist Church, which, led by its charismatic leader John Goldie, was also relying on copra to sustain the mission. Villages across the New Georgia Group were required to provide "gift copra" to the mission. As the congregation grew on Simbo, the church, located at that time in Masuru village, needed a larger building, so part of the coconut plantation was cleared, and a new, more substantial church was built.

Japan's invasion of the Solomon Islands in 1942 and its subsequent occupation of the islands was a major turning point in the history of the country. Luckily, Simbo's isolated location to the south of the infamous "slot" running between the major islands of the Solomons chain meant that it was almost completely spared from the conflict. My older interlocutors recounted stories from their parents about planes buzzing through the skies in dogfights and warships passing through the inshore waters, but life on Simbo changed little. After the Americans overtook Guadalcanal, the Japanese retreated to Munda and Kolombangara, where they built airbases. Munda in particular saw fierce fighting in 1942 when Allied forces mounted an offensive and retook the region.

The postwar period began with booming commercial copra development across the Solomon Islands, followed by a frenzy in logging after independence in 1979. Since the 1980s, commercial logging has dominated the Solomon Islands economy as mainly Malaysian and other Asian multinational companies have extracted tropical hardwoods from the untapped forests, selling the logs to the growing economies of Asia.[34] New Georgia as well as Vela Lavella and Kolombangara all have large inland forests, and they became a central focus for commercial logging through the 1990s and 2000s.[35] The Asian logging companies negotiated directly with landowners, promising large royalties as well as social development and infrastructure such as schools, clinics, and roads. The injection of royalties into rural communities caused much internal strife as the various landowning groups and their leaders struggled over reconciling ownership rights to the trees of these uninhabited inland areas. At the same time, the agendas of outsiders were also leveraged by local groups to advance their own visions of development.[36]

In large measure, however, commercial and economic activity was absent on Simbo. Its small size and lack of large forests meant that commercial resource extraction ventures were nonstarters. For this reason,

Simboans describe their island as poor, a characterization echoed by Simboans to Harold Scheffler during his visit in 1960.[37] This lack of significant commercial activity, however, has not inhibited the penetration of the cash economy and the logics of capitalism. Today most Simbo households intermittently participate in commercial activities such as copra production, shell-diving, or the marketing of fruits and vegetables in the market town Gizo, although subsistence fishing and gardening remain the mainstays of island life.

In many respects Simbo is only weakly enmeshed in the global economic system and is underdeveloped; it has no electricity and few amenities except a small clinic in Lengana and government-run schools. Without a steady and broadly shared source of income such as timber royalties, access to cash varies widely, and income-generating opportunities are disproportionately skewed in favor of those who have been educated. There is a visible, educated elite on the island, who have been able to pursue salaried employment in Honiara or Gizo, primarily as government employees, or are employed locally as teachers or nurses. Shopkeepers, too, tend to have more education than other villagers. This has generated a marked contrast between the majority who depend on the subsistence economy and those who have access to some cash or capital.

Growing inequalities on the island, however, have not undermined a dedication to change and deep desire for Western goods and lifestyles. In many areas of their lives the Simbo people reject Indigenous practices and assume the Western analog is morally and practically superior. Frequently my interlocutors negatively evaluated their less-educated and subsistent-dependent kin for being too "local" or "buskanaka" (hillbilly). Likewise, Indigenous technology and practices are thought to be chronically inadequate, disparagingly referred to as "village." This yearning for modernity means the good life is defined in terms of material possessions and conspicuous consumption of foreign goods. Households with access to cash will invariably build a raised, tin-roofed house with saw-cut lumber, instead of a traditional sago palm leaf house. Other material markers of affluence include a water tank fed by a rain catchment system from the tin roof, an outboard motor, and a fiberglass canoe or boat.

In addition to these material possessions, food consumption ideals also reflect the desirability of money and yearning for economic development.

Rice stands out as one of the most symbolic markers of modernity. As noted by Dureau, the Simbo people have a keen desire for rice: "Rice tasted good; it filled the stomach, it meant rested bodies and comfortable joints for those who need not garden."[38] They also adore ramen noodles, tea (especially tea bags), sugar, and freshly baked buns. Fishers prize tinned fish over their regular hauls of fresh, delicious tuna, mackerel, rainbow runner, or snapper. These dietary preferences for processed foods are common across the Pacific, resulting in an epidemic of obesity in many wealthier Polynesian countries where households have more disposable income.[39]

Simbo's fervent pursuit of modernity, however, has some important nuances. Beneath their keen desire for a Western lifestyle and embrace of Christianity, my consultants also spoke highly of kastom. A broadly shared anxiety was that encroaching modernity is undermining sharing and working for mutual benefit. These notions of generosity and reciprocal obligations are known in the local vernacular as varivagana (sharing of food and labor) or *varivaia* (sharing of nonedible items such as land, house, trees, etc.) and continue to underpin basic norms and values of sociality on Simbo. These words connote not only exchange but also love, compassion, and empathy (*tataru*), a feeling of concern for other people, and maintaining community relationships. Households on Simbo continue to share food and other resources, yet many describe how these sharing relations have narrowed from broader corporate kin groups or clans (bubutu) to more closely related sibling groups (*tamatasi*) and extended household members (*tavitina*).

As it is for many societies in Melanesia, reciprocal exchange and sharing of goods and labor is a central feature of Simbo social life and is a mode by which the vitality and potency of land and sea is equalized across households and across gusu.[40] Varivagana parallels a sense of personhood that anthropologists have noted in Melanesia that privileges the sociocentric "fractal" person over egocentric selfhood.[41] Relationships with kin and the wider community tend to be valued positively over self-centered activities such as profit making, resource accumulation, and entrepreneurship directed toward individual or household benefit. Indeed, on Simbo generosity is what constitutes a "good person" (*tinoni zonga*) and ensures cherished aspects of Simbo sociality.

The condition of bulo poata in many ways is the antithesis of variva-gana and indexes Simboan's complex and contradictory relationship with the market economy. Although modern goods such as rice and tin roofing are highly valued, Simboans also demonstrate apprehension about modern currency and the logics of capitalism, a sentiment noted across Melanesia and among Indigenous societies more generally.[42] In Fiji, for example, rural people contrast themselves with urbanites, Indo-Fijians, and tourists in that they follow the "way of the land" rather than a "path of money."[43] In the Tanga Islands of Papua New Guinea the Tok Pisin word bisnis is contrasted with kastom as a means to differentiate balanced, long-term exchanges and relationships from the isolated transactions of the cash economy that do not bind the transactors in continuing relations.[44] Similarly, on Simbo purchasing items or labor from close kin with Solomon Islands dollars is anathema to cherished sharing relations. As Joel Robbins suggested in his discussion about transactions in Melanesia: "When people buy from each other, they risk losing their connection as kin."[45] Trade stores in particular are sites where Simbo kin struggle to manage the cash economy. Typically, the relatives of a store owner insist that they receive credit rather than pay cash. This strategy avoids directly purchasing items and transforms the modality of the exchange toward generalized sharing rather than socially shunned cash transactions.

Despite the contrasts Simboans and other Oceanic peoples draw between reciprocal exchange and relations and the market economy, modern currency has entered exchanges that the Simbo people also evaluate positively and seeps into what is generally understood as kastom. "Payments," for example, usually coins, are placed in ancestor shrines to appease them, and "compensation" (*ira*) is paid with currency when opposite-sex siblings (*luluna*) breach social prohibitions or a person fails to show respect to their affines. At the same time, those with money employ the Pijin term wantok bisnis (one-talk business) to speak disparagingly of the obligatory sharing and social obligations that stymie economic development.[46]

In this context, the epithet "bulo poata" that was leveled at those who died from the tsunami was a comment that they had forgotten not only about their own lives and well-being but about their kin, too, and the wider community. Thus, to be bulo poata is not only to deny one's well-being; it also is a denial of the very core of Simbo sociality.

SHOCKED INTO SHARING

In contrast to the behavior of those who perished during the tsunami, something astonishing occurred when survivors fled up the hills to seek higher ground: the desire for money receded, and those cherished aspects of kastom, mutual help and sharing, blossomed. After the tsunami, survivors climbed the hills behind Tapurai to the highest, cleared gardens that sit nearly 150 meters above sea level. There was enormous uncertainty and unease about the possibility of even larger waves coming.[47] As aftershocks rocked the island, news trickled into the camps that another large earthquake and tsunami might strike.

Many villagers remained in these provisional camps for weeks, and some stayed three or four months. Aid began to reach the island within a few days, but prior to that the Simbo people demonstrated remarkable self-reliance and coping skills. The camps were established in gardens, so no one went hungry. As one man stated, "If you were hungry, you just reached over and pulled up a sweet potato!" Although for a few weeks after the tsunami people were terrified of entering the ocean and little fishing occurred, one of the species of canarium nut on the island, *vino* (*Canarium salomonense*), was just beginning to ripen, and nuts were plentiful.[48] These delicious nuts are high in protein and fat and can be cracked open with a stone and eaten raw, and the two species found on the island, *ngari* (*Canarium indicum*) and the larger vino, ripen six months apart, providing a year-round supply of nuts.

Dead fish were found strewn across the coastal areas inundated by the tsunami. Some of these were collected and cooked but ultimately not eaten because they had a peculiar and offensive taste. The fish were not wasted, however; they were fed to the dogs, cats, pigs, and chickens that had also survived the tsunami.

Enough bush knives (machetes) were retrieved from the wreckage to build provisional huts from sago palm thatch and wood from the surrounding forest. Cooking pots and other utensils were scarce, so food was roasted over fires or cooked in pit ovens, two common cooking practices that, prior to the arrival of Europeans, were the only modes of cooking.

Edible wild foods were also tapped, such as mushrooms, ferns, and the shoots of certain plants. Although it was not necessary, the Simbo people could have lived for months if not years in these camps without external assistance. Survivors, rather sarcastically, did note that there was a lack of certain highly sought-after luxury items: tobacco and betel nut. Drinking water was also difficult to get, although drinking coconuts (bulo) are abundant and were relied upon.

The survivors of Tapurai and all the other less-damaged villages established temporary camps in active gardens that were clear of dense tropical foliage. Like the broader concept of gusu, active gardens (poki) connote more than just a site to produce food and other provisions. They are locales of deep intimacy and immediacy for Simbo households where the traces of human action and the embodied relational entangling of shared substances is ever present. Gardening for Simboans is quintessentially a form of dwelling, where the world comes into being through immersion in the soil, clippings, pests, and tools employed to bring into and sustain human and nonhuman life.[49]

In their practice of swidden agriculture, the labor of the living and the recently deceased have intermingled through time as the garden plots cycle through periods of cultivation and lying fallow (see figure 15). Just like household members in the past, women and their daughters spend nearly every day in the gardens weeding, planting, and harvesting the sweet potatoes, bananas, yams, and other produce while also socializing. For a garden to be productive, it is carefully managed through different stages of preparation, cultivation, and lying fallow. The first is zazu, in which it is cleaned, followed by hoeing and planting (piki). As the sweet potato vines grow the garden reaches a stage called ukagore. Then the tubers are harvested (gori kamu); after two or three years of harvesting the garden it is left to lie fallow (bubusa).

It is important to note here that this garden intimacy is related to a critical distinction made on Simbo between ground or land (peso) and property (isisongo). The ground of a gusu is imbued with ancestral beings who impose themselves on their living descendants. Isisongo, on the other hand, a term I gloss as "property," is conceived of as a more direct product of the land that has been produced through the labor of household members and their immediate grandparents.[50] This immediacy of household property grants them control over the consumption and distribution of the garden's products.[51] At the same time, a household's ability to create

Figure 15. Hoeing a new garden that will be planted with sweet potatoes. The volcanic soils of the island are highly fertile. (Photo by author.)

property by farming on any particular plot is regulated by the clan that has ancestral entitlement to and guardianship responsibilities for the land of the gusu in which the garden is situated.

Since gardens are considered a household's property, household members are sensitive about any intrusion into the space. And the most vulnerable and critical stage of a garden, in terms of both the garden's attachment to the owner and the crops themselves, is ukagore. At this point in the gardening cycle the clippings of the vegetatively propagated sweet potato (*Ipomoea batatas*) have been carefully placed in their mounds, and new runners are just beginning to sprout and grow. If the delicate vines are disturbed the clippings will typically fail to take root and die. For this reason, the proprietor of an ukagore garden is particularly sensitive if nonhousehold members enter their garden. Failure to show respect for an ukagore garden is equivalent to disrespecting the crops, its proprietor, their family, and their ancestors, all of whom collectively bring forth life in the garden.

Even just walking through a garden breaches a serious norm and brings the transgressor into disrepute.

For these reasons, my interlocutors were surprised that social friction was absent even though the relocation camps were established in ukagore gardens. Gideon, my close collaborator from Meqe who was traveling from Gizo to Simbo on the morning of the tsunami, narrated to me his arrival in Simbo after the tsunami and how surprised he was to see his family in an ukagore garden with many of the mounds and plantings torn up:

> After landing our boat we made our way up the steep path behind Meqe and came upon my family and most of the village huddled together in an open garden area. Relieved that my family was unscathed it struck me right away. Everyone was sitting in a garden that was in ukagore, when the sweet potato vines are just starting to sprout. Normally if someone without permission were to enter a garden at this stage there would have been a row. But the owner was sitting there and hadn't complained at all. I couldn't believe my eyes!

Owners of gardens across the island relaxed their normally stringent oversight and allowed the relocation camps to be formed in them. Moreover, the owners offered the tsunami survivors ripe crops from their gardens as well as the produce and other forest products from trees in the surrounding area. Like gardens, important trees such as canarium nuts, coconut, pandanus, and sago palm are considered property. These trees, like gardens, have specific and recognized owners whom they belong to. In normal times, a person from outside the owner's kin group must consult with and be granted permission by the owner before harvesting. But when villagers occupied the relocation camps, everyone freely harvested the trees across the island without seeking permission.

This shift in sentiments toward household "property" that occurred in the relocation camps was described by my interlocutors as the blossoming of their most cherished kastom practice: varivagana. Thus, villagers took pride that while in the relocation camps their lives were filled with love for each other, and the pressures to enter market relations and earn cash vanished. They were all "good people" sharing their food and labor.

As noted earlier, varivagana is not simply the exchange of objects, food items, or labor; it also connotes notions of love and empathy between those who share and the intermixing human and nonhuman substances.

Indeed, a variant of varivagana, *vaiaia*, translates directly as "make it place/home." In this sense, garden products and forest resources are not actualized as inert objects but rather are ontologically enmeshed with the giver, whereby the essences of the land and the people who devoted their time and labor to cultivate them are intermixed. Land, people, food, and tree crops, and the history of cultivation all intermingle and are expressed and reproduced through mutual help and exchange.

Many on Simbo, however, commented on and lamented the decline in varivagana over their lifetimes and the rise of selfishness and self-serving behavior, in which villagers accumulate wealth without redistributing it for the benefit of the wider community. One middle-aged man from Masuru described the situation this way:

> In the past varivagana was strong. If you needed a sweet potato you could go to any garden and take the potatoes. You didn't even have to ask. You could take any food, any sago palm, anything without asking and no one would be offended. Now people still share vegetables or copra but you must ask the owner. The owner can refuse if he has a good reason. He can't make up a reason: it must be something important, like the sago palms aren't producing very well, or that the owner is also making a house and needs the palm fronds. Many people refuse now because they need more for school fees. This is a strong and legitimate excuse to refuse someone access to your crops or copra because everyone must pay the school fees. So today people share if you ask them, but it is slowly eroding because of the need for cash. Everyone needs cash for legitimate reasons. The key is to have a legitimate reason, not a self-interested one. That is grounds to refuse to share.

For these reasons, many survivors were surprised by the outpouring of sharing across households as people occupied the relocation camps. Even shop owners freely distributed the goods of their stores across the island. In normal times, small shops on Simbo are a constant site of contestation as the owners struggle to demonstrate the legitimacy of their profits to kin who accuse them of accumulating ill-gotten gains.

The surge in sharing and the relaxation of property attachments meant that no one went hungry before aid reached the island. Survivors glowed when they talked about the strength of kastom and how "people loved each other," "we all shared food," and "there was sharing, giving to each other, accepting. We stayed together and prayed together" or "everyone helped each other and lived quietly." The looting, violence, and price gouging that are sometimes witnessed after disasters in other parts of the world were nonexistent on Simbo.

ALCHEMIC VULNERABILITIES

Jerry Jacka, in *Alchemy in the Rainforest*, provides an illuminating and richly embroidered account of development and change in the highlands of Papua New Guinea.[52] He invokes the imagery of "alchemy" to suggest that change and transformations transpiring on colonial frontiers involve material, conceptual, linguistic, and ecological redistributions and trans-mutations that parallel the practices of medieval alchemists who sought to alter metals into gold. Alchemists employed special elixirs not only to convert stones into precious metals, they also applied them to the body to prolong life, enlighten the soul, and improve the human condition. It is this alchemy that Jacka traces through an examination of Pogera, a region famous for its enormous alluvial gold deposits. The glittery deposits in the riverbeds of the region became a source of eye-popping wealth when a large mine was established in 1990. Pogerans, however, benefited little from it. Nevertheless, the inhabitants of the region continued to avidly engage with and seek out the wealth and technology of outsiders. As on Simbo, foreign objects such as steel were initially absorbed through ritual and other means, but later, as Pogerans learned that outsiders desired gold, they began panning for the alluvial riches. They, like Simboans, adopted Christianity for spiritual improvement. In a far more extreme case than Simbo, however, Pogerans simultaneously desired and actively pursued the benefits of capitalism and development while also lamenting the ero-sion of some of their most cherished practices such as reciprocal exchange. The vulnerabilities spawned by colonial and postcolonial processes pro-duced not just "social" or "ecological" shifts but alchemic "socioecological" transformations. The large-scale mining, conversion to Christianity, and later the arrival of firearms transformed the Pogerans' world and undercut their capacity for reciprocity so drastically that they referred to their new condition as a situation in which "the land is ending." Rather than having fertile crops, healthy people, and placated spirit beings, the Pogeran world underwent a radical and tragic breach.

As we have learned in this chapter, the transformations have been much less dramatic on Simbo. Without significant resources such as minerals or timber that attract outsiders, Simboans to a large degree have been able to reshape and adapt to colonial impositions, capitalist relations, and new cosmologies. But similar to Pogera, when Simboans refract and appropriate external influences through their own practices, this produces uneven, complex, and unexpected outcomes, many of which were dramatized during the tsunami. As we have learned in this chapter, the emergence of twentieth-century vulnerabilities joined with the 2007 tsunami in such a way that some Simboans, tragically, remained in the path of the tsunami.

But in another surprising twist, a wave of social solidarity took hold during the immediate aftermath of the tsunami while survivors lived in the relocation camps high up in the hills. This flowering of sharing surprised many and was interpreted as an effervescence of kastom, those pre-Christian practices such as sharing and mutual self-help that, unlike Pogerans, Simboans continue to engage in to compose their world. To understand these varied and contradictory responses to the tsunami, this chapter has traced the material and conceptual transformations that have occurred on Simbo over the last century. As we have learned, these shifts generated a new repertoire of vulnerabilities, including an anxiety on the island over modern currency, capitalist relations, and the perceived erosion of Simbo life. In particular, colonization precipitated a radical spatial reorganization of the island in which villages were moved from inland areas to the coastal zone. It was in this way that the two villages most severely affected by the tsunami were established on tsunami-vulnerable sites, and capitalist systems of exchange and logics were extended into Simbo.

Even though Simboans do not lament that their "land is ending" as do Pogerans, we will learn in the next chapter that the tsunami disaster produced a new form of land that would ultimately be at the center of disputes that erupted during the reconstruction of Tapurai. Rather than the land ending due to gold mining, there was the emergence of "tsunami-land," a sociotechnical alchemy that was brought into existence by government experts and humanitarian workers. The coastlines would be deemed dangerous again, as they were during precolonial times. But this time the threat of danger was engendered by professionals with machine-washed shirts and mobile phones, armed with scientific instruments, who arrived in 23-foot fiberglass Ray Boats propelled by 75 horsepower Yamaha

Enduro motors, rather than lime-painted warriors wielding hatchets and paddling canoes with intricate inlays of mother of pearl. Instead of traces of Simbo being taken away in the form of heads and captives, these new arrivals left the island with computers, notebooks, and GPS instruments filled with photographs, inundation height measurements, and the narratives of tsunami survivors.

5 Assembling Reconstruction

The initial social solidarity and amicability described by Simboans as they occupied the provisional relocation camps high up on the mountains after the tsunami were short lived. Within just two days aid began to reach the island, and as the rehabilitation and reconstruction phase of the disaster unfolded, conflicts and tensions arose. News of Simbo's plight spread quickly across the country and through the international news media. It was the only island where villages suffered a total loss and nearly every structure was swept away. This tragic news attracted much attention to the island from the national government and humanitarian organizations, and within days even the governor general of the Solomon Islands paid a visit to Simbo via helicopter to show his moral support and assure the island that more aid was on the way. By December 2007 a combination of donated and government funds totaling US$4.8 million had been deposited in a government-managed earthquake and tsunami relief fund, although it is unknown how much of those funds was directed to Simbo.[1]

Despite the shock and trauma caused by the tsunami, many on Simbo commented on how they were dazzled by the humanitarian effort. Gathered in their mountaintop refuges, they had a clear view of the huge US Navy Seahawk helicopter buzzing overhead and landing on the island, delivering bottled water and bags of rice. Small cargo ships anchored just offshore delivering relief supplies, and a US Navy supply ship, the USS *Frederick W. Stockton*, could even be seen lumbering off in the distance. For many Simboans it was their first time witnessing this kind of material wealth, and as one woman stated, the first time she "smell[ed] a helicopter." Some of the first visitors were teams of geoscientists. In total seven different groups conducted "post-tsunami reconnaissance," measuring the wave's height and other physical indicators as well as interviewing survivors. Later officials from humanitarian NGOs as well as authorities from the Solomon Islands National Disaster Management Office and international disaster organizations all paid visits to the island to assess the damage and organize the relief effort.

The early aid distribution proceeded smoothly. The first ship to arrive was chartered by the Don Bosco Technical Institute, a Roman Catholic organization in Honiara, and it sent rice, tea, sugar, canned tuna, bales of used clothing, tents, mosquito nets, bottled water, medicine, cooking pots, and utensils. In many cases after disasters local people reject food aid and other assistance on the grounds that it represents foreign oppression and control over local affairs.[2] After the 1970 Great Peruvian earthquake, for example, survivors were offended by donated used clothing and declared that prior to arrival of food aid they had had to live "like people without civilization," subsisting only on the produce provided by surrounding Indigenous communities.[3] On Simbo the aid was embraced. The massive influx of goods enabled many of the survivors, for the first time in their lives, to continuously consume highly desired canned tuna and rice over several weeks. One man's response was typical: "We ate lots of rice! We even had tea with sugar. It made us feel good and calmed our nerves. We ate like you white people." To the Simboans, rice and other store-bought goods constituted desirable manifestations of modernity and economic development.

The survivors also ate well before the arrival of food aid. Households reported that root crops from their gardens and canarium nuts from the orchards were plentiful, so the supplies provided by the relief effort were considered a perk that had positive psychological benefits but was not necessary for survival. The only real hardships involved drinking water. Most villages today lack, and prior to the tsunami lacked, access to potable water systems; they depend on roof-collected rainwater as their source of drinking water. In Tapurai all the rain tanks were destroyed. Luckily there is a small freshwater lake in the hills above Tapurai, and survivors tapped into that source while living in the camps. That did, however, require laborious treks down and then back up steep trails lugging the water in plastic jugs.

To receive, account for, and distribute the incoming relief aid three well-educated Simboans formed a committee called the Simbo Disaster Management Central Committee (SDMCC). They based themselves in Lengana near the island's sheltered harbor and produced a detailed damage assessment and tracked the incoming aid. When aid started to arrive, however, there was some grumbling from the SDMCC that much of it was delivered directly to the Tapurai survivors, circumventing the SDMCC. They argued that Tapurai, despite bearing the brunt of the tsunami, was receiving a disproportionately large amount of relief relative to other villages that had sustained some damage, the members of which were living in temporary camps, too. Members of the SDMCC criticized Tapurai for developing a "severe mania for hoarding" and acting like a "cargo cult," a pointed example of how the concept of the cargo cult now circulates in Melanesian political debates and can serve negatively to denigrate and ridicule.[4]

More disruptive conflicts emerged in the months and years after the tsunami as displaced villagers from Tapurai sought out a locale where they could permanently resettle. Their reluctance to rebuild on the destroyed Tapurai site was buttressed by the geoscientists and the parade of aid workers and disaster authorities who visited the island and described the destroyed village land as "vulnerable" and "risky," concepts that were foreign to Simboans but gained traction quickly and became common in the local discourse. These external influences combined with their lingering trauma led Tapurai's households to resettle a flat area known as Rupe, while others settled in the nearby hamlets of Patu Belama and Qeoro. Rupe and the other hamlets were just a kilometer from the original Tapurai village site and high enough above the coast that visiting disaster experts were confident they would be safe from future tsunamis. Survivors nevertheless found Rupe far from ideal. Access to the sea required negotiating a steep and slippery trail, and the coast was mainly large boulders, which meant there were almost no suitable sites to store their dugouts. In contrast the old destroyed village was highly desirable: it was large and flat and had a gorgeous ribbon of beach where villagers could easily board their dugout canoes and haul them up on the beach when they were not in use. Some households did contemplate returning to the much more desirable old site, but many remained fearful, especially after the visiting experts warned them that the Tapurai site was "disaster prone."

International aid agencies including World Vision, Save the Children, Oxfam, Red Cross, and UNICEF, in collaboration with the Solomon Islands NDMO, established their hub in Gizo, the administrative seat of the Western Province, where they coordinated the relief effort. Luckily, most of Gizo's infrastructure survived the earthquake, and the town's location inside the lagoon meant the tsunami's impact was less severe; the water rose only a few meters. The intact port and airport were quickly put into action to receive aid and distribute it to the more affected islands and communities. In the immediate relief effort, the NGOs worked across the region, taking on different roles. Save the Children, for example, worked on water purification and also set up "play safe areas," tented areas with toys and children's games, staffed with trauma counselors who attended to the children's needs. World Vision distributed rainwater tanks and food. Dozens of large white tents bearing the UNICEF logo were delivered around the region, and on Simbo they became the main shelters for those staying in the relocation camps.

As the initial relief effort shifted toward reconstruction and rehabilitation, the NGOs and the NDMO decided to divide the region into sectors where one NGO would be responsible for delivering aid. World Vision was designated as the NGO responsible for Simbo, Ranongga, and Kolombangara, and it donated corrugated tin sheeting and lumber to the Tapurai families so that they could rebuild their houses.

Soon after relocating to Rupe, however, villagers from Narovo and core members of one of its principal clans that had recognized attachments to the Rupe area demanded that they be monetarily compensated by the NGOs and national government for the use of their land for the proposed new village. At one point, villagers from Narovo stormed into Rupe and unstaked the UNICEF tents used by some of the Tapurai families as their dwellings. To resolve the land dispute, a series of heated community meetings involving NGO staff were held. In those meetings it became clear to the Narovo clan that the NGO did not have funds to compensate them for the use of their ancestral homelands. Eventually the

Narovo people relented and granted the Tapurai survivors permission to rebuild in Rupe.

However, tensions flared up again a year later in 2008 when the Solomon Islands government offered to rebuild Tapurai's grammar school. Excited about the opportunity to again have their own grammar school, Tapurai villagers identified several parcels of level land that were large enough for the school and near the new settlement of Rupe. When Tapurai announced their decision to build the school they again ran afoul of a clan in Narovo, who protested and demanded monetary compensation for the use of their land. The Narovo clan sent letters to the government detailing their complaints and declaring that they were the true landowners and deserved to be remunerated. Tapurai responded with counter letters, endorsed by the NGOs, that the Tapurai site was dangerous and too risky to be reinhabited. After months of tense community meetings, the government declared that the project would be revoked if the land disputes were not resolved. Desperate, Tapurai reluctantly elected to rebuild the school on the old Tapurai village site, the same exposed and vulnerable beach flat that was wiped clean by the tsunami (see figures 16 and 17). The old site was the only location near Rupe where historic attachments had been resolved in the distant past and villagers from other parts of Simbo could not make ownership claims.

Many of Tapurai's survivors were frustrated by their inability to find a safer site for the new grammar school. Instead of praising their kastom, as they had in the immediate wake of the tsunami when attachments to property relaxed and sharing flourished, they instead expressed consternation about their inability to effectively harness opportunities presented by outsiders. This sense of despair was exacerbated by the unmet promises of Christianity that emphasize unity and brotherly love. Tensions and conflicts over land, like the one witnessed over building the school, have been common on Simbo, as they have been across Island Melanesia when external agents introduce different kinds of projects such as logging initiatives, conservation schemes, or infrastructure projects.[5]

To shed light on these tensions and conflicts, in this chapter I focus theoretical and empirical attention on the role of place and especially land during the reconstruction phase of the disaster. As I discussed in chapters 2 and 3, on Simbo, and across much of Island Melanesia, places

Figure 16. Satellite images of Tapurai village taken in 2002 before the tsunami and three years after the tsunami in 2010. (Images by IKONOS and GeoEye-1.)

Figure 17. The new Kalaro Elementary School, rebuilt on the vulnerable flat area where Tapurai village stood before the community was destroyed by the 2007 tsunami. (Photo by author.)

are experienced in ways that confound modernist assumptions about the relations between humans and the nonhuman world.[6] The Simbo people actualize their island neither as a mute landscape upon which the dramas of sociopolitical contestations are played nor as "ecological services" abiding by universal biophysical mechanisms. Rather, the island is composed of spaces produced through the movements and intermingling of persons, spirit beings, plants, animals, and other nonhumans. How do we begin to grasp Simbo notions of place and land during the reconstruction without provincializing it as a specific, contingent, "cultural" phenomenon or cognitive framework of meaning being overlaid on a biophysical substrate? This certainly is not how Simboans talk about, engage with, or experience their landscapes and seascapes.

One approach to apprehending the various modes of composing place is to focus on *performativity*. From this perspective, accounts of place are not simply representations of external reality; they actively participate in its making. Science and technology scholar Ann Marie Mol developed a similar approach when she employed the concept of *enact* to delineate those practices, discourses, and materialities that constitute multiple versions of atherosclerosis.[7] Through an examination of patients', clinicians', and pathologists' practices at different sites in a Dutch hospital, the disease emerges as a different entity at different sites and in many cases under conditions that patients or health practitioners do not choose or expect. Rather than being a single entity that people represent differently, the body is multiple; it is more than one and less than many. In the lab it emerges under the microscope as clotted arteries, while during office visits the disease is an irritating leg pain. What Mol's work and that of others suggest is that reality is always in the making through dynamic assemblages of heterogeneous entities and actors.[8] Capable of fixity and sedimentation, yet open to surprise and complexity, assemblages require discursive and material work as they are made and reenacted, sometimes in ways that are not always intended by the actors involved. This approach is grounded in a relational philosophy developed by scholars such as Tim Ingold, Bruno Latour, Donna Haraway, and Gilles Deleuze and Félix Guattari, who posit that life is a process that unfolds through the emergence and shifting of relations between humans, nonhumans, technologies, and institutions.[9]

Importantly, a focus on performativity and the relationality of land parallels Simboans' discussion of their land and also Indigenous Oceanic scholars' writings. Fijian anthropologist Ilaitia Tuwere, for example, noted Ratu Sukuna's statement that land "is something he must explicitly serve: but something that would also help him in his difficulties."[10] Thus I consider here how Simboans *do* place or more precisely how they assemble it in practice, especially land. I seek to analyze the contradictions, coexistence, and consequences of how landscapes and seascapes were enacted in practice during the reconstruction phase of the disaster.

Land, we should note, has the rather unique materiality that its usefulness is difficult to share and thus depends on exclusion.[11] You cannot cultivate a plot where a school is built. At the same time, land's life-giving qualities lie at the core of human life as well as that of terrestrial nonhumans. For these reasons land, as Tanya Li notes, tends to spark moral arguments about its use.[12] Karl Polanyi weighed in on this topic and argued that treating land as a commodity for which the proprietor is conferred with the absolute right to ownership is corrosive to society.[13] Everyone has to have a place to dwell, and for the Simbo people, grow their food; thus, any claims to exclude others from land requires scrutiny. The question that arises is how exclusion occurs. Why do some arguments and modes of assembling land prevail while others fail?

The goal in this chapter, then, is to elucidate the heterogeneous elements and the manner in which they are arranged and deployed by different kinds of actors during the disputes over land. I ask: What kinds of practices did different actors engage in to actualize land as the reconstruction process unfolded? Approaching land through a lens of performative engagement helps focus attention on the reasons that some enactments of place succeed and others do not during disaster recovery, in a context where different assemblages derived from fundamentally different precepts are deployed.

COMPOSING SIMBO PLACES

For the Simbo people, "gusu" is the term that most closely approximates "place," although it could also be glossed as "country." Many scholars refer to these spaces as "land/sea district," but this inappropriately narrows the concept to a political boundary. Gusu not only bounds a territory; it also encompasses land (peso) and all the terrestrial beings and spaces such as nut groves, gardens, habitation sites, and other physical features that contribute to its existence. The gusu does not stop at the water's edge but instead extends across the seascape to include a myriad of specified spaces, including coastal zone (poana), island (nusa), lagoon reef (mati), and open ocean reef (gasaru) (See figure 6 in chapter 2.) Not only is place a composite of what we define as landscapes and seascapes, but gusu also connotes an amalgam of what we would define as historical, political, economic, and cosmological processes whereby human beings and the physical world are actualized as intermingled and sharing substance. Similar to Jamon Halvaksz's notion of "placepersons" or Donna Haraway's "naturecultures," on Simbo landscapes/seascapes and human beings are human/nonhuman collectives.[14] As the Bougainville author Regis Stella declared, "Land/place is regarded as an extension of the Indigenous self."[15]

An important practice to compose place is through naming. The reefs and lagoon areas are demarcated into seventeen spaces, which have specific kastom histories (see chapter 2 for the history of the two important reefs to the south of the island). Moreover, the land is demarcated at a surprisingly high spatial resolution. I learned this early on during my fieldwork when I had trouble understanding Simboans when I asked where they were going. A common exchange when you see someone on a walking path is to ask: "Where are you going?" Yet many of the responses were places I was not familiar with. Common village names such as Lengana, Nusa Simbo, or Masuru were rarely mentioned. I learned that Lengana is divided into at least six areas of habitation, and my interlocutors were providing those more specific destinations. All areas of the island and the surrounding reefs are named, and often they have overlapping names where a nut grove or coconut plantation has a different name than the land upon which it grows.

These everyday terms that Oceanic peoples like Simboans employ to describe the different spaces on their island are critical practices in which they perform place. The terms enable Simboans to speak about their island with authority that non-Simbo speakers lack, as do all languages for their native speakers. It is a mechanism that enables them to uniquely identify and actualize certain dimensions, lay claim to, and generate place. The fact that Simbo speakers maintain an autochthonous vernacular is critical to their sense of being and their sense of place. Gusu as a living concept would cease to exist without the Simbo language.

As I described in chapter 3, there is more than one gusu on Simbo. This is reflected most conspicuously in the name employed by the Simbo people when they speak to each other about their island: Madegugusu (four countries). The four gusu are Karivara, Ove, Simbo, and Narovo, and their boundaries are marked by rocks, points, mountains, bays, or other biophysical features. So instead of partitioning the fabric of reality between a universal biophysical domain on the one hand and heterogeneous meaning making of human beings on the other, the most salient and durable discontinuity on Simbo is *between* each gusu.

How, then, is this partitioning between gusu done in practice? One way is through narratives or what we call "myths," a term that immediately provincializes what Indigenous people say about their etiology as a flimsy layer of meaning overlaid on "material reality." As Fijian scholar Ilaitia Tuwere, noted: "The questions of whether the myth is an explanation of what was already existing or whether it became the social charter upon which the Fijian community was built in the first place is superfluous."[16] Similarly, the Simbo people do not conceive of their origin stories about the "time before" (*kama rane*) as "cultural constructions" or just tall tales. This was impressed upon me during my participation in a recent archaeological project on Simbo. To launch the project, the archaeologists and I organized several community presentations at which we discussed our goals and archaeological methods. We also outlined contemporary archaeological theories about the deep history of Simbo, including the Austronesian expansion and the more recent Lapita migration. Our Simbo audiences were inquisitive and open to our discussion about the history of their island. However, after the presentation, Goldie, one of Nusa Simbo's leaders, first praised me for helping educate the Simbo people about archaeology and the island's history, but then added, "It's nice what you say about the time before (kama rane), but we (mifala, exclusive "we") have our own kastom stories."

It is important to point out that Simboans make a distinction between fictional stories and their true history about the past. There is a large corpus of folktales (*pitopito liligan*) about the people-eating *liligani* (Hocart:

Iliganigani), which Hocart glossed as "giant."[17] Similar legends are found throughout the New Georgia Group, and they are typically recounted to children in highly dramatized narratives and also to tourists or other outsiders who would like to hear "custom stories."[18]

These tall tales are contrasted with "real history," narratives about the origins of the clans who emerged within each gusu. Through these narratives the primordial partitioning of the island is evidenced most clearly by the fact that there is not a common history describing the origin of all Simbo's inhabitants. Instead, leaders of the clans from each gusu recount specific narratives chronicling the genesis of the ancestral proto-human beings to which today's descendants owe their specific existence. These clan histories have a similar form and resemble those told on other islands in the New Georgia Group as well as Makira in the southeast Solomons, in that the original proto-humans of each clan were fundamentally distinct classes of beings who emerged from distinct places and times.[19] On Simbo each gusu today has two major clans, each with a distinct origin story. For example, Narovo's two main clans, Vunagugusu and Katapana, recount how a proto-male and proto-female emerged from a hole on top of Mt. Patu Kio. Ngari Lulumi, one of Ove's main clans, involves three angel-like spirit beings called mateana who appeared near a large stone at the summit of Mt. Watidingi (see chapter 4 for a more detailed version). Another clan emerged from a proto-woman who was thrown from the ocean by a sea being.[20]

Michael Scott insightfully noted how these narratives describe a past that is polyontological, in contrast to the more familiar monontological assumptions of Genesis as told in the Bible or the creation stories of the Society Islands of French Polynesia, where a single God, Ta'aroa, created the universe.[21] The origin stories of each of Simbo's clans describe how proto-humans within each district engaged in a process of humanization whereby they intermingled with the proto-humans of other clans to produce human lineages and assemble a human and nonhuman territory with nut groves, gardens, shrines, burial sites, settlements, named places, totem beings, and ancestor spirits. The narratives detail not only the genealogy of the clan's descendants, usually ten to twelve generations deep, but also important place-names, nut groves, shrines, or other sites of significance within the gusu inhabited by the descendants. Similar spatially explicit narratives are found across the Austronesian world.[22] For the Simbo clans that originated on the mountaintops, the narratives describe progressive movements down the mountainsides, creating their gardens, entombing their dead, planting nut trees, and building ancestor shrines, eventually reaching those habitation sites where the elder recounting the clan's history was born. Those who tell these stories are discursively providing the form and character of the respective territories and at the same time fusing the truly human ancestors' agency into the terrain.

These narratives are also highly charged political documents, as the names of the taboo sites, places, people, and other beings involved in these movements through space form the basis of each group's claims to authority to manage access to the land and resources of the gusu. These past movements inform a specific temporality of place, wherein the gusu are partially controlled by the past. This temporality is informed not only by the agency of ancestral human and nonhuman movements but also by cyclical markers of changing wind and ripening nuts.[23]

Ancestral movements and places depicted in these accounts are not simply disembodied, intergenerationally transmitted information but rather form the central corpus of Simbo kastom, the idealized reconstruction of past events, genealogies, or other aspects of history deemed important. As has been pointed out by anthropologists working in many Austronesian contexts like the Solomon Islands, the history of land use and the movements of people are inseparable from identity and political positioning.[24] This is the case here because all Simbo land and the surrounding reefs, except for the parcel "purchased" by European trader Jean Pratt at the turn of the twentieth century, are under the guardianship of clans (bubutu) rather than individuals or households with formal, government-registered titles.[25]

Clan membership is based on a bilateral system of kin reckoning that is an inherently flexible social organization in which status is contextual.[26] Cognatic descent systems, unlike unilineal ones, do not favor the maternal or paternal side, so in theory, most Simboans have a traceable, linked pedigree. Each gusu has a number of recognized clans led by recognized bangara (chiefs) who serve as stewards of the land and sea and monitor their uses. When asked about clan membership, my interlocutors said they give preference to kin traced through the maternal side and that rights passed through the mother to the child are "stronger," but in practice membership tends to be determined by principles of cognatic bilateral descent since, as my consultants noted, "your father was born from a mother" and thus a child can claim rights through his or her father's side, too.

Adept individuals are able to exploit others who are less skilled at expressing their land rights or simply do not know their rights.[27] Thus the question "Who were your ancestors and where did they live?" is intrinsically political. For it is through the identification of previous habitation sites, shrines, nut tree groves, and genealogical history that members of a clan lay claim to the landscape and adjacent seascape. Households who have established genealogical links to a clan are free to establish gardens, build houses, or plant trees in that gusu. Important for our understanding is the Simboan distinction mentioned in chapter 3 between property (isisongo) and land (peso). Property includes those possessions produced by the labor of recent ancestors, such as gardens, nut groves, coconut plantations, and land cleared for settlements, while land is that which was populated and humanized by the mythical ancestors. Those who do not have strong genealogical links to the landholding clan must seek permission to create property on the land.

COLONIALISTS AND CHRISTIANS

Over the course of the twentieth century there were demonstrable shifts in how the Simbo people assembled place. First, the materiality of narratives mentioned previously transformed from strictly aural and verbal to include paper. Over the course of the twentieth century, as many Simboans became literate, certain details of the oral narratives were inscribed into notebooks or onto sheets of paper. I learned this during my first interview about a clan's history. I interviewed an elder named Harold from the village of Bulolo, who is widely recognized as a principal leader of the Katapana clan. I asked him to recount his clan's origin stories, and after a few minutes he paused and with an inquisitive expression on his face he tapped his temple with his index finger while stating forlornly, "I'm old, my head is soft." He then asked one of his sons who was sitting nearby to fetch him "papers." A few minutes later his son appeared with a heavily worn manila folder. Inside were stapled sheets of equally worn and soiled paper with the names and habitation sites printed out by what appeared to be a dot matrix printer. I asked him if he knew how to operate a computer, and he laughed and stated that he barely knew how to read. His son who lives in Honiara, he went on to explain, had done him the favor of compiling the genealogies and typing them into a computer.

This shift in the materiality of the clan origin stories has meant that clan leaders' skills are no longer based solely on memory and oratory skills but also on their literacy or the literacy of their family members. After interviewing many of the clan leaders I noted a wide variance in written documents; some were handwritten, others were typed lists of names, and some, like Harold's, were computer generated, with detailed notes about each relative and place-name.

The coherence and details of these written accounts have emerged as critical markers of authenticity as they now circulate through the Solomon Islands courts where land disputes are adjudicated.[28] Even the acceptance of a court case by the local courts requires several written documents detailing the specifics of the dispute. Thus, literacy and paper documents are vital elements for contemporary Simboans to actualize land.

Similar to the paper charts and diaries of the European ship captains who visited Simbo in the eighteenth and nineteenth centuries, these paper documents are what science and technology scholars refer to as "inscription devices," in that they transform and create traces of an entity, in this case narratives about land, into another material form. But rather than just being a new method to record land claims, I suggest they actively participate in their remaking. First, the materiality of paper enables a spatiality that land does not have. Land, unlike paper, "is not a mat: it cannot be rolled up and taken away."[29] Paper documents enable traces of Simbo land to circulate much faster and more widely. Crucially, the documents can circulate through state bureaucratic institutions such as courts and render traces of land into a form that is more legible and more vulnerable to corrosive forms of external bureaucratic and capitalistic control such as expropriation.

The first traces of Simbo land to appear on paper were after the "sale" of land around the head of Narovo harbor to the trader Jean Pratt in December 1893. Transactions like this between European traders and local people were documented and registered with the Department of Lands

and Surveys in Honiara. According to these records, a chief named Si-
lanana sold a parcel of 100 acres called Tubi to Jean Pratt in exchange for
"trade goods."[30] When I inquired about this sale my Simbo interlocutors
were convinced that it involved a process known as *pajuku*. Typically, in
pajuku shell money (*bakia*) is given by guests to a landholding clan not
simply as an exchange of wealth but also to appease the land and all its
imminent historically constituted ancestral relations. According to my interlocutors, before the widespread use of Western currency, arrangements
like this were effective and enabled guests from other districts to reside on
another's land to build interdistrict alliances, especially in headhunting
times when districts cooperated to mount large raids on other islands.

But because the transaction was registered with the protectorate, the
parcel was in effect alienated from Simbo's inhabitants and pulled into
capitalist relations of commodification that assume land is an entity that
can be bought, sold, rented, and held in perpetuity. This parcel is known
colloquially as "LR 60" and eventually was sold to the Methodist Church.
Later, in the 1970s, the protectorate began a process of repatriating dis-
possessed lands back to their original owners. Upon its release to the clans
of Narovo it became embroiled in a dispute that went to local courts, and
a Simbo man won the rights to the parcel.

As paper and literacy emerged as critical elements to actualize land,
colonial-imposed concepts of "land" and "landowners" may have resulted
in an even more radical shift in how Simboans compose place. Scholars
who have analyzed the evolution of landownership in the western Solomons have argued that the contemporary emphasis on clan identity as the
basis of ownership may have been refracted through the local category of
bubutu as Simbo and other islands in the region became entangled with
colonial institutions and concepts.[31] Joel Robbins suggests a similar process occurred during religious conversion in the highlands of Papua New
Guinea, where existing categories were employed to absorb the Christian
doctrine but were transformed in the process.[32] Careful historical analysis
of the concept of bubutu describes how prior to European contact land-
group relations were more focused on place-focused notions of land such
as gusu than on clan-based land ownership.[33] Indeed, in Hocart's unpublished and published writings bubutu is only mentioned briefly; he defines
it as "a descendent" and makes no reference to kin groups or categories.[34]

Instead of describing their kin affiliations through genealogically defined bubutu groupings, Hocart's interlocutors identified with their particular gusu and would refer to themselves as tinono Narovo (Narovo person), tinono Ove (Ove person), and so forth. Today district membership continues to be a salient category by which people self-identify, but only in a generalized sense. The people of Tapurai, for example, continue to refer to themselves as "Ove people," but they will also emphasize that family groups within the village are members of specific clans.

The contemporary emphasis on genealogically derived landownership emerged during the colonial era as local categories were repurposed to fit European concepts of land and notions of social organization. In the 1920s a major shift occurred regarding the protectorate's treatment of landownership when native courts were established to enable Solomon Islanders to adjudicate their own claims through "customary" mechanisms. Most protectorate administrators, however, had only a shallow grasp of Melanesian social organization. These courts invoked notions of unilineal descent and primogeniture, models of social organization that were found in Africa but not in Melanesia. Indeed, early anthropologists working in Melanesia, who were also influenced by African, descent-based models of social organization, struggled to understand Melanesian cognatic systems, in which affiliations can be traced through either the mother or father.[35] Influenced by the African descent models, native courts assumed genealogical claims were the basis of determining landownership conflicts.

An informative example of this colonial-induced shift on Simbo is the current divisions within Narovo district. During Hocart's time these groups self-identified as Narovo people (tinoni Narovo), and there was little mention of descent group identification. But by 1960 when Harold Scheffler visited the island, Narovo's inhabitants described to him how Narovo was divided into two segments, Vunagugusu and Katapana, which were and continue to be the names of the landowning clans.[36] At that time, members of Vunagugusu claimed that they were the originary lineage of the entire island and that from their apical ancestors all the other lineages emerged. Indeed, the term "Vunagugusu" means "base" or "bottom" clan. Yet Scheffler noted how leaders from clans in the other gusu did not describe their lineages branching off from Vunagugusu. During my research the lineage leaders of Vunagugusu no longer asserted that their clan was the founding lineage of the entire island, and members of the other districts adamantly disavowed that Vunagugusu was the founding clan.

With the rise of these new material and institutional modes of composing place, formal ritualistic practices that dominated life prior to the arrival of Europeans have been displaced. As detailed in chapter 3, skull repositories (tabuna), tuna shrines (inaru), dance circles (*kokobara*), and canoe houses (paile) dotted the landscape. Skull repositories in particular were focal points of ritual practices in which ancestor spirits (tomate) were provided burnt offerings of fish, puddings, and other foods, to channel their mana for the benefit of the community. Garden shrines (*tagoro*) were also built and were the sites where the first fruits of new gardens were burned as offerings to help ensure the land's fertility.

Even though Christian practices have supplanted these pre-Christian rituals, ancestral mana and the associated spirit beings continue to inhabit the island as they did in ancestral times and to assert their agency. The presence of ancestor spirits is especially potent in the spaces around former ancestral shrines or other areas that were focal points of pre-Christian ancestor propitiation. In other words, it is not a situation in which the Simbo people simply replaced their old cosmology with a new one.[37] Rather, they practice Christianity to subdue the ever-present agency of ancestor spirits that imbue the land and influence daily life. When shrines or other sites of pre-Christian cosmological importance are approached today, it is with great caution, and those who enter these locales ask permission to do so from the residing spirit beings. Transgressors who fail to show respect and who disturb the spirits inevitably suffer retaliation and fall ill or experience mishaps, sometimes lethal ones. More generally the agency of the land affects those who are involved in land disputes. There is a widespread understanding on Simbo that repercussions, usually illness, will befall those involved in acrimonious land disputes. Far from being a mute backdrop, spirit-imbued Simbo land exceeds the capacity of Simboans to control it.

Those with close genealogical ties to an ancestral area, who show their respect by asking permission or placing a few coins at a shrine site, frequently have positive experiences. One particularly memorable case occurred while I was conducting the archaeological fieldwork mentioned earlier at a shrine site near Ove crater, where our goal was to search for

Figure 18. Aseri holding a seven-hundred-year-old potsherd he found at his ancestors' shrine. (Photo by author.)

and collect ancient ceramic potsherds. Our group was accompanied by Aseri, one of the most knowledgeable elders from Ove, whose parents are buried in cemented graves at the base of the volcano. Aseri is the father of Nickson's wife, Puso, and I have grown close to him over the years. He is a delightful man in his late seventies with thick, calloused hands and a wide, inviting grin.

The old shrine site now is not much more than a mound of rocks that sits above the active volcano on an exposed site that, because of the volcanic activity, lacks vegetation. We had shown Aseri samples of the potsherds we had found a few days earlier in Nusa Simbo. Simboans were unaware that their ancestors used pottery and that these little pieces were from old, broken cooking pots. The sherds we found were, at their largest, only a few centimeters across, so they were difficult to spot in the cracks between the stones and rubble of the shrines. We searched this site for over an hour until Aseri located a sherd. Excited that we had found something, the archaeologists and I moved closer to Aseri, expecting to find more sherds near where he had located the first one. Within a minute he spotted another, this time within my field of vision just beside my feet. I, for some reason, was unable to see it. When I commented to Aseri that he had keen eyes, he responded matter-of-factly, "It's not my eyes only, it's my ancestors too, this is my place, this is my land, they are looking after this place." Indeed, Aseri's eyes, like those of most elders on Simbo, are clouded with cataracts! Sharp eyesight was most certainly not the reason he had spotted the sherds between our legs. Only later did the rest of the team begin to find the sherds (see figure 18).

TSUNAMILAND

The waves that slammed into Simbo not only caused destruction and horror on Simbo; they also provoked, through the myriad visits of scientists, disaster experts, NGOs, and government officials, a novel repertoire of concepts and material practices by which to enact place. As mentioned earlier, the international humanitarian disaster relief apparatus began descending on Simbo within days of the tsunami. One of the first groups of visitors was a Japanese team of geoscientists accompanied by representatives of the NDMO. They visited Simbo to conduct assessments or "post-tsunami reconnaissance." Deploying GPS instruments, leveling rods, tape measures, and cameras, they carefully measured the local tsunami heights, its peak run-up, and inundation distances.[38] While conducting the surveys they interviewed Simbo eyewitnesses about the physical characteristics of the wave and in many cases relied on local people to judge the inundation levels. Another team, this time Americans, arrived a few weeks later and carried out similar rapid assessments, deploying their instruments at dozens of locales around the island.[39] These physical assessments carried out on Simbo, as well as those conducted on the surrounding islands, were then transported as inscriptions to calculation centers at universities like Georgia Tech in Atlanta to be re-represented through geophysical models that depicted the tsunami's characteristics and be published in scientific papers. Traces of Simbo's graceful coast areas were now contributing to the extension and durability of geophysicists' knowledge.

Ironically, the first trace of Simbo's tsunamiland was produced by Nickson, one of my closest Simbo associates. Prior to the tsunami he was Simbo's email station operator for the UNDP-sponsored People First Network (PFnet), a system of rural email stations that used solar-powered high-frequency radios with modems. Within twenty minutes of the tsunami, Nickson emailed a report to PFnet's central office in Honiara describing the size of the tsunami waves and the distance the water traveled inland, along with an estimate of the damage. He became somewhat of a local celebrity because his report contained the first direct observations of the 2007 tsunami's effects and was passed to the Pacific Tsunami Warning Center in Hawaii, which within thirty minutes of the earthquake issued a tsunami warning for the entire Pacific basin.

The scientists and Nickson enacted the island's coastal lands through technoscientific practices that were quite foreign to most Simboans. By identifying the tsunami-prone areas and inscribing their data into reports and research papers, they not only rendered Simbo land visible to the scientific community and government bureaucracies but also imposed novel forms of assembling land on Simboans. My interlocutors related to me how they learned during the visits of these experts and presentations of NDMO staff geophysical explanations of tsunamis and the future risks they pose for the old Tapurai site and other low-lying areas. Simboans found a Simbo term, *tapata*, which I gloss as "problem" or "hardship," to describe the new concepts they had learned from the tsunami experts that characterized the old Tapurai land as "vulnerable." In the local vernacular tapata also became a gloss for "disaster," although the Pijin-inflected English word disasta dominated local discourses about the tsunami, as did "sunami."

As described in chapter 3, prior to the earthquake Tapurai was considered an ideal locale for a village, with easy access to the sea for loading and unloading canoes and a large flat space for the village. In my interviews about the old site, Tapurai's survivors contrasted their rationale for not reinhabiting the old site as new and different compared to the traditional reasons that households make moves and build houses on new plots. As one middle-aged man stated:

> Our resettlement is different from when people normally go and build new houses. They move because their village is full or they just want to move to a different place, but for us here in Tapurai it is different. The village land was totally destroyed, it is a problem. The tsunami spoiled it. I've also seen the sea start to come up. Three or four years from now, Tapurai will be gone. Because the sea is coming up as you white man have told us and I have seen with my own eyes. When I was child there was much more beach.

Or as another man stated: "You scientists have been here and visited that place [Tapurai]. This prediction of future tsunamis cannot stop. It is non-stop. It will happen" (see figure 19).

Importantly, Tapurai survivors have not converted the old Tapurai site into orchards, gardens, or coconut groves. The Simboan survivors are not engaging in one of the key material practices by which land is assembled on Simbo. As described in chapter 4, gardening and planting coconuts or canarium nuts are some of the most intimate ways in which Simboans and their hoes, seeds, and bodies bring forth life from their island. When I asked my interlocutors why they were not growing produce or planting coconuts on the old site, they responded in similar terms that the land had a "problem" and would eventually be struck by another tsunami or be inundated by the rising sea.

In contrast to the land, the seascape around Tapurai was never evaluated in these terms.[40] Fishers were fearful about entering the water for several weeks after the tsunami, but within a month they resumed their regular fishing practices on the reefs adjacent to Tapurai and around the island. When I asked about this discrepancy, my interlocutors commented that the ocean did not have "problems," and that they had been told by the outside experts that it was the land rather than the sea that was vulnerable to tsunamis.[41]

The influence of outside experts was also evident in the naturalistic explanations that dominated local descriptions of the tsunami. When I asked survivors about the cause of the tsunami, many quite readily provided a

Figure 19. A geoscientist from Georgia Tech University, United States, using a survey rod to measure the tsunami "flow depth" of 5 meters above ground elevation in Tapurai two weeks after the tsunami. (Photo credit: Hermann Fritz.)

geophysical explanation, learned through workshops delivered by visiting experts, that the earthquake had moved the ocean floor and created the wave. There was, however, a far less prevalent narrative that attributed the tsunami to a curse (*pinamanga*) that was an outcome of steady and widely accepted decline in respect for elders as well as the frequent disputes over land. Interestingly, scientific explanations of the tsunami seemed not to displace local conceptualizations of other biophysical phenomena such as the island's active volcano that Simboans attribute to a spirit being known as Ratovo, although that explanation appears to now be in question. As one woman stated: "I'm not so sure if Ratovo is causing all that steam [laugh]."

The introduced yet locally refracted characterization of the Tapurai site as a "problem" was a critical conceptual resource in the Tapurai survivors' attempts to relocate their village on land that belonged to the Narovo clans. As I discussed in chapter 4, Tapurai's residents were the descendants of immigrants from Ove who made an unprecedented move away from their ancestral territories in the early 1900s and established Tapurai on the land of the Narovo people. Ove lacked flat land on the seaside suitable to establish a new village, so Tapurai's ancestors moved to the much more accessible Tapurai site. The northern half of Simbo, however, had since time immemorial been within the Narovo district. Narovo's clans, I was told, accommodated the migrants in the early 1900s through the process of pajuku mentioned earlier, whereby the Ove immigrants were granted access to Narovo land. Today, however, pajuku has largely been abandoned when the transaction involves extra-local entities and the building of infrastructure that is not conceptualized as "property," such as school buildings or mobile phone towers.

As Tapurai's survivors began relocating to Rupe, they asked permission from the Narovo clans to resettle and justified their move by arguing that the old site had "problems" with tsunamis as well as with sea-level rise. A man put it succinctly when he declared in Pijin that Tapurai was a "rubbish place." In other words, Tapurai's survivors had adopted the concepts of outside experts about the Tapurai land to make their case to the Narovo people. They attempted to bring land into being by assembling it with novel elements introduced during the recovery from the tsunami. Ultimately, the strategy of deploying technoscientific modes of assembling land and leveraging them to acquire new land failed in their attempts to rebuild Tapurai's elementary school on safer ground. Central to this failure were the ways in which capitalist relations have become entangled with composing Simbo land.

PLACE AND PROFIT

Although the Narovo clan denied Tapurai's survivors access to land to build the school, they did accept the rebuilding of houses. This decision was related to meetings with World Vision, the NGO that was donating the materials for the new houses, in which they made it clear to Simboans that donor funds were not available to purchase land. Hence the houses were outside of the capitalist relations that are considered so corrosive and antithetical to the practices of mutual self-help and sharing that Simboans cherish and reify as kastom. In addition, houses constitute property (isisongo) and are conceived, along with gardens and nut groves, as essential to life on Simbo. When land is used for "property," access is readily granted by the landholding clan to anyone, regardless of their clan affiliation, who needs the property for subsistence purposes outside of profit making. For these reasons, the Narovo clans dropped their disputes and allowed the NGO-funded houses to be built on their land.

The building of the school, however, was a fundamentally different dispute because externally funded infrastructure does not constitute "property." Although schools and schooling are highly valued by the Simbo people, a school is considered a permanent entity that will inhabit a site in perpetuity, and thus a clan's ancestral attachments are emphasized rather than a household's more ephemeral "property." When government-funded infrastructure like a school is built, the land underneath must be apprehended as a commodity: a mute, inert, indifferent surface upon which individual or collective rights are overlaid. This is the scenography assumed by capitalist relations, wherein human relationships to land are restricted to the relationship between owner and property.

The reticence to apprehend land in capitalist terms has arisen as a strategy of the Simbo people, and across Island Melanesia, to protect land from being alienated or exploited by commercial or government entities and also for inhibiting fellow islanders who seek to earn profit from their activities.[42] Tapurai's arguments that the old village land was a "problem" and that their resettlement was different than a "normal" relocation were ineffective in displacing this resistance to profit making and the encroachment of capitalist relations.

In fact, almost all government-funded infrastructure, including Simbo's community high school, primary school, market stalls, large hall and dormitory (Centenary Hall), wharf, and clinic, is located on LR 60, the land block that was alienated in the late 1800s and later formally titled, via a court adjudicated dispute, to a single Simbo family. Firmly anchored in capitalist relations and under the control of one family, these facilities have been built without disputes and have benefited Simbo, but at the expense of extending the entangling of Simbo land among external actors and governmental structures.

The resistance to individual profit making and commodification of land on Simbo has also had the effect of limiting economic development on the island. My interlocutors recounted numerous economic development projects initiated by ambitious Simbo entrepreneurs or external actors such as NGOs or the national government. These projects have included everything from aquaculture, women's sewing initiatives, cattle husbandry, and micro-grants for local shops, to copra cooperatives. Invariably these projects have collapsed due to disputes arising over the distribution of the financial benefits. The only commercial enterprises that endure on the island are small shops, yet typically they survive for only a year or so before going bankrupt.

The disputes that emerged over the installation of a mobile phone antenna on Simbo illustrate the difficulties of building public infrastructure.[43] In 2007 Solomon Telekom Company, the state-owned telecom, began expanding cellular phone service into the western Solomon Islands. It first established service in Gizo, which provided partial, unreliable coverage on Simbo. In 2008 a private company, Digicel, contacted landowners on Simbo and surveyed the island. The results determined an optimal site location that would provide the widest network coverage for Simbo as well as the southwest coast of Ranongga (the nearest island to the north). After a site was tentatively selected, disputes quickly arose over rights to the land. The key issue, as with rebuilding Tapurai's elementary school, was that the cell phone operator had to pay rent, and several people from Simbo insisted that they had rights to the land and thus should receive some of the rent income. Digicel eventually dropped its plans to build the tower, but in 2012 Solomon Telekom, the state-owned company, finally installed a cell tower on a different site within LR60, the only piece of registered land on Simbo. This new site, however, was suboptimal relative to the site slated for the original tower during the initial land survey. Much lower in elevation, the tower only provides partial coverage to Simbo and no coverage to Ranongga.

As with the school building in Tapurai, there is a certain level of ontological dissonance among Simboans about their kastom and their notions of land, in that they cannot capitalize on the benefits of economic development and government infrastructure programs that could provide desirable material benefits to the island.

HEALTHY OCEANS

The upshot of enacting land in ways that counter capitalist relations is that the land and sea resources on Simbo, the island's livability conditions, appear not to be overharvested. As noted by Paul Nadasdy, conceptions of land configure not just human-land relations but wider relations between human and nonhuman entities more generally.[44] Simbo gardens, for example, remain productive despite centuries of cultivation. In household surveys I conducted, 66 percent of villagers responded that over their lifetimes garden yields have not declined. To sustain this fertility farmers employ a number of practices. This includes mulching, terracing to control erosion, and intercropping nitrogen-fixing tree species (e.g., *Lysiloma latisiliquum*). In addition, several species of introduced, fast-growing vines such as mile-a-minute (*Mikania micrantha*) are allowed to cover gardens during fallow periods, providing a rapidly growing layer of humus-generating foliage that can be easily cleared by cutting and rolling up the thick mat of vines.

The marine environment also appears to be healthy.[45] One proxy of coral reef health is its ability to bounce back from a severe disturbance. The tsunami presented just such a scenario, and I worked with a marine ecologist from the University of Queensland in 2009 to assess the recovery. In conversations with Simbo fishers, we were told that prior to the tsunami the coral reefs on the northwestern side adjacent to Lengana and Tapurai were dominated by coral and had a diverse fish community that provided an abundance of food. The marine ecologist surmised that the earthquake and tsunami were likely to have had separate yet compounding impacts on the reef community. First, the powerful earthquake would have physically broken individual coral colonies and fractured the reef substrate. Second, the series of powerful waves would have completely destroyed fragile branching coral species (already weakened and fractured by the earthquake), leaving a handful of larger massive corals and a bare limestone substrate.

To assess the damage from the tsunami, we conducted underwater surveys of coral reef condition at four sites adjacent to Lengana and Tapurai villages. The assessments showed that the four reefs adjacent to Tapurai and Lengana had recovered well in the two years between the earthquake (2007) and the surveys (2009). Live coral cover ranged from 15 to 45 percent, with negligible dead coral and macroalgae (signs of stress) across all sites. This indicated that the reef structure and function were still intact, and coral larval supply was strong.

In our assessment we also found that the coral community was primarily a branching and massive species. The majority of the massive colonies ranged between 50 centimeters and 200 centimeters in diameter (twenty to one hundred years old), indicating that they had survived the tsunami. The branching corals, however, were all less than 30 centimeters in diameter and hence were likely new recruits after the tsunami (see figure 20).

The marine scientist I worked with surmised that the rapid recovery of the Simbo coral reef ecosystem was probably due to low local-scale human disturbance of the marine ecosystem. During the reef surveys he noted that the limestone substrate was dominated by coralline algae with minimal algal turfs. These coralline algae are known to provide the preferred substrate for coral recruitment and contributed to rapid recovery on coral reefs.[46] On reefs where herbivorous fish such as parrot fish (*Scaridae*) and surgeonfish (*Acanthuridae*) that consume algae are overharvested, algal turfs tend to flourish and outcompete corals. Poor water quality also

Figure 20. A Simbo diver above Simbo's recovering coral reef. Note the small size of the branching corals, an indicator that they had regrown after being destroyed by the tsunami. (Photo by author.)

contributes to turf algae. But because of the lack of landscape disturbance on Simbo, there are few terrestrially derived sediments and nutrients, resulting in high water quality around the island.[47] Hence the relatively low human pressures on the reefs surrounding Simbo prior to and after the tsunami provided the environmental conditions to allow for a rapid recovery of hard corals, which are the fundamental building block of a healthy and productive reef ecosystem.

LAND MOVEMENTS AND ACTIONS

This chapter has detailed that the tsunami humanitarian relief effort involved dozens of scientists, NGO personnel, and disaster experts descending on the island. They exposed the Simbo people to new discursive strategies, concepts, experiences, and technoscientific practices by which to assemble Simbo land into vulnerable tsunamiland. Through measurements collected during scientific assessments, interviews, and workshops, as well as with concepts such as "vulnerability" and "tsunami prone," the expert prognosis was that the old Tapurai was risky and unfit for rebuilding. By pulling these discourses, relations, and technologies together and aligning them, they assembled something quite novel for most Simboans: an island that had coasts vulnerable to tsunamis. Even the concept of "tsunami" was foreign to most Simboans. However, this did not stop the residents of Tapurai from attempting to leverage this technoscientific assemblage of land to their own advantage as they resettled in an area that from time immemorial had been under the guardianship of the Vunagugusu clan of Narovo. In response, members of the Vunagugusu employed their long-standing, yet historically transformed, ancestral entitlement to the land that is an outcome of regenerating their gusu through a repertoire of myths, spirit beings, ancestral mana, gardening practices, fishing, extensive knowledge of their territory's ecology, totems, and property taboos.

What I hope to have shown in this chapter is that the displacements experienced by the Simbo people after the tsunami were not simply the movement of Tapurai villagers to a new locale. Land was not, as Karl Marx argued, "the equivalent of a production platform . . . a substratum . . . , an interface between the mental and the material where the sheer physicality of the world comes hard up against the creativity of human endeavour."[48] Rather, land was a participant in the movement as it was mobilized through different forms of praxis.

But the rendering of Simbo coastal areas into vulnerable tsunamiland has an important effect: it redistributes expertise about Simbo toward centers of power in the global North.[49] Vulnerable tsunamiland is the product of and circulates within a technoscientific network of people, institutions, resources, and machines that extends across the planet. Collectively they compose an object that could then be contemplated and acted on by experts sitting at their computer screens in Atlanta or Oxford. Tsunamiland, like the gusu, was not passive; it was active and it would eventually circulate into the bureaucratic centers such as the UNDP to convince disaster experts to declare that Simbo, like many islands of the Pacific, was among the most vulnerable to natural disasters.

6 Vulnerable Isles?

January 12, 2019, was one of those magnificently calm days. The blustery peja winds had diminished overnight, leaving the ocean surface with just a hint of surface ruffle. I was a week into my most recent visit to Simbo, making my way by boat from Meqe around the east side of the island toward the old Tapurai site. Rather than heading out through the main passage of Narovo bay and motoring at full speed to Tapurai, we saved fuel and hugged the coast. Nickson carefully navigated our fiberglass canoe through the huge dome-like *Porites* coral heads that dot the shallow lagoon. Underneath us the now fully recovered gardens of branching and plating corals dazzled us with their glowing pinks, blues, and greens. January is when the high tide peaks midday, so there was enough water on the reef that we could run faster without much fear of the propeller striking the coral. As we cleared the reef, we increased our speed and passed Rupe, the village where most of Tapurai's members had relocated. It sits 50 meters above the coast on one of the few flat spots on the northern end of the island. Down the slippery path from the village, at the water's edge several young boys were jumping off the branches of an enormous tree that grew over the water. On the other side of us, with the mountains of Ranongga forming a picturesque background, a young boy and girl, probably siblings and no older than ten or eleven, sat calmly 100 meters or so from shore in a dugout, their right hands gently tugging on small fishing lines in anticipation of a strike and possibly their morning snack of fresh reef fish. As we passed by, I raised my hand and waved. They responded with a burst of laughter and then timidly waved back; the white underside of their hands contrasted sharply against their dark skin. It was a Saturday, so most children were not attending school and were either working in the gardens or, if they were lucky, free to roam the village or paddle the lagoon.

I was on my way to Kalaro Elementary School, the school discussed in chapter 5 that was at the center of post-tsunami disputes and was eventually rebuilt on the vulnerable, tsunami-prone beach in old Tapurai. Earlier in the week I had learned from my Simbo consultants that the Solomon Islands NDMO had sent a group of government experts on several visits to Simbo in 2018 to conduct meetings and workshops about tsunami preparedness. Later I was able to interview two of the NDMO's staff who carried out the workshops. Both were young Solomon Islander professionals with college degrees who had undergone training. The leader, Danny Ruel, was a pleasant, soft-spoken man from Guadalcanal who was the provincial disaster officer for the Western and Central Provinces. Since the 2007 tsunami, the Solomon Islands has received funding from a number of international agencies, and the Gizo office was an outcome of the government's efforts to expand the NDMO's reach into the provinces. Danny was the only staff member, and he was provided with a desk in the Western Province's government building in Gizo as his office. Prior to Danny and his team's visits to Simbo in 2018, he and other colleagues from the NDMO were funded by the UNDP to visit India's Tsunami Earlier Warning Center in Hyderabad India for a two-week training session, where they learned the techniques and methods they would employ in Simbo. Later Danny attended six more weeks of "community-based disaster reduction risk" training in Japan.

Danny detailed to me that he and his team made two visits to Simbo. The first was to collect information from tsunami survivors through a "consultation" that would inform their tsunami risk assessments. During this first trip they focused their efforts on the three main elementary schools on the island, interviewing survivors from Tapurai, Lengana, and Nusa Simbo about their experiences with the 2007 tsunami. In a report the NDMO team created to document their work on Simbo, the staff were well versed in the discourse of the UNDP and stated that their goal was to "identify and assess vulnerability and risk of the schools to tsunami and strengthen their preparedness and capacity to respond to the hazard." They also demonstrated the technical skills necessary to carry out a number of field methods including interviews, participatory mapping, GPS data collection, and transect walks to identify vulnerable areas, evacuation routes, and the most suitable locations for signage. Danny stressed that the approach was guided by a philosophy of "community participation" in which "local knowledge" was combined with "technical input."

GPS data collection and mapping played a prominent role in their work. They used handheld GPS receivers to validate "tsunami safe areas" by measuring the sites' elevations and determining if they were high enough to avoid inundation during a tsunami event. Escape routes were also mapped with the GPS receivers and displayed on the maps in the report. When I inquired about the demarcated inundation areas, Danny responded that local knowledge was used to verify the maps they had produced from geophysical analysis that predicted the spatial extent of the low-lying areas of the island.

On the second trip to Simbo several months later, the team presented freshly printed and laminated large format posters to the schools, then gave several "capacity building" talks about the "science of tsunamis" and the risks of living near the water's edge. The second visit culminated with several practice drills to test the schools' tsunami response plans, in which NDMO staff, schoolchildren, and teachers carried out an exercise simulating an earthquake; they directed students to first shelter under their desks and then evacuate along the escape routes to the designated safe zones in the hills behind the schools.

These workshops were part of a region-wide effort organized by UNDP and funded by the Japanese government called Strengthening School Preparedness for Tsunamis in the Asia-Pacific Region. In fact Simbo's workshop was featured on the UNDP webpage, including excerpts from an interview that Danny conducted with one of Simbo's schoolteachers.[1] The stated objective of these workshops was to "mitigate the impact of tsunamis by enhancing school preparedness in high-risk communities in the Asia-Pacific region." The eighteen-month, $1.6-million project funded

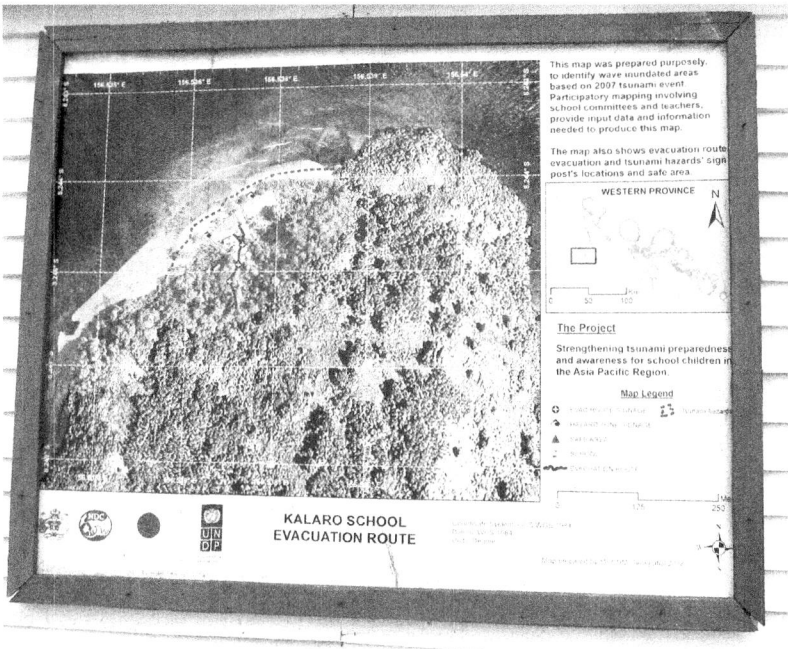

Figure 21. A poster mounted on the wall of Kalaro Elementary School in Tapurai that was created from knowledge collected in a participatory tsunami preparedness workshop conducted on Simbo in 2018. (Photo by author.)

programs like the one on Simbo in more than 155 schools in eighteen countries. As one official from UNDP stated: "Drills in schools will ensure that younger generations are prepared for a future tsunami, . . . Natural disasters like tsunamis cannot be prevented. It is in our best interest to work together to be prepared and have the knowledge to save lives."[2]

On my visit to Tapurai in 2019 I snapped a photo of Danny's "visual product," a large poster titled in English "Kalaro School Evacuation Route." It was nailed to the outside wall of the school building (see figure 21). The poster, already faded and a little moldy, had been carefully designed by Danny's team with an inset of the Western Province indicating the geographic location of Simbo, a scale bar, north arrow, UTM coordinates, and legend. Most of the poster was a satellite image of Tapurai with a thick dashed line in red demarcating the "tsunami hazards" zone and another blue line designating the evacuation path into the hills behind the village, to an officially designated safe zone. There were also icons indicating where signs, translated into Pijin, had been installed to designate the tsunami hazard zones near the coast and evacuation route signs leading up the hill to the safe areas. In Tapurai the evacuation route was precisely the one used by the survivors of the 2007 tsunami.

As I stared up at the poster with Nickson and another man who had come down from his garden to join us, I asked if they thought this poster was needed, considering that Tapurai's children had fled before the 2007 tsunami destroyed the village. They both looked at me, a little confused. Nickson then spoke up and said: "We need things like this to be safe. People from big places like yours know a lot. We're still in the dark about these things." When I noted the irony that these tsunami experts were informing people who for the most part had successfully saved their own lives during the tsunami, Nickson just shrugged his shoulders. His statement and attitude captured how many Simboans understood the workshops and their position in the world, and it underpins why most of my Simbo interlocuters were excited and enthusiastic about the visits made by the tsunami mitigation experts. Capacity workshops given by NGOs, the national government, or international organizations on topics ranging from cooperatives, to community-based resource conservation, to economic development initiatives occur with some frequency on Simbo, and many find them to be an entertaining break from the regular routine even though some aspects may be incomprehensible.

I poked around to see if any of the "hazard zone" or evacuation route signage was present, but I could not find any. Nickson said he had never seen any signs. Danny confirmed that his team did not install the signs since they wanted the communities to take ownership of the project and had asked the teachers, school principals, and headmasters to organize the installation of the signs as well as to form community disaster committees that would conduct regular disaster drills. Danny was well aware that the signs were never installed and that these committees rarely functioned as they were intended by his staff. He told me in Pijin: "Hey, these communities, they are a little bit of a challenge. They are remote and monitoring their progress is hard."

This chapter, then, reflects on this visit by disaster experts and relates it to what we have learned from Simbo's experience of the tsunami and how it might reshape our understandings of vulnerability and disaster recovery in a world that is progressively construed as riskier. Indeed, the arrival of disaster experts on Simbo is symptomatic of a wider shift in how the concept of vulnerability has been drawn into major international governance structures and deployed around the world to delineate certain regions, communities, and coastlines as vulnerable to biophysical threats.

FROM CONCEPT TO PRACTICE

It probably comes as no surprise that despite the miraculous response to the tsunami on Simbo, major international bodies such as the UN, World Bank, and IPCC consistently characterize small island nations like the Solomon Islands as some of the most vulnerable nations in the world to natural disasters and climate change.[3] Understandings of small islands in these organizations follow a consistent discursive pattern that describes vulnerability as attributes that nations like the Solomon Islands lack: "Major constraints to adaptation . . . [include] lack of technology and human resource capacity, serious financial limitations, lack of cultural and social acceptability, and uncertain political and legal frameworks."[4] Based on composite metrics such as the UNDP's Human Development Index, the Solomon Islands ranks second to last among Pacific Island nations (Papua New Guinea is the lowest).[5] The Solomon Islands has emerged as a prototypical "vulnerable" place, like many other small island nations such as Kiribati or Tuvalu.[6]

What is critical for our purposes here is how vulnerability, as a concept, has become mobilized and deployed in specific sites by these international organizations and to register the material-semiotic effects. Rather than construing vulnerability as an underlying condition waiting to be explicated, my approach here is to describe ways in which vulnerability as a concept was put into practice. I elucidate the collection of forces, things, and imaginings that resulted in a team visiting Simbo and conducting disaster mitigation workshops.

There is little doubt that vulnerability has emerged as an enticing boundary object that enrolls many different actors, from policy makers to academics to Indigenous people, and it has increasingly been absorbed into powerful international organizations such as the IPCC and UNDP. Within disaster anthropology the concept of vulnerability was mobilized in the 1970s and 1980s to denaturalize disasters and focus attention on current and historical structural inequalities that distributed harm unevenly through the communities impacted by catastrophes.[7] This remains one of the key achievements of vulnerability approaches.

However, during roughly the same period in which vulnerability research emerged there were parallel developments in ecology, and to some extent psychology and engineering, that spawned what has become one of the most prevalent, cross-cutting, and policy relevant approaches to disasters and climate change: *resilience*. Even more so than vulnerability research, resilience thinking has progressively gained traction over the last several decades to permeate much scientific and popular debate not only in disaster research, but also in the arenas of global environmental change and environmental management.[8] Within disaster studies, major international frameworks like the United Nations International Strategy for Disaster Risk Reduction (UNISDR)'s adoption of the Sendai Framework for Disaster Risk Reduction 2015–2030 have embraced resilience as a means to conceptualize disasters and socio-environmental relations more generally as well as to organize applied programs to aid vulnerable communities.

Like many widely adopted concepts, resilience is highly contested and variable in its application. In disaster research, however, most definitions center on the idea that resilience is "the ability of social entities (for example, individuals, households, firms, communities, economies) to absorb the impacts of external and internal system shocks without losing the ability to function, and failing that, to cope, adapt, and recover from those shocks."[9]

Overviews of resilience point to the influential work conducted in the 1970s by the ecologist C. S. Holling as providing the theoretical inspiration for the concept.[10] In his groundbreaking 1973 article, Holling drew from his research on predator-prey relations to show that their dynamics do not follow a predictable abstract pattern of carrying capacity that leads to an optimal balance between the two populations.[11] Instead, the populations fluctuate, with one population spiking and remaining stable while in other cases both populations remain high. In other words, rather than a single, predictable equilibrium point, there are multiple configurations and possible equilibriums as the system responds to external perturbations. Resilient ecosystems, he argued, were those that could absorb disturbances and change and still maintain their basic structure and functioning.

At the time, Holling's arguments were a radical departure from mid-twentieth-century systems ecology that understood ecosystems as mechanistic, and perturbations as aberrations from an optimal and predictable ecosystem state.[12] Systems ecology, for example, assumed that a forest ecosystem that had undergone a disturbance such as fire would return to a climax state with a predictable assemblage of species. Holling's work opened ecologists to the possibility that ecosystems reorganized after disturbances in myriad unpredictable ways. Rather than attempting to determine the optimal, stable state of an ecosystem, the central research questions shifted to determining how much disturbance (i.e., the thresholds or tipping points) an ecosystem could withstand before it lost its capacity to self-organize and maintain system identity and function. Moreover, perturbations were no longer framed as aberrations that negatively impacted an optimal norm, but rather as inherent, necessary, and even beneficial if managed properly. Holling's work inspired what later became known as "new ecology," a recharacterization of ecological systems as inherently nonlinear, stochastic, and highly indeterminate with a multiplicity of stable ecosystem states.[13]

Beginning in the 1980s resilience scholars began to theorize that not only ecological but social change demonstrated these nonlinear patterns of complexity. Proponents of resilience began to conceptualize ecological and social dynamics as social-ecological systems, and reminiscent of vulnerability research, resilience scholars emphasized that complex interactions and changes occur at different temporal and spatial scales, from the local to the regional to the global. These various interacting dimensions of social-ecological systems are conceptualized as complex adaptive systems, wherein emergent properties, nonlinear change, and unpredictable dynamics are all emphasized as core properties of social-ecological systems.[14] Resilient social-ecological systems are defined as persistent, adaptable, and transformable, a suite of properties that enable them to absorb shocks, avoid crossing thresholds into new states, and regenerate after disturbances.[15]

As resilience thinking has progressively permeated both policy circles and academic thought, it has absorbed the concept of vulnerability and

shifted its meaning away from those promulgated by more critical political ecologists and disaster anthropologists who theorize vulnerability
as born out of the cascading effects of colonization, underdevelopment,
and capitalism. Take Neil Adger's highly influential article that reviewed
vulnerability approaches and attempted to articulate the concept more
coherently with resilience.[16] Adger defined vulnerability as "the state of
susceptibility to harm from exposure to stresses associated with environmental and social change and from the absence of capacity to adapt."[17]
He then went on to advocate for a conceptualization of vulnerability as a
"property of a social-ecological system" and outlined a precise formula in
which vulnerability is an outcome of the exposure and sensitivity of a system to hazards and the adaptive capacity of the system to cope and recover.
Indeed, most of the major international organizations such as the IPCC
follow this definition and seek to operationalize its various components.[18]

This refocusing of the vulnerability concept that downplays the exogenous structural determinants of vulnerability has resulted in an emphasis on building local capacities to live and cope with vulnerability. Indeed,
the Solomon Islands national disaster strategy and the UNDP program
that funded the workshops on Simbo were organized around these principles of "building local community resilience to disasters." The tsunami
mitigation workshops mentioned previously reflect a "cultures of safety"
approach that has now permeated many disaster management agencies
around the world.[19]

The intention of the workshops was to build Simboans' local capacity
to mitigate tsunamis by increasing their awareness of tsunami-prone
areas on the island and enabling them to respond more effectively by
educating them about the link between earthquakes and tsunamis and
about early warning signs of impending tsunamis, like ocean drawback.
The established escape routes were also conceived as building local capacity
to manage the early stages of disaster response. The assumption of these
resilience-inspired disaster management strategies is that local people lack
cultural or institutional capacity to effectively manage disaster and that
through expert-guided interventions adaptive capacity may be increased.
This conceptualization of vulnerability rests on a functionalist view of
social formations that presupposes the inherent cohesion of society built
on interrelated parts that function to maintain the stability of the whole

system.[20] This kind of functional, systems thinking closely parallels that of ecological anthropology in the 1960s that assumed rituals and other social practices had adaptive functions to maintain a society in balance with the surrounding environment.[21]

VULNERABILITY GONE BUREAUCRATIC

The problem of this conceptualization of vulnerability should now be plainly evident by Simbo's experience with the tsunami. The workshops on Simbo were not designed as platforms to discuss the history of colonization or the power structures of global capitalism that drew Simboans to build their villages on vulnerable coastal sites like those of Tapurai and Riquru. Instead, they focused on shifting Simboans' sense of their coastlines as areas that are disaster prone and risky. When vulnerability is assumed to be an *internal* condition of communities like those on Simbo, the vulnerable themselves are the targets of capacity building while wider structures of power remain unchallengeable. These workshops normalized and depoliticized disasters not by naturalizing them as "natural" as previous hazard approaches to disasters have done, but by naturalizing precarity and insecurity and possibly reinforcing rather than ameliorating the imbalances of power that are the source of the turbulence.[22]

Critical scholars have rightly noted how the rise of resilience thinking paralleled the neoliberal political and economic reforms of the late 1970s that have increased the precarity and risk of marginalized peoples around the world.[23] Neoliberalism emerged as a political and economic practice in response to economic stagnation in the 1970s. As policy sought out new strategies to fuel economic growth, scholars began to embrace the idea that human well-being was best advanced by liberating individual entrepreneurialism.[24] State institutions that regulated the economy or redistributed wealth through social safety nets were cast as impediments to entrepreneurial freedom since they were thought to be shaped by powerful interest groups who distorted those interventions toward their own interests. Instead of the state, the market was understood to provide a neutral mechanism to guide policy making, and thus the reach of the state needed to be limited to a minimum. As these reforms took hold in the 1980s and state-directed programs such as welfare, unemployment and job retraining, and environmental regulations were rolled back, the end result was heightened precarity and insecurity for communities, especially for the working class and populations of color.[25] Resilience thinking promulgates a strategy to manage these conditions, normalizing vulnerability and naturalizing instability as an inherent dimension of living in an interconnected, globalized world rather than as products of specific political economic policies.

Yet if we bracket the effects of these workshops in terms of "social processes," "culture," or "meaning making," we foreclose the possibility that disaster mitigation programs and disasters more generally may involve more than just different yet complex perspectives about a single object, which in this case, as with the dispute discussed in chapter 5, is land. Rather what is at stake here is the possibility that land is actualized differently with different consequential effects. A raft of recent scholarship in anthropology, as well as science and technology studies, has begun to analyze these kinds of postcolonial encounters by focusing empirical attention on the "continuous enactment, stabilization, and protection of different asymmetrically entangled ontologies or worlds."[26]

One of the key practices employed by outside experts to stabilize land as vulnerable to tsunamis was the use of a powerful inscription device, a satellite image. Inscription devices are items or apparatuses that produce traces of an entity in another material form.[27] Satellite images, for example, transform traces of the ground into pixels. But there are many other transcription devices related to land, such as titles and deeds, as well as ancestral shrines or nut groves. Importantly, transcription devices do not just record the land; they are modes of ordering that render it legible and stabilize it in certain forms while displacing others. That the poster was in English, with geographic coordinates, and oriented with north as "up," all can be interpreted as ordering processes that enable tsunami experts, not necessarily Simboans, to solidify their claim that the ontological status of Simbo's coastal areas is a hazardous zone. These workshops, however, exceeded the motives and intentions of the experts. It was not their intention to displace Simboan practices of stabilizing and coordinating their gusu, where land is composed as an entity intermixed with ancestral mana, spirit beings, nut groves, church buildings, villages, and all the living and nonliving beings upon which the Simbo people depend for life. These experts did not see themselves as displacing difference and other ways of knowing and being; their concern was to build capacity and make Simbo a safer place to live. Nevertheless, the experts and their posters and satellite images were assembling land in new ways that were discordant with Simbo ways of knowing and being.

An important intended and unintended effect of displacing the Simboan sense of land, beyond just foreclosing the possibility that it might be something other than hazardous, is that it also instituted new forms of governing and the extension of state and bureaucratic control. For if coastal Simbo is hazardous, this new apprehension of land renders Simboans' capacities and strategies to manage and live on their island inadequate and intermeshes Simbo lands into bureaucratic, state, and international institutional assemblages. And conversely, reconfiguring land as hazardous deterritorializes it from the shrines, subsistence gardening, fishing, and all those other relations and entities that Simboans know well, rendering the Simbo people, at least partially, more reliant on the knowledge and capacity of experts to mitigate future tsunamis. Moreover, these capacity building and disaster awareness programs have the effect of narrowing the possibility that vulnerabilities may be reduced through strategies that are outside of state and bureaucratic systems. Vulnerability, when conceived of as an internal condition of communities, may ultimately render places like Simbo *more vulnerable* rather than less, all the while accelerating the entanglement of the island into bureaucratic systems of control and surveillance.

The tsunami and the arrival of new modes of composing land as vulnerable are similar but also different from the mode that Simboans have come to know quite well through centuries of entangling with global capitalism, in which land is also constituted as a thing, but rather than rendered vulnerable, it is instead composed as a commodity that can be freely bought, sold, or rented. This ontology of land is something that Simboans, and Island Melanesians more generally, have rejected despite the benefits it might enable.[28]

As I have attempted to show in this chapter, Simboan practices of navigating the tsunami recovery produced their own vulnerabilities, but these workshops quite possibly may worsen local capacity to manage disasters rather than enhance them while also rendering the Simboans more dependent on external institutions rather than less. Instead of creating space for radical difference and focusing attention on root causes of vulnerability in times of catastrophe, this particular deployment of the vulnerability concept and its attendant material and semiotic practices, like those witnessed in the disaster mitigation workshops, further the neoliberalization of social-ecological relations. Nevertheless, vulnerability has the potential, depending on how it is deployed in response to specific problems, for multiple political effects that may preserve the status quo or open possibilities that the world could be otherwise.[29] Much work in the anthropology of disasters has mobilized vulnerability as a means to transgress bureaucratic structures and technocratic solutions or a version of vulnerability, like the IPCC's, that emphasizes exposure to hazards rather than externally imposed political and economic processes that produce risk.[30] In this sense, vulnerability is *politically polyvalent*.

7 Sensing Disaster Compositions

How can one not be inspired by the astonishing achievements of the Simbo people? Their ability to flee the tsunami, not to mention to sustainably inhabit their island for thousands, possibly tens of thousands, of years, is something to cherish and celebrate. Learning about the island has been an inspirational journey, which included more than a few harrowing boat trips to reach Simbo across a rough ocean and through tempestuous wind! During this journey my exposure to Simbo concepts like mulongo and the diverse lines of inquiry they required produced within me a personal paradigm shift of sorts. I was weaned as a graduate student primarily in the more "ecological" version of environmental anthropology inspired by Julian Steward, and this book reflects the challenges posed by the Simbo experience to that style of thought. Over my many visits to Simbo, listening to and conversing with survivors discussing their tsunami experiences and spending hundreds of hours participating in their day-to-day activities, I reached the limits to what I, with my human ecologist hat on, could measure and understand about Simbo's "environment" and "practical activities."

The Simbo people demonstrated a remarkable openness, a sensitivity, to their surroundings that led to effective and split-second judgments about how to act as a massive wave swept toward their villages. Here, drawing on Timothy Morton's notion of attunement, and similar to Donna Haraway's "response-ability," I suggest that Simbo's response might have emerged through a process of *attuning*, wherein the relationality and interdependence between humans and nonhumans enables a certain reflexive sensitivity and caution when confronted with unordinary circumstances. This aesthetic, if we apply the older etymological sense of the term to "perceive" or "learning to be sensitive," enabled at least some of the survivors to detect odd shifts in the ocean and act on them appropriately with little codified, intergenerationally transmitted knowledge about the phenomenon. This book has been an attempt to illuminate the various heterogeneous elements and processes involved in this attunement. In writing it, I have followed a repertoire of entities, skills, and myths as well as interrelatings with sharks, fish, insects, birds, crocodiles, fish, spirits beings, benthic organisms, reefs, and ocean waves that Simboans implicated in their ability to sense the impending danger of the approaching tsunami.

Far too often some of these elements of Indigenous lifeways have been bracketed out by anthropologists and other social scientists as distorted beliefs or forms of irrational thought. Yet others, in their attempts to celebrate non-Western ways of life, might promote the Simbo mode of existence by fantasizing it and other Indigenous lifeways as a truer expression of the human condition. In both cases, however, the effects of other modes of being are not really taken seriously, leaving our own analytics beyond the reach of reflexive engagement.

As we have learned in this book, local theorizations of the disaster response are not just expressions of other modes of thought; they also urge us to accept that the world might be composed in different ways, or as Povinelli puts it, as "forms of life that are at odds with dominant, and dominating, modes of being."[1] Here I am referring to the important shift in anthropology and cognate fields from an emphasis on epistemology, our understanding of what knowledge is and how it may be generated, to ontology, our understanding of what exists.[2] This shift requires that we take seriously, in the sense outlined by Vivieros de Castro, what our interlocutors say to us, not to highlight just the ethical importance of respecting Indigenous lifeways or to signal that Indigenous modes of being are superior to Western thought, but rather as a means to alter our own thinking.[3]

Reflecting back to when I first began visiting Simbo in 2008 to investigate the tsunami disaster, I came to the island ready to interpret Simboans' response as a case of IEK. This widely popular concept not only has made inroads into general awareness but continues to be avidly mobilized by experts to explain disasters as well as many other dimensions of Indigenous lifeworlds. A broad aim of this book has been to place Simboans' descriptions of their remarkable response to flee the incoming waves in conversation with IEK. We have learned that in some respects IEK, as it is conventionally interpreted, is productive. If we define IEK as "knowledge acquired by Indigenous peoples over hundreds or thousands of years through direct contact with the environment and that is transmitted intergenerationally," then there were elements of the response that are understandable in this register. Some of Simbo's survivors did indeed discuss how their parents and grandparents warned them to stay away from the seaside after earthquakes. Nevertheless, much of the scholarly literature interprets Indigenous disaster response within these parameters and the analytical vocabulary it provides and goes no further. Indeed, the first two published academic papers written about Simbo's response to the tsunami were in this mold.[4]

The limitations of IEK, in my view, are related to its rise in popularity. As IEK research has gained steam across the social and natural sciences, scholars have tended to rely heavily on scientific knowledge to bolster IEK's validity. Some researchers go so far as to disparage IEK research that fails to validate it against scientific knowledge. Anthony Davis and Kenneth Ruddle, for example, claim that most cited IEK literature lacks scientific validation, rendering it problematic because of the "need for researchers to be held accountable to their knowledge claims" through "systematic evaluation."[5] These researchers remain committed to Western science as providing a privileged access mode to phenomena, and "like it or not, until replaced at some future time, Western science is the dominant paradigm that sets the prevailing standard."[6] This commitment is a continuation of processes beginning at least as far back as the eighteenth century of subjugating non-Western knowledges through the disciplinary tactics that Michel Foucault described as "selection, normalization, hierarchicalization, and centralization."[7]

In addition to this overt scientism, much research into the local knowledge and Indigenous adaptation to climate change relies on similar yet more subtle modes of scientific validation. Susan Crate, for example, work-ing among the Viliui Sakha of northeastern Siberia, discussed in detail how local elders lament the disappearance, due to warming temperatures, of winter, which they describe as a "white bull with blue spots, huge horns, and frosty breath."[8] The warming observed by the Sakha is assumed to be an outcome of "unprecedented global climate change."[9] However, many climate scientists fiercely deny the possibility that global climate change is locally visible.[10] As discussed in detail by Peter Rudiak-Gould, research such as Crate's accepts climate change science as a means to legitimize local ecological knowledge and emphasize that it is a viable and empiri-cally sound body of knowledge.[11] Moreover, by validating IEK, the voice of marginalized communities tends to gain more traction in bureaucratic and state decision-making apparatus.

Indeed, I too have pursued similar lines of inquiry. In chapter 2 I dis-cussed how I conducted studies comparing Roviana villagers' assess-ments of environmental change before and after the tsunami to scientific surveys. My team and I found that villagers detected tsunami-induced changes that we could verify through benthic surveys. To Western science this is a highly legible facet of Simboans' IEK. From Harold Conklin's early pathbreaking work among the Hanunóo people in the Philippines to Robert Johannes's pioneering marine-focused research in Palau, scientific knowledge is positioned hierarchically with IEK to justify its worthiness as a body of knowledge.[12] Through similar modes of inquiry much of the scientific community has become convinced that IEK is not inferior or de-ficient compared to expert, scientific knowledge and can serve as the basis of disaster response or sustainable resource management.

Scientism relies on the assumption that scientific knowledge is open, universal, and improvable, while IEK or any other form of nonexpert knowledge is more closed, place-based, and less dynamic.[13] Michael Howes and Robert Chambers, for example, state that "science is an open system whose adherents are always aware of the possibility of alternative perspec-tives to those adopted at any particular point of time. ITK [Indigenous technical knowledge], on the other hand, as a closed system, is character-ized by a lack of awareness that there may be other ways of regarding the world."[14] But for decades anthropological studies of science in action have shown that scientists produce knowledge that is just as situated, partial, embodied, and locatable in the world as IEK and involves a heterogeneous "mangle" in the production of facts, instruments, and concepts, influenced by certain epistemic commitments, value-laden assumptions, and political positions.[15] As Donna Haraway provocatively has taught us, scientists do not have a magical ability to occupy a godly transcendent positionless position or "view from nowhere."[16] The key difference is a matter of scale. Scientific knowledge is not everywhere or universal. Instead it extends and is produced and maintained through networks of institutions, machines, practitioners, and interest groups, not to mention large sums of money, that enable its circulation and combinability and hence the durability of the knowledge that pulses through its circuits.[17] Scientists produce knowledge just as locally as Simboans do; the difference is just that scientific knowledge is extended much further and thus acts on the world more widely. And as we have witnessed with climate change science and its deniers, scientific networks are fragile and need the utmost care or they may be overrun and the knowledge they have accumulated rendered feeble.

One of the broad goals of this book has been to rethink the relationship between IEK and scientific knowledge and to seek new ways for both forms of knowledge production to flourish. The first step, I argue, is to interpret all knowledges, scientific or Indigenous, expert or nonexpert, as produced and generated through *situated, localized practices.* Here I am in full agreement with Arun Agrawal that the terms "scientific" and "Indigenous" would best be banished from our analytical vocabulary, since "all, knowledge can be useful or useless, politically salient or meaningless, socially relevant or irrelevant, empirically testable or irrefutable, and ideologically open or blind, without reference to whether it is indigenous or scientific."[18]

This symmetrical localization of knowledges, however, should not be interpreted as a call that all knowledges are justified, nor am I encouraging antiscience thinking. To democratize knowledges is not a move to dispose of objectivity. The argument of many Indigenous rights activists that all science is a corrosive expression of neocolonial or misogynist power, for example, is as flawed as that of those who claim that science should, without question, be "the dominant paradigm that sets the prevailing standard," since both appeal to absolutisms about the nature of knowledge production.[19]

Approaching all knowledge as generated through situated practices not only encourages us to begin to critically examine, recognize, and research how knowledge claims are constructed, but also can serve as a means to rebuild the legitimacy of scientific knowledge while not denigrating IEK. Opening up all forms of knowledge production, especially science, to democratic scrutiny and detailing step by step the processes involved will stabilize the most durable knowledge claims rather than diminish them. In an age of climate change and pandemics, we need scientific knowledge more than ever. But hardening the walls of contemporary centers of scientific knowledge production such as universities or government agencies to public scrutiny will only exacerbate distrust in science. We need more diversity in science and more open institutions rather than fewer.[20] I agree with Kim TallBear when she states, "I seek scientific coconspirators who don't think they have the gospel truth but who want to challenge the social and ethical norms of their fields not only in order to make them more inclusive but also to make the science more robust, more strongly objective."[21]

Conceptualizing Simboans' IEK and their response to the tsunami as a situated practice also enables other productive gains in understanding. First, it provides a theoretical basis for addressing the hybrid and contested dimensions of disaster response. Indigenous peoples like the Simbo people are at the intersection of many knowledge practices, and their knowledge of the local environment is constantly recombining with new innovations, outside knowledge, and changing environmental conditions. Indeed, a handful of Simbo survivors had learned about tsunamis from radio and TV programs, and they attributed their response to flee after the earthquake to this knowledge they had picked up from the media. And as is discussed in chapters 5 and 6, disaster experts instituted discursive and material practices on Simbo that constituted its coastal areas as tsunami-prone, a kind of knowledge practice that was foreign to most Simboans prior to the disaster.

A more sympathetic view of disaster responses must accommodate this variety of practices and overlapping knowledges. Indeed, the notion of a knowledge "system" is problematic, for it implicitly stresses the coherent, smooth boundedness of knowledge rather than rhizomatic or tentacular qualities of entangling through time and space. Instead of attempting to differentiate which knowledge "system" provides the clearest representation of reality, approaching knowledge as situated practices shifts attention to how knowledge is produced in practice and then is spread and propagated through and by instruments, concepts, and human and nonhuman actors.

Another advantage of a practice approach to disaster response is that it facilitates lines of inquiry into tacit, unarticulated, or informal ways of knowing, aspects of knowledge that cannot be separated from the activities or contexts in which they are applied. As eloquently discussed by James Scott, tacit, improvised capacities tend to be sidelined by Western science or the state because of a long intellectual tradition that privileges formal, abstract knowledge over ways of knowing that are experiential and constituted through embodied engagement.[22] Julie Cruikshank made a similar argument in her analysis of glacial surges that destroyed villages in the mountains of northwest Canada.[23] She documented how local knowledge about glaciers, like Simboans' ocean knowledge, has tacit dimensions that are continually produced during encounters. It stands to reason that these sorts of capacities are central to understanding and characterizing a successful disaster response like the one discussed in this book.

RELUCTANT KNOWLEDGES

Despite such widespread celebration of IEK, a second important lesson we can learn from the Simbo disaster is about the potential modes of domination that are engendered when IEK is put into action by experts. Here I am referring to strategies of *participation* and *integration* that were central to the disaster preparedness workshops carried out on Simbo. These forms of knowledge production reflect a shift not just in disaster mitigation programs but in numerous forms of intervention, such as community-based resource management and sustainable development, in which participation is now de rigueur.[24] In the workshops, disaster experts asked Simboans to delineate the coastal areas that were inundated by the 2007 tsunami and to identify appropriate escape routes. Rather than denying the validity of IEK, as has been the practice of top-down, state-led schemes, IEK was embraced as a critical component of the workshops that could be harnessed and made useful for specific disaster mitigation needs.

The rise of participatory strategies has been propelled across the applied environmental sciences by interest in and acceptance of IEK.[25] Even bureaucratic and state structures like the IPCC and the United Nations now positively evaluate IEK as an essential ingredient to effectively reduce vulnerability to environmental hazards and mitigate the impact of disasters. This decentering of scientific knowledge can be linked to an outgrowth of the "new ecology" and resilience perspectives that acknowledge the complexity of the social-ecological where a totalizing understanding of social-ecological systems can never be fully attained. Resilience theorists no longer assume that a privileged, overarching view of any social-ecological system is obtainable and that precise quantification of variables enables predictive control over it. Indeed, this was the premise of what scholars call "command-and-control" environmental management, wherein experts armed with complex statistical models assumed that management problems were tractable, "well-bounded, clearly defined, relatively simple, and generally linear with respect to cause and effect."[26]

Most advocates argue that through learning from IEK and then pairing and synthesizing it with Western scientific and management knowledge, more effective disaster management can be achieved. It is this kind of framework that Jessica Mercer and colleagues encourage when they argue that the integration of Indigenous and scientific knowledge can not only reduce a community's vulnerabilities to environmental hazards but also help reduce disaster risk through planning and increase collaboration of stakeholders.[27] This literature exemplifies a broader emphasis on "knowledge coproduction" that has gained popularity in some segments of the scientific community where IEK and scientific knowledge are envisioned as combinable information in which new and innovative forms may be created.[28]

Although I fully welcome this decentering of scientific knowledge and growing acceptance of nonexpert and Indigenous modes of thought and action, the disaster mitigation workshops conducted on Simbo exemplified an assumption about knowledge that has the potential to foreclose the possibilities of difference and reduce space for modes of thought that are outside of bureaucratic structures. The disaster experts leading the workshops embraced Simboan knowledge of the 2007 tsunami, but knowledge in the workshops was treated as if it was *information* that, through its capture in participatory mapping, could then be rendered functional through abstraction. This process of decontextualization and abstraction is the method by which it then can be combined with scientific knowledge and generate new knowledge and insights about complex social-ecological systems.[29] However, the implicit assumptions that IEK is solely a form of information and that social-ecological systems are information-processing arrangements significantly reduces the possibilities for registering difference. So many aspects of Simboan IEK overflow the boundaries of what we consider "information." How, for example, can Simboans' creation stories, an important dimension of their IEK, be effectively located in Euclidean space? How might the communication that goes on between Simboans and insects or the will of ancestor spirits that imposes on Simboans be abstracted and synthesized? More broadly, when knowledge is equated with information, affective nonrepresentational dimensions of knowing and being remain illegible and thus marginalized or worse, are thrown, a priori, into the dustbin of "beliefs."

Moreover, when we presuppose that IEK is information it opens the possibility that Indigenous lifeways are subjected to novel forms of what Jean Baudrillard refers to as "cybernetically controlled participation."[30] Participatory workshops like the ones conducted on Simbo construe participants primarily as producers of data that can be abstracted during the participatory exercise and circulated as signs, eventually making its way back to the community as a map with instructions about where to run for safety after earthquakes or even as, I recently learned, a children's storybook.

While finishing up this manuscript in April 2022 I learned about a UNDP-published children's book entitled *Durie, the Tsunami Teacher*.[31] The illustrated book featured Durie Hickie, a Simbo woman from Lengana who was washed into the roots of mangroves by the tsunami but luckily survived with only minor injuries (see the prologue for her account). The book was part of UNDP's series of illustrated real-life accounts of tsunami survivors aimed at raising awareness of and enabling children to protect themselves from tsunamis. The last time I visited Simbo, in 2019, Durie was the teacher of Kalaro Elementary School and was a participant in the tsunami mitigation workshops I discussed in the previous chapter. In an article published online by the UNDP she was quoted as stating that the tsunami preparedness workshops were helpful: "Now, our school has an emergency plan, we have done evacuation drills and we know where the safe zones are near school. This all has made our future evacuations much faster and more organized."[32] Yet neither the storybook nor the on-line article refers to the Simbo people's ability to save their lives and flee the tsunami. Instead, the final page of the book depicts Durie instructing the classroom about the "signs" of tsunamis and the words "feel, hear, see, here, run." I was shocked: Why was the Simboans' successful response not included in the storybook? Why was it forgotten?

Rather than integrating IEK with scientific knowledge to produce storybooks and maps, might it be better to experiment with practical approaches that enable both to go along "together in difference," wherein one knowledge is neither absorbed nor denied by the other?[33] If Simboans' achievement in fleeing the tsunami is deleted from the "official" story of the tsunami circulated by the UNDP, is that not just an extension of scientific networks that displaces Simboan modes of being? As Elizabeth Povinelli has noted in Australia, even when aboriginal modes of being are accepted and embraced as a basis for Indigenous Australian identity and territorial claims, they have been funneled toward specific forms of "animism" that are compatible with capitalist relations and markets.[34] Rather than reannex IEK into dominant scientific discourses and circulate it after disqualifying what is not appropriate, why not strive to create conditions in which it might thrive? Rather than unifying IEKs with some kind of theoretical edifice, why not enable Indigenous peoples, if they so desire, to sustain their knowledge practices as reluctant, heterogeneous, patchy, polymorphous, and able to struggle against capital, colonial, bureaucratic, and scientific control? We need diversity not only *within* scientific networks but also *outside* of them.[35] I suggest that we should seek to sustain diverse knowledge production conditions by enabling the coexistence of science with IEK rather than attempting to combine the two.

With the widespread recognition that Indigenous peoples may have effective practices to sustainably manage their resources and reduce their vulnerability to hazards, the problem for state rule is no longer that indigenous people need to be taught; it is that their knowledge and practices have emerged autonomously from bureaucratic structures of centralization and homogenization. IEK remains a threat to state-directed forms of resilience, adaptation, and disaster mitigation in its potential to subvert state control through alternative modes of sensing disasters. Simbo IEK retains that capacity to be insurrectionist, to be a "subjugated knowledge" to use Foucault's term, to transgress and reveal the ongoing socio-natural warfare that is chronically waged against Indigenous peoples.[36]

THE CONTOURS OF DISASTEROLOGY

It was in quite a different setting than an uncomfortable Simbo dugout or the lovely leaf house that I typically rent in Meqe that the contrast between contemporary understandings of disasters and the Simbo experience with the tsunami was revealed quite starkly. I was inside a stuffy conference room named "Franklin" somewhere deep in the bowels of a plush hotel in downtown Philadelphia, attending the 2018 Society for Applied Anthropology annual meeting. A few rows from the front in a session titled "Disasters and Epistemology," experts of all stripes sat around me with the requisite conference nametags dangling around their necks as they listened to a series of talks (or checked their phones!). Indeed, the SfAA prides itself on attracting to its conferences experts outside of the academy who work in applied settings.

Midway through the session, under bright fluorescent lights, a Turkish scholar had just provided an intimate and fascinating account of the massive and highly monitored North Anatolian Fault, a seismic area that stretches across Turkey. Her presentation focused on the discourse and practices of geoscientists who, we were told, all agree that a large 6.0 earthquake will inevitably strike Istanbul. The big debate for the scientific community and a source of much uncertainty was when it would occur. The threat of future quakes has been of widespread concern in Turkey ever since the county was rocked by two devastating tremblers in 1999 that killed more than eighteen thousand people.

The young, smartly dressed presenter with jet black hair was suggesting that the fault was best understood not as a single phenomenon that different scientists viewed differently, but rather as a complex multiplicity that was brought into being through the practices of different groups of geoscientists. Through their conceptual and practical work earth scientists were laboring away in their offices to bring into existence not a single fault system, nor many different ones, but a fault system that was "more than one less than many." This was not a question, the scholar argued, of different descriptions and theories of the same object. Instead, the arguments and debates around predicting a future quake were due, at least partially, to the ways in which they delineated and composed geological fissures in multiple and divergent yet connected forms.

After concluding her talk the moderator opened the floor for questions. One gentleman a few rows behind me, who was struggling to understand the Turkish scholar's argument, made a brief comment about the importance of understanding the physical aspects of earthquakes so that better planning and construction practices could mitigate the impact of natural disasters like earthquakes. Although the comment was directed at the presenter, someone from the back of the room spoke up and stated firmly without concealing their aggravation: "Disasters aren't natural, they are socially constructed!"

This brief exchange between audience members encapsulates the axis of debate that has dominated disaster scholarship over the past fifty years. Among many disaster experts, like the one attending the SfAA meeting, as well as the wider public, the term "natural disasters" remains tenaciously ingrained. Our reference to calamities using names such as "Superstorm Sandy" or the "2004 Indian Ocean Tsunami" or the "1908 San Francisco Earthquake" is symptomatic of the wide appeal of locating the nexus of causality inside a universal nonhuman agent, "roped off" from the rest of human-environmental relations in what Kenneth Hewitt provocatively described as an "archipelago of disaster."[37] In the scholarly literature, research that normalizes disasters as a natural outcome of uncontrollable physical forces is known broadly as "hazards" approaches. Such analyses privilege the hazard, and the arrow of causation and explication tends to run in one direction from the geophysical event to society. The agent of disaster is assumed to reside in an uncontrollable "nature," which determines, due to its impact, strength, intensity, and so forth, which segments of society it will destroy and cause harm to. In short, disasters are assumed to be abnormal, extreme events, but natural.

Hazards approaches dominated until the 1970s and 1980s, when social scientists began to shift the nexus of causality from the hazard to social, cultural, and economic processes that produce vulnerability. As stated by Susan Hoffman, a prominent disaster scholar: "No matter if the happening is an earthquake, flood, volcanic eruption, cyclone, wildfire, drought, nuclear meltdown, oil spill, or other pollutant, the underlying determinant is social. We ourselves are creating the hazards and the calamities."[38] Many anthropologists who study disasters articulate their research in these terms and argue that disasters are not due to acts of God, natural events, or bad luck. Instead, they are produced from within society, through the current and past practices of colonial agents, state apparatuses, or even NGOs that unequally distribute harm along lines of gender, race, ethnicity, or class

A 1976 paper by O'Keefe and colleagues entitled "Taking the 'Naturalness' out of Natural Disaster," published in the journal *Nature*, was an early and influential analysis establishing the social nature of disasters.[39] It documented how the increasing frequency and magnitude of disasters was not accompanied by a similar rise in the number of extreme physical events. Moreover, the growing death toll was disproportionately felt in poorer, underdeveloped countries. The paper reflected a growing upsurge in environmental anthropology and disaster research toward political economic thinking and the importance of analyzing capitalism and colonialism's roles in shaping social and ecological dynamics.[40] By harnessing new Marxist-derived analytical tools such as surplus value, commodity fetishism, and modes of production, a proliferation of new frameworks with a critical bent and a commitment to social justice emerged, such as dependency theory, world systems theory, and Marxist feminism.

Hewitt's highly influential 1983 edited volume *Interpretations of Calamity* extended these insights and marked a decisive break from early hazards research paving the way for political ecology, a critical approach to disasters and human-environmental relations that places power and inequalities at the center of the analysis.[41] Vulnerability was not an inevitable outcome of untoward natural events, but rather produced and distributed through uneven power structures. This literature drove home the key insight that naturalizing disasters has a potent depoliticizing effect. When the ultimate cause of catastrophe is outside of human control, the cures can be construed as neutral, technocratic solutions best left to engineers and other experts rather than to political projects of social change.

Motivated by an explicitly political project of social change, political ecological studies of disasters proliferated, and an extensive literature now documents the wider historic and structural underpinnings of catastrophes. For example, in what has become a classic study in disaster anthropology, Anthony Oliver-Smith scrupulously describes how one of the largest disasters in human history, the 1970 Ancash earthquake and landslide that killed nearly seventy thousand people in central Peru, was prefigured five hundred years earlier during the Spanish conquest and subsequent colonization that severely underdeveloped the region and undermined pre-Columbian adaptations.[42] With the arrival of the Spanish, the pre-Columbian settlement pattern of establishing villages outside of flood- and landslide-prone canyons was ignored, a shift that haunted the Peruvian communities after the 1970 earthquake, as avalanche debris roared down the canyons, burying many towns including Yungay, the community where Oliver-Smith conducted his research.

The emergence of the "social" framing of disasters can also be traced to developments within human ecological anthropological analyses. These approaches have a long pedigree of theorizing about the relationships between humans and the nonhuman world. Many point to Julian Steward as the lodestar of human ecology; he developed a "cultural ecology" approach in the 1950s. At that time he was writing against environmental determinism, a simplistic and often racist current of thought with a long and influential history within anthropology and cognate fields that views broad environmental influences such as temperature or geographic latitude as "mainsprings" of cultural formation. In Steward's groundbreaking work among the Shoshone people of Nevada's Great Basin, he theorized that "environmental factors" only influenced those aspects of a culture's subsistence and economic activities.[43] He posited that these "core" aspects were limited by local ecologies but not constitutive of them. The Shoshone, for example, were inhibited from farming intensely or practicing shifting cultivation in the arid, resource-patchy Great Basin. Within those limits, however, he envisioned the human-environmental nexus as a creative potentiality that could generate differing material and semiotic formations.

Although Steward's cultural ecological approach was a decisive break from early environmental determinists, its use of culture as an analytic unit and its narrow focus on productive activities was later deemed too constrictive, and it was felt that it underdetermined the role of ideological, religious, and political factors. But contemporary ecological anthropological approaches that have extended Steward's insights and adopted systems ecology or more recently complex adaptive system frameworks continue to assume that practical activities such as subsistence or resource extraction patterns play a more fundamental role in life than meaning making.[44] Moreover, human ecologists assume "environmental factors" are a stable domain of reality that has universal characteristics and dynamics rendered accessible and most accurately through scientific measurements and instruments. The whole scenography relies on the universality of the environment, albeit broken down into different ecozones, so that analyses can judge the adaptive or maladaptive nature of subsistence activities or livelihood practices. Others interested in the semantic rather than the practical dimensions of culture, such as those who profess to study emics, otherwise known as ethnoscience or ethnobotany, rely on a similar universal natural order. For only by assuming there is one botany can all the other *ethno*botanies be compared and contrasted. On one side knowledge is assumed to be independent of society, and on the other side the knowledge of the ethnoscientist's interlocutor is embedded in society.[45]

BEYOND BIFOCALS

Simboan tsunami survivors, however, interpreted the disaster in ways that did not conform to those who presuppose a universal nature that shapes culture, nor did they conform to the long-running debate between hazards approaches and political ecology that continue to animate discussions like the one I heard during the 2018 SfAA meeting. Rather than approaching it as an experience that can be divided between "natural" and "social" processes, Simboans intermixed these categories at every point. I was taught this most explicitly when I learned about the Simboan notion of gusu and the role land played in the conflicts during reconstruction. Many Oceanic peoples employ concepts similar to gusu when they discuss the land upon which they and their ancestors dwell. In Tonga they speak of their islands in terms of distinct *fonua*, which the Tongan scholar Hufanga Okusitino Māhina defines as meaning both "land" and "people," which "espouses the 'unity' deriving from the ongoing exchange between people and land."[46] Or as Christina Toren put it when interpreting the Fijian concept of *vanua*, it "is constituted as much by the land to which people belong as by the people to whom that land belonged."[47] Like the Simbo people, these authors describe land not as a thing to be occupied but as co-constitutive of life.

Whereas Simboans discern a continuity between land and persons (i.e., clans) that belies the modernist essentialist distinction between the natural world on the one hand and culture on the other, the essentialized disconti-nuity on Simbo is between gusu, that is between different land-sea-human collectives. As we learned in chapter 3, Simboans call their island Made-gugusu, or "four places": Ove, Karivara, Narovo, and Simbo. And members of the clans from each of these gusu attach and reproduce themselves and their gusu through praxis: planting crops, burying their deceased, fishing the local waters, planting nut trees, encountering spirit beings, observing sanctions imposed by ancestor spirits, and recounting stories about their unique histories. In this sense, meaning is not overlaid onto the gusu; it is woven into its essence. And it was these distinct semiotic and material repertoires of praxis that Simbo's clans debated during the controversies engendered by the tsunami. These debates were not simply about their cul-ture or society, or about how to manage, demarcate, or "own" a biophysical landscape; rather, the disaster dramatized cosmopolitical questions about *the kind of world in which Simboans wish to live and how it might be com-posed or assembled through particular forms of praxis*.[48]

From this starting point, we may glean new insights into a long-standing argument put forth by researchers that disasters expose under-lying socioeconomic structures of the societies that undergo catastrophe.[49] Oliver-Smith, following Marshall Sahlins, for example, famously theorized disasters as "revelatory crises," in that "fundamental features of society and culture are laid bare in stark relief by the reduction of priorities to basic social, cultural, and material necessities."[50] Although I fully acknowledge the gains political ecologists have made toward denaturalizing disasters, my sense is that describing catastrophe as an event that peels away less important layers of significance and "reveals," "unmasks," or, "undrapes" more basic forms might well have quite the opposite effect. Arguably, it provides a space for Steward-inspired social scientists interested in "prac-tical activities" or natural scientists concerned with biophysical processes to develop their lines of inquiry without being troubled by what people say about their world. When we presuppose that the world is a series of layers with more real, solid, and universal biophysical entities supporting contingent, ephemeral, and localized cultural or ideological processes, then we have already structured our analysis with a particular epistemological shape. Might we have something to learn from Simboans when they describe their experiences of the tsunami, rather than just assuming what they say is a cultural curiosity or an outcome of some mechanism hidden from Simboans but visible to anthropologists? We certainly would not apply that explanation to scientists who assert that the Simboan coastlines are vulnerable to tsunamis.

The ways in which Simboan survivors described their experiences, especially the relocation process, did not unfold as a peeling away of nonpractical layers of meaning from some deeper, more authentic, or basic form of life that was already present; rather, the tsunami wave engendered new actors and processes that required creative work to figure them out. Simboans had to add something to specify and digest their own response and the tumult that occurred in the aftermath. Thus, it might be more productive to think of the effects of the tsunami as discursively and materially *catalytic* rather than as a process that reduced Simbo's inhabitants to some more basic practical existence. Simbo's experience with the tsunami involved an overflow of new and novel actors, concepts, technologies, and discourses. Indeed, the tsunami wave itself was an entirely unknown phenomenon to nearly everyone on the island before that calm, cloudless morning in April 2007. The catastrophe did not diminish the ebb and flow of life to a bare minimum; the tsunami merged with the preexisting fabric of life and produced an outpouring of local theorizations and speculations to explain and digest it, not to mention an efflorescence of reciprocal sharing (varivagana). Similarly, the tsunami wave that destroyed Simboan villages did not eliminate the timbers and palm thatching; it transformed these materials into a mass of splintered timbers and rubble. The disaster did not *reduce* the Simboan houses to rubble; it transformed them—just as it did not strip away their capacity for meaning making but engendered new and unexpected forms. If anything, the tsunami waves were multipliers, albeit in ways that were not so pleasant. In this sense vulnerabilities are not produced through a scraping away of discourses, materialities, and practices, but instead are an outcome of novel reconfigurations that place some at a disadvantage compared to others.

Take the recovery and reconstruction period as another example. The tsunami attracted disaster experts and NGO officials from all over the world, including myself, to a tiny island in western Oceania. These outsiders introduced a new repertoire of concepts, entities, and activities by which to assemble land on Simbo and make it visible as a risky and tsunami-vulnerable place. This was an unintentional challenge to Simboan notions of place and land. Indeed, the survivors in Tapurai, most of whom were descendants of immigrants from the Ove gusu, attempted to mobilize this new "vulnerable land" in their bid to claim new territory and engage in a fundamental place-engendering practice: building a new village.

The possibilities that this novel technoscientific actualization of "vulnerable coastline" were recognized by Tapurai's residents and were central to their arguments with the clans of Narovo as a means to justify relocating their village to a new, safe locale. Ultimately Tapurai's survivors were only partially successful in their rebuilding efforts; they were allowed to rebuild their village but were blocked from building their elementary school at the new village site. The question of inalienability trumped "vulnerable land." Since colonization, Simboans have refused to accept that land is a mute "thing" or simply a background to human affairs that can be bought, sold, or rented out willy-nilly to the highest bidder. When land is inseparable from human beings and impinges on day-to-day life, an exchange of cash or the illegitimate building of an elementary school has ramifications across the Simbo lifeworld. These land disputes illustrate that the disaster did not reduce the possibilities of action among those involved; it reordered them, albeit unequally. It did not reduce human existence; it generated new material and semiotic admixtures.

The technoscientific production of vulnerable tsunamiland, however, presents a new and possibly more insidious challenge to the Simbo lifeworld. In the coming decades islands like Simbo will be faced with rising sea levels, bleached corals, droughts, and all the other consequences of a planet warming to 2.0 degrees Celsius above preindustrial levels. Choices will be made about altering the coasts and building seawalls or seeding tropical coastal areas with "super corals," some of which may undergo "accelerated evolution" or be genetically altered so that they can withstand warming oceans.[51] The ways in which Simbo struggled with the novelty of "vulnerable land," in which the coastal area was assembled through technoscientific praxis as vulnerable, is a harbinger for much more dramatic struggles over "atmospheric management," coastal alteration, and ocean geoengineering. Just as the land disputes on Simbo were not simply questions over what local land means, future controversies will involve choices that will have physical, biological, and social effects at every point.

ANTHROPOCENE CATASTROPHE APPROACHES

There is no doubt that disaster research has made substantial gains toward grasping the complex and intertwined social and ecological ramifications of catastrophes, yet the vast majority of the disaster literature continues to pass analyses rather too neatly through the analytical sieve of nature and culture that dominates the Western intellectual tradition. Both the hazards and political ecological approaches, with a few notable exceptions, presume that the world is self-evidently partitioned between universal material regularities on the one hand and social formations on the other.[52] But as the previous pages have shown, Simbo's tsunami experience challenged these root assumptions about how the world operates.

Might it be prudent to describe contemporary disasters without the sturdy hooks of "nature" and "culture" and be open to the possibility that Simbo islanders' mode of existence is grounded in radically different precepts about the nature of things? The scientific community itself seems to be coming around to the idea that the relations between humans and nonhumans need to be rethought. Likewise, the shift toward exploring ontological postulates in anthropology signals the current destabilized moment of modernity. Of course the Simbo people, like many Indigenous peoples around the world, have been teaching those patient enough to listen that other modes of existence are possible.[53]

Within the broader biophysical sciences, the inspiration propelling a reevaluation of the nature-culture dichotomy has not been, symptomatically I would emphasize, inspired by Indigenous modes of being but by an off-the-cuff remark made by a prominent atmospheric chemist. Here I am referring to Paul Crutzen's statement that we no longer live in the

Holocene but have entered the age of humans and are living in the An-thropocene.[54] Progressively the concept has overflowed the tight circle of geologists and has come to signify a realization that human beings have the capacity not just to radically degrade and alter biological ecosystems, but also to redirect geological history and shape physical processes that threaten life as we know it, forcing a conceptual leap that challenges the foundations of the modern world. Rather than a fragile Christmas tree or-nament or a blue marble floating in space, the earth system might be bet-ter equated to nitroglycerin—if we shake it too much we do so at our own peril!

Just as Simboans describe their land in ways that breach our distinctions between nature, culture, and the supernatural, geoscientists and others in the natural sciences are now grappling with understanding "hazards" as nature-culture imbroglios. Seismologists are starting to consider the activi-ties of human beings in addition to plate tectonics as they compose their analyses of earthquakes.[55] For many decades mining and dam-induced earthquakes have been recognized and documented, but geoscientists are progressively realizing that human-induced seismicity is much wider than previously thought. Climate change–induced typhoons, for example, appear to be triggering earthquakes as the sudden reduction of atmo-spheric pressure nudges faults deep within the earth's crust.[56] Huge vol-umes of rainfall associated with tropical hurricanes and cyclones may also be linked to earthquakes such as the devastating 2010 Haitian quake, which followed an exceptionally wet hurricane season.

Although there remains much scientific debate about the fusion of an-thropogenic processes and seismic activity, in other domains empirical evidence is mounting that gives the lie to any sense that the earth is an inert backdrop to human affairs. Take plastiglomerates. Geologists' con-ventional analytic tools and categories such as the term "rock" lose their power to explain the materiality of these novel plastic and rock amalgams or the more than two hundred new Anthropocene minerals.[57] Stymied by the indeterminacy of these entities, geologists employ scare quotes to dis-tance themselves from their meaning; thus plastiglomerates are "stone" or minerals become "mineral-like compounds" or "human-mediated mineral-like compounds." Rocks (and of course the chemistry of the atmosphere) that were once considered inert forms impervious to the agency of human beings are now imbued with human intentionality and politics. What modernism took for granted as stable and inert has been revealed to be much more contingent, plural, and reactive to our impositions. As Timothy Norton has noted, what we assumed to be the background has merged with the foreground, forcing us to think about what kind of planet, from the lithosphere to the atmosphere, our politics will engender and bequeath to our children.[58]

Moreover, the Anthropocene era unsettles the conventional distribution of labor between the natural and social sciences. It is not the case that specialists have failed to increase our understanding of phenomena such as climate change, vaccines, genetically modified foods, geoengineering, or disasters; rather, these issues breach the distinction between what we consider natural phenomena and social ones, and thus our disciplinary divisions contribute to rather than diminish these controversies. When a climate scientist pronounces that CO_2 concentrations continue to rise above the preindustrial levels or a seismologist asserts that earthquakes are related to human activities, these are not just descriptions of the atmosphere or the earth's crust: they are also political comments on a society that promotes internal combustion engines. Experts alone, whether they are natural scientists, social scientists, engineers, or government planners, are ill equipped to resolve these kinds of disputes since they involve questions of how collective life should proceed as much as they involve technical questions about the nature of the world.

Acknowledgment that physical entities such as rocks and earthquakes may now be intermixed with social and political processes has not only disrupted the natural sciences, it has also compelled researchers in the social sciences and humanities to rethink their object of study as fundamental notions of the "human" and the "social" have been destabilized.[59] As Dipesh Chakrabarty detailed, the Anthropocene imaginary collapses the distinction between geological, biological, and historical timescales that is so central to historical and social science analysis.[60] No longer can human history be effectively disentangled from geological history, let alone biological processes, since the human species has become a geological force in its own right. Although this may signal how human agency has been magnified to a planetary scale, it also poses a real threat that we, as a species, will be responsible for our own extinction.[61] Thus, the modernist

telos that innovation and creative thought would lead to collective better-
ment and improvement has unraveled.

Many have pinned the climate crisis on capitalism, arguing that we live
in the Capitalocene rather than the Anthropocene, yet the socialist ideals
of increasing autonomy, freedom, and equality built on growing material
wealth also appear problematic.[62] As David Chandler notes, if the dreams
of a more evenly just and prosperous world had been realized earlier, and
the poor had had larger carbon footprints, the climate crisis quite possibly could have been even worse.[63] Although capitalism most certainly is
disproportionately responsible for the demise of the planet, both social-
ism and capitalism developed from the Enlightenment notion of freedom,
wherein humans could transcend constraints and we eventually could free
ourselves from depending on nonhumans. Modern science, however, has
revealed the opposite—rather than being more independent from nature,
we have become more entangled with biophysical processes. As a result,
humans can no longer be seen at the center of the conceptual world, but
rather as actors entangled with many others. Human history and politics
no longer can be envisioned as operating in a distinct sphere of autonomy
and freedom. Instead, we must come to grips with Anthropocene politics
that involves "putting the nature of entangled being at the center of the
politics rather than the designs or goals of the human subject."[64]

In an era of ecological crises, the indeterminacy of the world has scram-
bled our fundamental notions of nature, and of the human. Thus questions such as "Are tsunamis human or nonhuman?" and "Are we humans
historical or geological?" seem to miss the point. Might it be time to for-
mulate new modes of sensing the ontological status of humans and the
nonhuman world? Most political ecologists who study disasters, however,
continue to ground their analyses in dichotomous human-nature terms.
Social scientists have made enormous gains by denaturalizing disasters
and focusing attention on the structural inequities that asymmetrically
distribute suffering in times of calamity. Yet the framing of disasters as
"socially constructed" or at the "human-environment nexus," in which it
is presupposed that "agents operating according to physical processes . . .
are ultimately prediscursive, 'outside' the text, no matter how many
texts be constructed about them after the fact," does not call into question nature-culture dualism; rather, it tends to reinforce it.[65] As Philippe

Descola notes, "If one agrees that human experience is conditioned by the coexistence of two fields of phenomena that are accessible through two distinct modes of understanding, one inevitably approaches their interface from the starting point of one aspect rather than another."[66] For this reason hazards scholars who naturalize disasters and political ecologists who socialize them continue to prosper as they mutually legitimate their confrontation.

If we have already decided in advance that disasters are "social constructions" or outcomes of "political-economic structures" or that our interlocutors' activities and descriptions are "cultural processes," are we not positioning them in such a way as to foreclose the possibilities and potentialities of other modes of sensing disasters? Moreover, these same analytics are undeniably inadequate to describe the production of scientific knowledge. Only a brazen postmodernist would assert that gravity is simply a cultural construction. Yet it was upon this asymmetry that anthropology and other social sciences were founded. As Mario Blaser points out, much contemporary anthropology has asserted that Indigenous peoples project their contingent culture or worldviews (i.e., symbols, politics, cosmologies) onto a presumably stable and universal, biophysical reality.[67] When we describe the Simboan experience as something either social, natural, or a mixture of the two, we also smuggle in a hierarchy of knowledge, for only Western scientific practice is assumed to definitively access and describe what is "outside the text," those biological or physical entities upon which the cultures of the world project their meaning.

Eduardo Viveiros de Castro has focused on this hierarchy of knowledge in his project to decolonize thought.[68] He argues that in order to enable alterity to flourish, we must take seriously the beings and entities taken seriously by our Indigenous interlocutors. To do so, he argues, anthropologists must maximize their ability to register what Indigenous peoples say exists and how those entities relate on their own terms rather than through the filter of nature and culture. The goal is not to elevate Indigenous modes of being as somehow universally superior to Western philosophy or science, nor simply to sentimentally support non-Western peoples, but to enable shifting our thinking and research inquiries. This is achieved not by assuming anthropologists have the capacity to transparently describe other modes of knowing and being like beads on a string, but rather by reflexively destabilizing and contaminating our own analytics as we coproduce anthropological knowledge, however indeterminate, with our interlocutors.

Might the seeds of our contemporary environmental crisis lie in the way in which we, since the Enlightenment, have composed a world based on a dichotomy of nature and culture?[69] Rather than creating a planet where we progressively have "fuller comprehension of the world," we instead have inserted our agency into every corner of the planet, creating a torrent of nature-culture hybrid entities, many of which are unintended and that continue to multiply.[70] The promise that science and technology would dramatically decrease uncertainty and risk in the world now appears grossly inflated since most contemporary hazards such as climate change, nuclear meltdowns, toxic environments, and possibly earthquakes and tsunamis are products, albeit indirect and mostly unintentional, of science and technology.[71] This does not deny the enormous accomplishments of modernity; it just forces a humbler sense of its gains and limits and a frank acknowledgment of not only the atrocities committed in the name of scientific and technological progress but also the limits of scientific rationality and its unintended capacity to increase uncertainty in the world.

My argument is that it is no longer sufficient just to assert, as many political ecologists do, that disasters need to be contextualized and that dominant narratives, especially the naturalization of disasters, be exposed as partial and contingent. Instead, we need conceptual tools that bring into view and generate new meanings, concepts, and material processes. The first step, and the one adopted in this book, is to listen closely to those involved in disasters without shortcutting to nature and culture as our conceptual resources. Not only could this lead to a greater appreciation of the entangledness of the Anthropocene condition, but it might also enable our interlocutors' practices and descriptions to unsettle our own assumptions more effectively.[72] Rather than lamenting the demise of modernity, we need to stimulate our noticing in our new precarious condition, while always acknowledging and being keenly attuned to how many of our Indigenous or marginalized interlocutors are chronically forced to adapt their worlds to the destructive forces of domination.[73]

If anthropology's goal is to understand and create space for these kinds of diverse experiences of disaster rather than explicating them based on our own analytical assumptions, then Arthur Hocart's famous statement is particularly trenchant: "How can we make any progress in understanding . . .

Figure 22. The author next to a memorial dedicated to those who perished in Tapurai during the 2007 tsunami. Some of the children in the photo fled to safety just before the waves destroyed their village. The monument sits near the center of Rupe village, where most of Tapurai's survivors have taken up residence. (Photo by author.)

if we persist in dividing what the people join and in joining what they keep apart?"[74] Approaching disasters in this way may enable us to sense the ontological multiplicity in catastrophic times (figure 22).

Or as Epeli Hau'ofa eloquently penned many years ago about the possibilities that contemporary Oceanians engender in their practices of "world enlargement":

> Oceania is vast, Oceania is expanding, Oceania is hospitable and generous, Oceania is humanity rising from the depths of brine and regions of fire deeper still, Oceania is us. We are the sea, we are the ocean, we must wake up to this ancient truth and together use it to overturn all hegemonic views that aim ultimately to confine us again, physically and psychologically, in the tiny spaces which we have resisted accepting as our sole appointed place, and from which we have recently liberated ourselves. We must not allow anyone to belittle us again, and take away our freedom.[75]

Notes

NOTES ON THE SIMBO LANGUAGE
AND SOLOMON ISLANDS PIJIN

1. D. T. Tryon and B. D. Hackman, *Solomon Islands languages: An internal classification* (Canberra: Australian National University, 1983); and Peter A. Lanyon-Orgill, *The language of Eddystone Island (Western Solomon Islands)* (Balmains, Stanley, Perthshire, Scotland: Crichton Press, 1969).

2. J. H. Lawry Waterhouse, *A Roviana and English dictionary, with English-Roviana index and list of natural history objects* (Guadalcanal: Melanesian Mission Press, 1928); J. H. Lawry Waterhouse, *A Roviana and English dictionary, with English-Roviana index and list of natural history objects and appendix of old customs*, rev. and enl. by L. M. Jones (Sydney: Epworth Printing and Publishing House, 1949); and Karen Davis, *A grammar of the Hoava language, Western Solomons* (Canberra: Australian National University, Pacific Linguistics, Research School of Pacific and Asian Studies, 2003).

3. Christine Jourdan and Ellen Maebiru, *Pijin: A trilingual cultural dictionary; Pijin-Inglish-Franis, Pijin-English-French, Pijin-Anglais-Français*, Pacific Linguistics, 526 (Canberra: Pacific Linguistics Research School of Pacific and Asian Studies Australian National University, 2002).

4. Lanyon-Orgill, *Language of Eddystone Island*.

5. Harold W. Scheffler, "Kindred and kin groups in Simbo Island social structure," *Ethnology* 1, no. 2 (1962): 135–57.

PROLOGUE: "SOMETHING WAS NOT RIGHT"

1. UNDP, *Durie, the tsunami teacher* (Bangkok, Thailand: UNDP, 2021).
2. UNDP, *Durie*, 3.

INTRODUCTION

1. See, for example, Ting Chen et al., "Slip distribution from the 1 April 2007 Solomon Islands earthquake: A unique image of near-trench rupture," *Geophysical Research Letters* 36, no. 16 (2009); and Ashar Muda Lubis and Nobuhiro Isezaki, "Shoreline changes and vertical displacement of the 2 April 2007 Solomon Islands earthquake Mw 8.1 revealed by ALOS PALSAR images," *Physics and Chemistry of the Earth, Parts A/B/C* 34, no. 6 (2009).

2. Hermann M. Fritz and Nikos Kalligeris, "Ancestral heritage saves tribes during 1 April 2007 Solomon Islands tsunami," *Geophysical Research Letters* 35, no. L01607 (2008); Brian G. McAdoo et al., "Solomon Islands tsunami, one year later," *EOS, Transactions—American Geophysical Union* 89, no. 18 (2008); and D. McDougall, I. Barry, and S. Pio, *Disaster and recovery on Ranongga: Six months after the earthquake in the Western Solomons* (Perth: Bergen Pacific Studies Group Initiative, 2008).

3. Kevin P. Furlong, Thorne Lay, and Charles J. Ammon, "A great earthquake rupture across a rapidly evolving three-plate boundary," *Science* 324, no. 5924 (2009).

4. Anne-Maree Schwarz et al., *After the earthquake: An assessment of the impact of the earthquake and tsunami on fisheries-related livelihoods in coastal communities of Western Province, Solomon Islands* (Gizo, Solomon Islands: WorldFish Center-Solomon Islands, WorldFish Center-Penang, WWF-Solomon Islands Program, Western Province Fisheries, 2007).

5. Michele Ruth Gamburd, *The golden wave: Culture and politics after Sri Lanka's tsunami disaster* (Bloomington: Indiana University Press, 2013).

6. J. Telford, J. Cosgrave, and R. Houghton, *Joint evaluation of the international response to the Indian Ocean tsunami: Synthesis report* (London: Tsunami Evaluation Coalition, 2006).

7. "Did island tribes use ancient lore to evade tsunami?," *National Geographic News*, January 24, 2005.

8. Karnjariya Sukrung, "Andaman sea gypsies heeded pre-tsunami signs," *Bangkok Post*, January 17, 2005, www.rense.com/general62/pretsn.htm.

9. Fikret Berkes, Johan Colding, and Carl Folke, "Rediscovery of traditional ecological knowledge as adaptive management," *Ecological Applications* 10, no. 5 (2000).

10. UNDRR, *The human cost of disasters: An overview of the last 20 years (2000–2019)* (New York: United Nations Office for Disaster Risk Reduction, 2020).

11. ChiChing Liu, Alan T. Linde, and I. Selwyn Sacks, "Slow earthquakes triggered by typhoons," *Nature* 459, no. 7248 (2009).

12. Julia Becker et al., "Use of traditional knowledge in emergency management for tsunami hazard: A case study from Washington State, USA," *Disaster Prevention and Management* 17, no. 4 (2008); Roy F. Ellen, ed., *Modern crises and traditional strategies: Local ecological knowledge in island Southeast Asia* (New York: Berghahn Books, 2007); and Jessica Mercer et al., "Framework for integrating indigenous and scientific knowledge for disaster risk reduction," *Disasters* 34, no. 1 (2010).

13. Sandra Díaz et al., "The IPBES Conceptual Framework—Connecting nature and people," *Current Opinion in Environmental Sustainability* 14 (2015).

14. Anna Lowenhaupt Tsing, *Friction: An ethnography of global connection* (Princeton, NJ: Princeton University Press, 2005).

15. Matthew Lauer, "Changing understandings of local knowledge in island environments," *Environmental Conservation* 44, no. 4 (2017).

16. Linda Tuhiwai Smith, *Decolonizing methodologies: Research and indigenous peoples* (London: Zed Books, 1999), 28.

17. Fikret Berkes, Carl Folke, and Johan Colding, *Linking social and ecological systems: Management practices and social mechanisms for building resilience* (Cambridge: Cambridge University Press, 1998), 14.

18. See Jamon Alex Halvaksz, *Gardens of gold: Place-making in Papua New Guinea* (Seattle: University of Washington Press, 2020); Edvard Hviding, *Guardians of Marovo Lagoon: Practice, place, and politics in maritime Melanesia* (Honolulu: University of Hawaii Press, 1996); Harold W. Scheffler, "Kindred and kin groups in Simbo Island social structure," *Ethnology* 1, no. 2 (1962); Geoffrey M. White, *Identity through history: Living stories in a Solomon Islands society,* Cambridge studies in social and cultural anthropology (Cambridge: Cambridge University Press, 1991); and Paige West, *Conservation is our government now: The politics of ecology in Papua New Guinea,* New ecologies for the twenty-first century (Durham, NC: Duke University Press, 2006).

19. David Welchman Gegeo, "Cultural rupture and indigeneity: The challenge of (re)visioning 'place' in the Pacific," *Contemporary Pacific* 13, no. 2 (2001): 495.

20. Although I prefer "Oceania" and "Oceanic peoples," I employ "Indigenous," "Oceanian," "Pacific," and "Islander" interchangeably to refer to the autochthonous peoples of the Pacific Islands region.

21. Epeli Hau'ofa, *We are the ocean: Selected works* (Honolulu: University of Hawaii Press, 2008), 73, 74.

22. James Weiner, "Between a rock and a non-place: Towards a contemporary anthropology of place," *Reviews in Anthropology* 31, no. 1 (2002): 21; and Steven Feld and Keith H. Basso, *Senses of place* (Santa Fe, NM: School of American Research Press, 1996).

23. Tim Ingold, *The perception of the environment: Essays on livelihood, dwelling and skill* (London: Routledge, 2000).

24. Here I am following Tim Ingold, "Epilogue: Towards a politics of dwelling," *Conservation and Society* 3, no. 2 (2005).

25. Tania Murray Li, "Indigeneity, capitalism, and the management of dispossession," *Current Anthropology* 51, no. 3 (2010); Judith Butler and Athena Athanasiou, *Dispossession: The performative in the political* (Cambridge, UK: Polity, 2013); and David Harvey, *A brief history of neoliberalism* (New York: Oxford University Press, 2005).

26. Marisol de la Cadena, "Indigenous cosmopolitics in the Andes: Conceptual reflections beyond 'politics,'" *Cultural Anthropology* 25, no. 2 (2010); and Mario Blaser et al., "Ontological conflicts and the stories of peoples in spite of Europe: Toward a conversation on political ontology," *Current Anthropology* 54, no. 5 (2013).

27. Annemarie Mol, *The body multiple: Ontology in medical practice* (Durham, NC: Duke University Press, 2002).

28. Roberto E. Barrios, "What does catastrophe reveal for whom? The anthropology of crises and disasters at the onset of the Anthropocene," *Annual Review of Anthropology* 46 (2017).

29. Re: "forms of noticing," see Andrew S. Mathews, "Anthropology and the Anthropocene: Criticisms, experiments, and collaborations," *Annual Review of Anthropology* 49, no. 1 (2020); and Nils Bubandt, "Anthropocene uncanny: Nonsecular approaches to environmental change," in *A non-secular Anthropocene: Spirits, specters and other nonhumans in a time of environmental change*, ed. Nils Bubandt (Aarhus: Aarhus University Research on the Anthropocene [AURA], 2018). Re: "beliefs," see Jean Pouillon, "Remarks on the verb 'to believe,'" in *Between belief and transgression: Structuralist essays in religion, history and myth*, ed. Michel Izard and Pierre Smith (1979; Chicago: Chicago University Press, 1982).

30. Here I use the terms "disaster," "calamity," and "catastrophe" interchangeably. I should point out, however, that some disaster scholars prefer to use "catastrophes" when discussing nonanthropological understandings that depict disasters as the inevitable outcome of unusually hazardous events. "Disasters" is used to describe the phenomena more diachronically in which social-ecological preconditions and human practices enhance or dampen the effect of the triggering perturbation or sociotechnical breakdown.

31. See these now classic accounts: Susanna Hoffman and Anthony Oliver-Smith, eds., *Catastrophe and culture: The anthropology of disaster*, School of American Research advanced seminar series (Santa Fe, NM: School of American Research Press, 2002); Anthony Oliver-Smith and Susanna M. Hoffman, *The angry earth: Disaster in anthropological perspective* (New York: Routledge, 1999); and Benjamin Wisner, *At risk: Natural hazards, people's vulnerability, and disasters* (London: Routledge, 2004).

32. W. Neil Adger, "Vulnerability," *Global Environmental Change* 16, no. 3 (2006); A. J. Faas, "Disaster vulnerability in anthropological perspective,"

Annals of Anthropological Practice 40, no. 1 (2016); and Elizabeth K. Marino and A. J. Faas, "Is vulnerability an outdated concept? After subjects and spaces," *Annals of Anthropological Practice* 44 (2020).

33. Aletta Biersack and James B. Greenberg, *Reimagining political ecology* (Durham, NC: Duke University Press, 2006); and Raymond L. Bryant, "Political ecology: An emerging research agenda in Third-World studies," *Political Geography* 11, no. 1 (1992).

34. Mark Schuller, *Killing with kindness: Haiti, international aid, and NGOs* (Rutgers, NJ: Rutgers University Press, 2012).

35. Arun Agrawal, *Environmentality: Technologies of government and the making of subjects* (Durham, NC: Duke University Press, 2005).

36. Carl Folke, "Resilience: The emergence of a perspective for social-ecological systems analyses," *Global Environmental Change* 16 (2006); and C. S. Holling, "Understanding the complexity of economic, ecological, and social systems," *Ecosystems* 4, no. 5 (2001).

37. Kai N. Lee, *Compass and gyroscope: Integrating science and politics for the environment* (Washington, DC: Island Press, 1994).

38. Nigel Clark, *Inhuman nature: Sociable life on a dynamic planet* (London: Sage, 2011); see also David Chandler, "Beyond neoliberalism: Resilience, the new art of governing complexity," *Resilience* 2, no. 1 (2014); and Paul Nadasdy, "Adaptive co-management and the gospel of resilience," in *Adaptive co-management: Collaboration, learning, and multilevel governance*, ed. D. Armitage, F. Berkes, and N. Doubleday (Vancouver: University of British Columbia Press, 2007).

39. Michel Callon, Pierre Lascoumes, and Yannick Barthe, eds., *Acting in an uncertain world: An essay on technical democracy* (2001; Cambridge, MA: MIT Press, 2009); and Timothy Mitchell, *Rule of experts* (Berkeley: University of California Press, 2002).

40. Barrios, "What does catastrophe reveal for whom?"

41. Here I am following Chandler, "Beyond neoliberalism." See Paul Nadasdy, "How many worlds are there?," *American Ethnologist* 48, no. 4 (2021) for a similar argument.

42. Arturo Escobar, *Designs for the pluriverse: Radical interdependence, autonomy, and the making of worlds* (Durham, NC: Duke University Press, 2018).

43. Michael L Cepek, "There might be blood: Oil, humility, and the cosmopolitics of a Cofán petro-being," *American Ethnologist* 43, no. 4 (2016).

44. Susanna M. Hoffman and Anthony Oliver-Smith, "Introduction to the second edition of *The Angry Earth*: From introduction to widespread reception," in *The angry earth: Disaster in anthropological perspective*, ed. Anthony Oliver-Smith and Susanna M. Hoffman (New York: Routledge, 2020), 18.

45. Shankar Aswani et al., *The Roviana and Vonavona marine resource management project, final report, 2000–2004* (Santa Barbara: University of California, Department of Anthropology, 2004).

46. "Tsunami wiped out entire island village," *Denver Post*, April 4, 2007, www .denverpost.com/2007/04/04/tsunami-wiped-out-entire-island-village/.

47. Kim TallBear, *Native American DNA: Tribal belonging and the false promise of genetic science* (Minneapolis: University of Minnesota Press, 2013).

48. Elenore Smith Bowen, *Return to laughter* (New York: Doubleday, 1964).

CHAPTER 1. THE RISE OF INDIGENOUS
ECOLOGICAL KNOWLEDGE

1. Michele Ruth Gamburd, *The golden wave: Culture and politics after Sri Lanka's tsunami disaster* (Bloomington: Indiana University Press, 2013), 1.

2. Deanne K. Bird, Catherine Chagué-Goff, and Anna Gero, "Human response to extreme events: A review of three post-tsunami disaster case studies," *Australian Geographer* 42, no. 3 (2011).

3. Tsunami science is quite unique in that "tsunami" is one of the few non-European words widely accepted as a scientific concept. Historians of science suggest that it only became widely used in Japan after Western scientists adopted it to describe the 1946 Alaska tsunami that devastated parts of Hawaii. In Japanese "tsunami" translates as "tsu" (harbor) and "nami" (wave), and its first use has been traced to historical Japanese documents written in the 1500s, although written descriptions of devastating waves occurring after earthquakes that sounded "like thunder" and the "sea mouth barking" date back to AD 684. See James Goff et al., "Defining tsunamis: Yoda strikes back?," *Earth-Science Reviews* 159 (2016).

4. Janice Sutherland, *Tsunami: Caught on camera*, video (Darlow Smithson Productions, 2009).

5. Sutherland, *Tsunami*.

6. UNISDR, "Leaders of Indonesia's Simeulue community receive a prestigious United Nations award," 2005, www.unisdr.org/news/v.php?id=5602.

7. Narumon Arunotai, "Saved by an old legend and a keen observation: The case of Moken Sea nomads in Thailand," in *Indigenous knowledge for disaster risk reduction: Good practices and lessons learned from experiences in the Asia-Pacific region*, ed. Rajib Shaw, Noralene Uy, and Jennifer Baumwoll (New Delhi: United Nations International Strategy for Disaster Reduction–Asia Pacific, 2008); W. Neil Adger, Nigel W. Arnell, and Emma L. Tompkins, "Adapting to climate change: Perspectives across scales," *Global Environmental Change* 15, no. 2 (2005); and Karnjariya Sukrung, "Andaman sea gypsies heeded pre-tsunami signs," *Bangkok Post*, January 17, 2005, www.rense.com/general62/pretsn.htm.

8. "Did island tribes use ancient lore to evade tsunami?," *National Geographic News*, January 24, 2005.

9. Neelesh Misra, "Stone age cultures survive tsunami waves," Associated Press, January 4, 2005, www.msnbc.msn.com/id/6786476/ns/world_news-tsunami_a_year_later/.

10. "Saved by tsunami folklore," *BBC News*, accessed March 10, 2007, http://news.bbc.co.uk/go/pr/fr2/hi/programmes/from_our_own_correspondent/6435979.stm; Paul Bishop et al., "Age-dating of tsunami deposits: Lessons from the 26 December 2004 tsunami in Thailand," *Geographical Journal* 171, no. 4 (2005); "Oral history saved islanders from tsunami," *Taipei Times*, March 2, 2005, www.taipeitimes.com/News/world/archives/2005/03/02/2003225170; and Herry Yogaswara and Eko Yulianto, *Smong, local knowledge of tsunami among the Simeulue community, Nangroe Aceh Darusallam* (Jakarta, Indonesia: Jakarta Tsunami Information Centre, 2008).

11. Yogaswara and Yulianto, *Smong*.

12. Sukrung, "Andaman sea gypsies heeded pre-tsunami signs."

13. Rebecca Leung, "Sea gypsies see signs in the waves. How Moken people in Asia saved themselves from deadly tsunami," *CBS News*, March 18, 2005, www.cbsnews.com/news/sea-gypsies-saw-signs-in-the-waves/2/; and Kevin Krajick, "Tracking myth to geological reality," *Science* 310, no. 5749 (2005).

14. Re: "ancestral knowledge," see Hermann M. Fritz and Nikos Kalligeris, "Ancestral heritage saves tribes during 1 April 2007 Solomon Islands tsunami," *Geophysical Research Letters* 35, no. L01607 (2008): 1. Re: "indigenous knowledge," see Brian G. McAdoo, Andrew Moore, and Jennifer Baumwoll, "Indigenous knowledge and the near field population response during the 2007 Solomon Islands tsunami," *Natural Hazards* 48, no. 1 (2009).

15. McAdoo, Moore, and Baumwoll, "Indigenous knowledge," 75.

16. Note that the name of the island of Ghizo is typically spelled with an "h". The letter is dropped when referring just to the town of Gizo.

17. B. G. McAdoo et al., "*Smong*: How an oral history saved thousands on Indonesia's Simeulue Island during the December 2004 and March 2005 tsunamis," *Earthquake Spectra* 22 (2006).

18. A. M. Hocart, "The cult of the dead in Eddystone of the Solomons," *Journal of the Royal Anthropological Institute of Great Britain and Ireland* 52 (1922): 277.

19. P. D. Nunn, "On the convergence of myth and reality: Examples from the Pacific Islands," *Geographical Journal* 167, no. 2 (2001); and Patrick D. Nunn et al., "Vanished islands in Vanuatu: New research and a preliminary geohazard assessment," *Journal of the Royal Society of New Zealand* 36, no. 1 (2006).

20. There are numerous words for "wave" in the Simbo language, including *tovogo* (breaking wave), *vate* (small lapping wave inside the lagoon), and *bou* (rogue wave), but none of these were employed to describe the tsunami waves.

21. Fritz and Kalligeris, "Ancestral heritage saves tribes."

22. Savanna Schuermann and Matthew Lauer, "Disaster recovery in the western Pacific: Scale, vulnerability, and traditional exchange practices," *Natural Hazards* 84, no. 2 (2016).

23. Kenneth E. Knudson, "Titiana: A Gilbertese community in the Solomon Islands" (PhD diss., University of Oregon, 1964); and Tammy Tabe, "*Ngaira Kain Tari*—'We are people of the sea': A study of the Gilbertese resettlement to Solomon Islands" (PhD diss., University of Bergen, 2016).

24. Hufanga 'Okusitino Māhina, "Ta, va, and moana: Temporality, spatiality, and indigeneity," *Pacific Studies* 33, no. 2 (2010): 170.

25. Regis Tove Stella, *Imagining the other: The representation of the Papua New Guinean subject* (Honolulu: University of Hawaii Press, 2007), 29.

26. A. F. Robertson, "Primitive society," in *International Encyclopedia of the Social & Behavioral Sciences*, ed. N. J. Smelser and P. B. Baltes (Oxford: Elsevier, 2004).

27. Edward Burnett Tylor, *Primitive culture: Researches into the development of mythology, philosophy, religion, art and custom* (London: John Murray, 1871), 2:424.

28. Émile Durkheim, *The elementary forms of religious life*, trans. Karen E. Fields (1915; New York: Free Press, 1995).

29. Émile Durkheim, "Review of Antonio Labriola, Essays on the materialist conception of history" (1897), in *Readings from Émile Durkheim*, rev. ed., ed. Kenneth Thompson (New York: Taylor & Francis Group, 2004), 15.

30. Bronislaw Malinowski, *The sexual life of savages*, 3rd ed. (London: George Routledge & Sons, 1932).

31. Bronislaw C. Malinowski, "Magic, science and religion," in *Science, religion and reality*, ed. Joseph Needham (New York: Macmillan, 1925), 29–30.

32. Bronislaw C. Malinowski, "Fishing in the Trobriand Islands," *Man* 18 (1918).

33. Harold C. Conklin, "The relation of Hanunóo culture to the plant world" (PhD diss., Yale University, 1954).

34. Charles O. Frake, "Cultural ecology and ethnography," *American Anthropologist* 64, no. 1 (1962).

35. Ian Saem Majnep and Ralph N. H. Bulmer, *Birds of my Kalam country* (Auckland: Auckland University Press, 1977).

36. R. E. Johannes, "Traditional marine conservation methods in Oceania and their demise," *Annual Review of Ecology and Systematics* 9, no. 1 (1978); and Robert E. Johannes, *Words of the lagoon: Fishing and marine lore in the Palau District of Micronesia* (Berkeley: University of California Press, 1981).

37. Kenneth Ruddle, "Introduction to the collected works of R. E. Johannes, publications on marine traditional knowledge and management," *SPC Traditional Marine Resource Management and Knowledge Information Bulletin* 23 (2008): 15.

38. Michael R. Dove, "Indigenous people and environmental politics," *Annual Review of Anthropology* 35 (2006).

39. Matthew Lauer, "State-led democratic politics and emerging forms of indigenous leadership among the Ye'kwana of the upper Orinoco," *Journal of Latin American Anthropology* 11, no. 1 (2006).

40. Kent H. Redford, "The ecologically noble savage," *Orion Nature Quarterly* 9, no. 3 (1990).

41. Tania Murray Li, "Articulating indigenous identity in Indonesia: Resource politics and the tribal slot," *Comparative Studies in Society and History* 42, no. 1 (2000).

42. Adam Kuper, "The return of the native," *Current Anthropology* 44, no. 3 (2003).

43. Arun Agrawal and Clark C. Gibson, "Enchantment and disenchantment: The role of community in natural resource management," *World Development* 27, no. 4 (1999).

44. Akhil Gupta, *Postcolonial developments: Agriculture in the making of modern India* (Durham, NC: Duke University Press, 1998).

45. Johannes, *Words of the lagoon.*

46. Fikret Berkes, "Traditional ecological knowledge in perspective," in *Traditional ecological knowledge concepts and cases*, ed. Julian Inglis (Ottawa, ON: International Program on Traditional Ecological Knowledge: International Development Research Centre, 1993), 3.

47. Stephen A. Tyler, *Cognitive anthropology* (New York: Holt Rinehart and Winston, 1969).

48. Dorothy C. Holland and Naomi Quinn, *Cultural models in language and thought* (Cambridge: Cambridge University Press, 1987).

49. Ralph C. Bulmer, "Why is the cassowary not a bird? A problem of zoological taxonomy among the Karam of the New Guinea Highlands," *Man* 2, no. 1 (1967).

50. Brian Wynne, "May the sheep safely graze? A reflexive view of the expert-lay knowledge divide," in *Risk, environment and modernity: Towards a new ecology*, ed. Scott Lash, Bronislaw Szerszynski, and Brian Wynne (London: Sage, 1996); Arun Agrawal, "Dismantling the divide between indigenous and scientific knowledge," *Development and Change* 26 (1995); and Erin L. Bohensky and Yiheyis Maru, "Indigenous knowledge, science, and resilience: What have we learned from a decade of international literature on 'integration'?," *Ecology and Society* 16, no. 4 (2011).

51. Johannes, *Words of the lagoon*, 131.

52. Bruno Latour, *Pandora's hope: Essays on the reality of science studies* (Cambridge, MA: Harvard University Press, 1999); and Sheila Jasanoff, *States of knowledge: The co-production of science and the social order* (London: Routledge, 2004).

53. Dipesh Chakrabarty, *Provincializing Europe: Postcolonial thought and historical difference* (Princeton, NJ: Princeton University Press, 2000).

54. Edward Said, *Orientalism* (New York: Vintage Books, 1979).

55. Paul Nadasdy, *Hunters and bureaucrats: Power, knowledge, and aboriginal-state relations in the southwest Yukon* (Vancouver: University of British Columbia Press, 2003); David Mosse, *Cultivating development: An ethnography of aid policy and practice* (London: Pluto Press, 2005); James Ferguson, *The anti-politics machine: "Development", depoliticization, and bureaucratic power in Lesotho* (Cambridge: Cambridge University Press, 1990); and Mark Hobart, *An anthropological critique of development: The growth of ignorance* (London: Routledge, 1993).

56. Said, *Orientalism*; Michel Foucault, *The history of sexuality*, vol. 1 (New York: Vintage Books, 1990); and Donna Haraway, "Situated knowledges: The science question in feminism and the privilege of partial perspective," *Feminist Studies* 14, no. 3 (1988).

57. Anna Lowenhaupt Tsing, *Friction: An ethnography of global connection* (Princeton, NJ: Princeton University Press, 2005), ix.

CHAPTER 2. OCEAN KNOWING

1. Milton Galokale Keremama, "Ethno-meteorological knowledge: Local indicators and perceptions of weather and seasons from Choiseul, Solomon Islands" (PhD diss., University of South Pacific, 2019).

2. The term *ia* also refers to "place," but it is a much narrower referent than gusu and closer to "home" in English. Both gusu and ia contrast with *kota*, another term for "place/area," but kota refers to a place to which one has no attachments. Christine Dureau, "Mixed blessings: Christianity and history in women's lives on Simbo, Western Solomon Islands" (PhD diss., Macquarie University, 1994), 309.

3. In Roviana Lagoon local fishers and I used GPS receivers to map over four hundred named fishing grounds. Shankar Aswani et al., *The Roviana and Vonavona marine resource management project, final report, 2000–2004* (Santa Barbara: University of California, Department of Anthropology, 2004). Within each fishing ground are more specific anchor points that fishers know by location and name. See Shankar Aswani and Matthew Lauer, "Incorporating fishers' local knowledge and behavior into geographical information systems (GIS) for designing marine protected areas in Oceania," *Human Organization* 65, no. 1 (2006).

4. Of the handful of fishers who spearfish, the most competent are Seventh-Day Adventists. The SDA community on Simbo is generally less fearful of pre-Christian spirit beings that command respect among fishers in non-SDA communities.

5. Edvard Hviding, *Guardians of Marovo Lagoon: Practice, place, and politics in maritime Melanesia* (Honolulu: University of Hawaii Press, 1996).

6. Tim Bayliss-Smith and Richard G. Feachem, *Subsistence and survival: Rural ecology in the Pacific* (New York: Academic Press, 1977).

7. Matthew Lauer and Shankar Aswani, "Indigenous knowledge and long-term ecological change: Detection, interpretation, and responses to changing ecological conditions in Pacific Island communities," *Environmental Management* 45, no. 5 (2010); and Matthew Lauer and Jaime Matera, "Who detects ecological change after catastrophic events? Indigenous knowledge, social networks, and situated practices," *Human Ecology* 44, no. 1 (2016).

8. Robert E. Johannes, *Words of the lagoon: Fishing and marine lore in the Palau District of Micronesia* (Berkeley: University of California Press, 1981).

9. Shankar Aswani and Richard J. Hamilton, "Integrating indigenous ecological knowledge and customary sea tenure with marine and social science for conservation of Bumphead Parrotfish (*Bolbometopon muricatum*) in Roviana Lagoon, Solomon Islands," *Environmental Conservation* 31 (2004).

10. Frederick W. Taylor et al., "Rupture across arc segment and plate boundaries in the 1 April 2007 Solomons earthquake," *Nature Geoscience* 1, no. 4 (2008).

11. For detailed technical descriptions, see Matthew Lauer and Shankar Aswani, "Integrating indigenous ecological knowledge and multi-spectral image classification for marine habitat mapping in Oceania," *Ocean and Coastal Management* 51, no. 6 (2008); Lauer and Aswani, "Indigenous knowledge"; and Shankar Aswani and Matthew Lauer, "Indigenous people's detection of rapid ecological change," *Conservation Biology* 28, no. 3 (2014).

12. Rebecca Leung, "Sea gypsies see signs in the waves: How Moken people in Asia saved themselves from deadly tsunami," *CBS News*, March 18, 2005, www.cbsnews.com/news/sea-gypsies-saw-signs-in-the-waves/2/.

13. J. H. Lawry Waterhouse, *A Roviana and English dictionary, with English-Roviana index and list of natural history objects* (Guadalcanal: Melanesian Mission Press, 1928).

14. Chris E. Gregg et al., "Natural warning signs of tsunamis: Human sensory experience and response to the 2004 great Sumatra earthquake and tsunami in Thailand," *Earthquake Spectra* 22, no. 3 (2006).

15. Indeed, the attribution of humanlike qualities to animals as well as inanimate objects was what nineteenth-century anthropologists such as E. B. Tylor described as "animism." Tyler's concept of animism was discredited by the early twentieth century for its blatantly racist assumptions that non-Western people lacked objective scientific observation and thus could not distinguish between humans and nonhumans. But over the last few decades there has been an upsurge of interest in what has been called "new animism" to distinguish it from the older pejorative formulation of the concept. As part of the broader shift toward ontological multiplicity, new animism attempts take seriously what Indigenous people say

about their relationships with nonhumans and especially how nonhumans are treated and acted toward. See Graham Harvey, *Animism: Respecting the living world* (New York: Columbia University Press, 2005); and especially Nurit Bird-David, "'Animism' revisited: Personhood, environment, and relational epistemology," *Current Anthropology* 40, no. S1 (1999).

16. Re: "Being with," see Tim Ingold and Gisli Palsson, *Biosocial becomings: Integrating social and biological anthropology* (Cambridge: Cambridge University Press, 2013). Re: "companion species," see Donna Haraway, *When species meet* (Minneapolis: University of Minnesota Press, 2008).

17. See Hviding, *Guardians of Marovo Lagoon*, 200–202, for a similar discursive practice in Marovo.

18. A. M. Hocart, "The canoe and the bonito in Eddystone Island," *Journal of the Royal Anthropological Institute of Great Britain and Ireland* 65 (1935): 102.

19. Hocart, "Canoe and the bonito in Eddystone Island," 103.

20. Hocart, "Canoe and the bonito in Eddystone Island," 103.

21. A. M. Hocart, "Warfare in Eddystone of the Solomon Islands," *Journal of the Royal Anthropological Institute of Great Britain and Ireland* 61 (1931): 308.

22. Simboans' relations to animals are also distinct from those in Amazonia, where animals and other organic elements of the environment, like manioc plants, are treated as persons. See Eduardo Viveiros de Castro, "Cosmological deixis and Amerindian perspectivism," *Journal of the Royal Anthropological Institute* 4, no. 3 (1998). Amazonians actualize a world that is populated by social subjects all with analogous humanlike institutions and where the critical difference is materiality (e.g., bodies). On Simbo humans and nonhumans who inhabit the same district share materiality in that both are hewn from the same primordial essence, but nonhumans are not thought of as human persons. Carl Georg von Brandenstein, *Names and substance in the Australian subsection system* (Chicago: University of Chicago Press, 1982).

23. In other domains, however, such as healing and property taboos, there are Simbo men and women who are widely recognized specialists and have the skills to channel metaphysical power.

24. Taylor et al., "Rupture across arc segment and plate boundaries."

25. Re: situated practices or strategies, see Roy Ellen, Peter Parkes, and Alan Bicker, eds., *Indigenous environmental knowledge and its transformations: Critical anthropological perspectives* (Amsterdam: Harwood Academic Publishers, 2000); Roy F. Ellen, ed. *Modern crises and traditional strategies: Local ecological knowledge in island Southeast Asia* (New York: Berghahn Books, 2007); and Matthew Lauer and Shankar Aswani, "Indigenous ecological knowledge as situated practices: Understanding fishers' knowledge in the western Solomon Islands," *American Anthropologist* 111, no. 3 (2009). Re: "metis," see James C. Scott, *Seeing like a state: How certain schemes to improve the human condition have failed* (New Haven, CT: Yale University Press, 1998). Re: performative

knowledge, see Paul Richards, "Agriculture as a performance," in *Farmer first: Farmer innovation and agricultural research*, ed. R. G. Chambers, A. Pacey, and L. A. Thrupp (London: Intermediate Technology Publications, 1989). Re: "motley" knowledge, see Andrew Pickering, *The mangle of practice: Time, agency, and science* (Chicago: University of Chicago Press, 1995); and David Turnbull, *Masons, tricksters and cartographers: Comparative studies in the sociology of scientific and indigenous knowledge* (Amsterdam: Harwood Academic, 2000). Re: situated learning, see Jean Lave, *Cognition in practice: Mind, mathematics, and culture in everyday life* (Cambridge: Cambridge University Press, 1988).

26. Arturo Escobar, "After nature: Steps to an anti-essentialist political ecology," *Current Anthropology* 40, no. 1 (1999); Tim Ingold, *The perception of the environment: Essays on livelihood, dwelling and skill* (London: Routledge, 2000); Virginia D. Nazarea, "Local knowledge and memory in biodiversity conservation," *Annual Review of Anthropology* 35 (2006); and Jean Lave, "The practice of learning," in *Understanding practice: Perspectives on activity and context*, ed. Seth Chaiklin and Jean Lave (Cambridge: Cambridge University Press, 1993), 7.

27. Mark Hobart, *An anthropological critique of development: The growth of ignorance* (London: Routledge, 1993), 17.

28. Bruno Latour, *Pandora's hope: Essays on the reality of science studies* (Cambridge, MA: Harvard University Press, 1999).

29. Lave, *Cognition in practice*.

30. Turnbull, *Masons, tricksters and cartographers*.

31. Donna Haraway, "Situated knowledges: The science question in feminism and the privilege of partial perspective," *Feminist Studies* 14, no. 3 (1988); and Latour, *Pandora's hope*.

32. Bruno Latour, *We have never been modern* (Cambridge, MA: Harvard University Press, 1993).

CHAPTER 3. ANCESTORS, STEEL, AND INLAND LIVING

1. Susanna Hoffman and Anthony Oliver-Smith, eds., *Catastrophe and culture: The anthropology of disaster* (Santa Fe, NM: School of American Research Press, 2002); Virginia Garcia-Acosta, "Historical disaster research," in *Catastrophe and culture: The anthropology of disaster*, ed. Susanna Hoffman and Anthony Oliver-Smith (Santa Fe, NM: School of American Research Press, 2002).

2. Anthony Oliver-Smith, "Peru's five-hundred-year earthquake: Vulnerability in historical context," in *The angry earth: Disaster in anthropological perspective*, ed. Anthony Oliver-Smith and Susanna M. Hoffman (New York: Routledge, 1999), 75.

3. Harold W. Scheffler, *Choiseul Island social structure* (Berkeley: University of California Press, 1965), 3.

4. James Weiner, "Between a rock and a non-place: Towards a contemporary anthropology of place," *Reviews in Anthropology* 31, no. 1 (2002); James Leach, *Creative land: Place and procreation on the Rai Coast of Papua New Guinea* (New York: Berghahn Books, 2003); and Hufanga Okusitino Māhina, "Ta, va, and moana: Temporality, spatiality, and indigeneity," *Pacific Studies* 33, no. 2 (2010).

5. Edvard Hviding and Cato Berg, eds., *The ethnographic experiment: A. M. Hocart and W. H. R. Rivers in Island Melanesia, 1908* (New York: Berghahn Books, 2014).

6. A. M. Hocart, "The cult of the dead in Eddystone of the Solomons," *Journal of the Royal Anthropological Institute of Great Britain and Ireland* 52 (1922); A. M. Hocart, "Medicine and witchcraft in Eddystone of the Solomons," *Journal of the Royal Anthropological Institute of Great Britain and Ireland* 55 (1925); A. M. Hocart, "Warfare in Eddystone of the Solomon Islands," *Journal of the Royal Anthropological Institute of Great Britain and Ireland* 61 (1931); and A. M. Hocart, "The canoe and the bonito in Eddystone Island," *Journal of the Royal Anthropological Institute of Great Britain and Ireland* 65 (1935).

7. Hocart, "Warfare in Eddystone," 303; Christine Dureau, "Skulls, mana and causality," *Journal of the Polynesian Society* 109, no. 1 (2000); and Shankar Aswani, "Changing identities: The ethnohistory of Roviana predatory headhunting," *Journal of the Polynesian Society* 109 (2000).

8. Classical anthropological interpretations of mana described it as an invisible medium of power or spiritual energy that was tapped through ritual behavior. However, early anthropologists appear to have misinterpreted the concept of mana as an abstract medium of supernatural power or energy. Closer inspection of Simbo narratives recorded by Hocart and other earlier anthropological writings do not support the idea that mana was a metaphysical substance or reservoir that existed independent of lived experience, but rather show that it was an achieved condition or state of being grounded in and inseparable from practical life and ritual activities. In the Simbo language, like many Pacific Island languages, mana typically functions as a stative verb rather than a noun. Things, people, or land do not have mana; they are actively coaxed into being mana. Roger M. Keesing, "Rethinking 'mana,'" *Journal of Anthropological Research* 40, no. 1 (1984).

9. Hocart, "Cult of the dead in Eddystone of the Solomons," 103.

10. Richard Walter, Tim Thomas, and Peter Sheppard, "Cult assemblages and ritual practice in Roviana Lagoon, Solomon Islands," *World Archaeology* 36, no. 1 (2004).

11. James J. Fox, "Place and landscape in comparative Austronesian perspective," in *The poetic power of place: Comparative perspectives on Austronesian ideas of locality*, ed. James J. Fox (Canberra: Australian National University, 1997).

12. Hocart, "Warfare in Eddystone," 302.

13. Michael Scott, *The severed snake: Matrilineages, making place, and a Melanesian Christianity in southeast Solomon Islands* (Durham, NC: Carolina Academic Press, 2007).

14. Aswani, "Changing identities."

15. Debra McDougall, "Paths of pinauzu: Captivity and social reproduction in Ranongga," *Journal of the Polynesian Society* 109, no. 1 (2000).

16. Hocart, "Cult of the dead in Eddystone of the Solomons," 105.

17. Dureau, "Mixed blessings: Christianity and history in women's lives on Simbo, Western Solomon Islands" (PhD diss., Macquarie University, 1994), 69–71.

18. Patrick D. Nunn and Ronna Pastorizo, "Geological histories and geohazard potential of Pacific Islands illuminated by myths," *Geological Society* 273, no. 1 (2007).

19. P. J. Sheppard, R. Walter, and T. Nagaoka, "The archaeology of headhunting in Roviana Lagoon, New Georgia," *Journal of the Polynesian Society* 109, no. 1 (2000); Tim Thomas, Peter Sheppard, and Richard Walter, "Landscape, violence and social bodies: Ritualized architecture in a Solomon Islands society," *Journal of the Royal Anthropological Institute* 7, no. 3 (2001); and Timothy Thomas, "Shrines in the landscape of New Georgia," in *Monuments and people in the Pacific*, ed. Helene Martinsson-Wallin and Timothy Thomas (Uppsala, Sweden: Uppsala Universitet, Department of Archaeology and Ancient History, 2014).

20. One of the goals of the archaeology project was to determine the antiquity of the hillside habitation sites and fortresses. Our team collected and then radiocarbon dated *Tradicna gigas* shell from a shrine just above the Ove crater as well as the fortress on Nusa Simbo. These were the first radiocarbon dates ever carried out on materials from Simbo. The oldest fragments were from the fortress and were dated to AD 200–400, while the youngest were from the shrine and dated to AD 1310–1450. These dates, however, are preliminary, and much more thorough archaeological work is needed to more firmly establish the antiquity of the settlement sequences.

21. Taylor et al., "Rupture across arc segment and plate boundaries in the 1 April 2007 Solomons earthquake." *Nature Geoscience* 1, no. 4 (2008).

22. Hocart, "Cult of the dead in Eddystone of the Solomons," 277.

23. R. Reeve, "Recent work on the prehistory of the Western Solomons, Melanesia," *Bulletin of the Indo-Pacific Prehistory Association* 9 (1989).

24. Debra McDougall, *Engaging with strangers: Love and violence in the rural Solomon Islands* (New York: Berghahn Books, 2016).

25. Epeli Hau'ofa, "Our sea of islands," in *A new Oceania: Rediscovering our sea of islands*, ed. Vijay Naidu and Eric Waddell (Suva: School of Social and Economic Development, University of the South Pacific, 1993).

26. Here I am following Arthur Phillip's detailed account drawn from Shortland's journals: *The voyage of Governor Phillip to Botany Bay*, comp. John Stockdale (London: Printed for John Stockdale, Piccadilly, 1789).

27. Phillip, *Voyage of Governor Phillip to Botany Bay*, 196–99.

28. K. B Jackson, "Tie hokara, tie vaka, black man, white man: A history of the New Georgia Group to 1925" (PhD diss., Australian National University, 1978).

29. Melinda S. Allen, "Three millennia of human and sea turtle interactions in remote Oceania," *Coral Reefs* 26, no. 4 (2007).

30. Edvard Hviding, *Guardians of Marovo Lagoon: Practice, place, and politics in maritime Melanesia* (Honolulu: University of Hawaii Press, 1996), 198.

31. Jackson, "Tie hokara, tie vaka, black man, white man."

32. Dorothy Shineberg, *The trading voyages of Andrew Cheyne, 1841–1844* (Canberra: Australian National University Press, 1971); and Andrew Cheyne, *The trading voyages of Andrew Cheyne, 1841–1844* (Honolulu: University of Hawaii Press, 1971).

33. Shineberg, *Trading voyages of Andrew Cheyne*, 303.

34. Timothy Thomas, "Axes of entanglement in the New Georgia Group, Solomon Islands," *Terra Australis* 51 (2019).

35. Hocart, "Warfare in Eddystone," 301.

36. Prior to the proliferation of firearms, the efficacy of hatchets and warriors who wielded them during headhunting was critical, and their combined vitality was the focus of ceremonial practices before and after raids (kana) held at *inatunu* shrines. Inatunu were shrines in each district, owned by chiefs, that served as focal points for offerings and blessings associated with headhunting. Just prior to boarding war canoes for a raid, the *votu manja* "clubs appear" ceremony was performed, in which each warrior would carry their hatchet and a shell ring valuable (ovala) to the inatunu of the chief leading the raid. The rings were brought as offerings and placed among the stone stele (*gele*) that typically adorn shrines. Then each warrior would present their club and summon ancestral power by stating "Grant me an enemy to slay, and let me club." Hocart, "Warfare in Eddystone," 308. Several days after returning from a successful raid, the enemies' hair and ears were sacrificially burned at inatunu. If the head was not brought back, the scrapings of hatchet handles would instead be burned and the spirits would be told "Here is yours, the spirits, this is yours the inatunu, Be efficacious and club men . . . be efficacious, let the people of this district club men." Hocart, "Warfare in Eddystone," 315. In many cases hatchet handles, like war canoes (geto) and other objects of spiritual potency, were heavily ornamented with inlaid mother of pearl shell and carvings.

37. Edward LiPuma, *Encompassing others: The magic of modernity in Melanesia* (Ann Arbor: University of Michigan Press, 2000).

38. Many of the names of the islands around Ghizo (e.g., Panapanga, Njari, Olosana) are from the Simbo language and suggest that Simboans guided the first Europeans through these depopulated islands.

39. J. M. McKinnon, "Tomahawks, turtles and traders: A reconstruction of the circular causation of warfare in the New Georgia Group," *Oceania* 45, no. 4 (1975).

40. McKinnon, "Tomahawks, turtles and traders"; Dureau, "Skulls, mana and causality"; Jackson, "Tie hokara, tie vaka, black man, white man"; and Sheppard, Walter, and Nagaoka, "Archaeology of head-hunting in Roviana Lagoon, New Georgia."

41. Thomas, Sheppard, and Walter, "Landscape, violence and social bodies."

42. Judith A. Bennett, *Wealth of the Solomons: A history of a Pacific archipelago, 1800–1978* (Honolulu: University of Hawaii Press, 1987), 378.

43. A. M. Hocart, "White men" (unpublished manuscript, n.d.), 2; and A. M. Hocart, "Trade and money" (unpublished manuscript, n.d.), 6.

44. David Russell Lawrence, *The naturalist and his "beautiful islands": Charles Morris Woodford in the Western Pacific* (Canberra: Australia National University Press, 2014), 52.

45. See Ian Alexander Scales, "The social forest: Landowners, development conflict and the state in Solomon Islands" (PhD diss., Australian National University, 2003), 63.

46. Jackson, "Tie hokara, tie vaka, black man, white man," 186.

47. Bennett, *Wealth of the Solomons.*

48. Lawrence, *Naturalist and his "beautiful islands."*

49. Here I am following Bruno Latour, *Science in action: How to follow scientists and engineers through society* (Cambridge, MA: Harvard University Press, 1987), 223.

CHAPTER 4. NEW VILLAGES, A NEW GOD, NEW VULNERABILITIES

1. Abandoning belongings has been identified as a key tsunami survival strategy by disaster researchers. See Brian F. Atwater, *Surviving a tsunami—Lessons from Chile, Hawaii, and Japan* (Denver, CO: United States Geological Survey, 1999).

2. The Simbo language has eight different terms for the various stages of the coconut, including a final germination stage known as *pidoko* or "coconut ice cream," when the meat expands to fill the interior, turns spongy and soft, and can be scooped out with a spoon. The fruits have myriad uses, including being the first food given to infants. Coconut water is thought to ease the nausea of pregnant women and also bolster a lactating woman's breast milk supply.

3. Another common locution involving bulo is bulo *rereko* (woman), which means "womanizer" or "excessive philanderer."

4. "Poata" is the generic term for shell and other valuables that include numerous different shell and clamshell rings of various sizes and colors, including

bakia (most valuable shell ring, usually with an orange or yellowish coloring and ground down from fossilized *Tridacna gigas* shells), *bareke* (unpolished shell ring), *hinuili* (small ring worn as protective amulet), *kalo* (sperm whale teeth), ovala (small shell ring), poata (pure white, less valuable shell ring), and *rango* (ring ground from pointed, spiral-shaped *Mitra mitra* shell). In the past many of these objects were employed both as currency for barter and in ceremonial exchanges and as a medium to transfer ancestral mana from one person to another. See Daniel Miller, *Report of the national sites survey, 1976–1978: Solomon Islands* (Honiara: National Museum, 1978). Bakia were and continue to be the most valuable and today are sometimes employed ceremonially as compensation given to a bride's parents during marriage (*vinarialava*).

5. Robert John Foster, *Social reproduction and history in Melanesia: Mortuary ritual, gift exchange, and custom in the Tanga Islands* (Cambridge: Cambridge University Press, 1995); and Joel Robbins and David Akin, "An introduction to Melanesian currencies: Agency, identity, and social reproduction," in *Money and modernity: State and local currencies in Melanesia*, ed. David Akin and Joel Robbins (Pittsburgh, PA: University of Pittsburgh Press, 1999).

6. Marilyn Strathern, *The gender of the gift: Problems with women and problems with society in Melanesia* (Berkeley: University of California Press, 1988).

7. Marshall Sahlins, "What is anthropological enlightenment? Some lessons of the twentieth century," *Annual Review of Anthropology* 28, no. 1 (1999).

8. See Jerry Jacka, *Alchemy in the rainforest: Politics, ecology, and resilience in a New Guinea mining area* (Durham, NC: Duke University Press, 2015). For other excellent case studies in Melanesia, see Paige West, *Dispossession and the environment: Rhetoric and inequality in Papua New Guinea* (New York: Columbia University Press, 2016); Deborah B. Gewertz and Frederick Karl Errington, *Emerging class in Papua New Guinea: The telling of difference* (Cambridge: Cambridge University Press, 1999); and Aihwa Ong, *Spirits of resistance and capitalist discipline: Factory women in Malaysia* (Albany: State University of New York Press, 2010).

9. Sahlins, "What is anthropological enlightenment?"

10. I. Scoones, "New ecology and the social sciences: What prospects for a fruitful engagement?," *Annual Review of Anthropology* 28 (1999); and C. S. Holling, "Resilience and stability of ecological systems," *Annual Review of Ecology and Systematics* 4 (1973).

11. Judith A. Bennett, *Wealth of the Solomons: A history of a Pacific archipelago, 1800–1978* (Honolulu: University of Hawaii Press, 1987).

12. David Russell Lawrence, *The naturalist and his "beautiful islands": Charles Morris Woodford in the Western Pacific* (Canberra: Australia National University Press, 2014).

13. A. M. Hocart, "Chieftainship" (unpublished manuscript, n.d.).

14. Hocart, "Chieftainship," 20.

15. Some scholars suggest that the cessation of warfare was not just due to the imposition of colonial power but was also an Indigenous adaptation to new circumstances. See Martin Zelenietz, "The end of headhunting in New Georgia," in *The pacification of Melanesia*, ed. Margaret Rodman and Matthew Cooper (Ann Arbor: University of Michigan Press, 1979). With the rise of copra at the end of the nineteenth century and traders taking up permanent residence on the island, Simbo commoners were no longer as dependent on their chiefs to gain access to trade goods. Commoners could trade their copra directly with the traders, weakening the position of chiefs as intermediaries.

16. The Methodist mission in the Solomon Islands eventually united with the London Missionary Society to form the United Church in Papua New Guinea and the Solomon Islands. In 1996 the United Church of Solomon Islands broke away from the Papua New Guinea branch. In local vernacular the church is typically referred to today simply as "United." David L. Hilliard, *God's gentlemen: A history of the Melanesian Mission, 1849–1942* (St Lucia: University of Queensland Press, 1978); and David L. Hilliard, "Protestant missions in the Solomon Islands" (PhD diss., Australian National University, 1966).

17. Frances Harwood, "The Christian Fellowship Church: A revitalization movement in Melanesia" (PhD diss., University of Chicago, 1971).

18. Christine Dureau, "Recounting and remembering 'first contact' on Simbo," in *Cultural Memory: Reconfiguring History and Identity in the Postcolonial Pacific*, ed. Jeannette Marie Mageo (Honolulu: University of Hawaii Press, 2001).

19. Hilliard, "Protestant Missions in the Solomon Islands," 295.

20. Dureau, "Recounting and remembering."

21. Geoffrey M. White, *Identity through history: Living stories in a Solomon Islands society*, Cambridge studies in social and cultural anthropology (Cambridge: Cambridge University Press, 1991); David W. Akin, *Colonialism, Maasina Rule, and the origins of Malaitan kastom* (Honolulu: University of Hawaii Press, 2013); and Robert J. Foster, "Commoditization and the emergence of *kastam* as a cultural category: A New Ireland case in comparative perspective," *Oceania* 62, no. 4 (1992).

22. Unlike in the past, the clan leaders I interviewed, except for those from Nusa Simbo, showed no hesitation or secrecy about their genealogical history. See Christine Dureau, "Mixed blessings: Christianity and history in women's lives on Simbo, Western Solomon Islands" (PhD diss., Macquarie University, 1994). The chiefs I interviewed from Nusa Simbo, however, were quite secretive and requested that I not record their narratives. This was not surprising considering that two chiefs of a major Nusa Simbo clan had been embroiled in an acrimonious power struggle over land that was sold for the purpose of building an SDA Church (see the introduction). On other islands in the Solomons, such as among the Arosi people of Makira (southwest Solomons), descent groups have moved into previously unoccupied land. Without well-established autochthonous

land-owning clans, knowledge about ancestral practices becomes deeply conten-
tious as different descent groups attempt to claim authority. See Michael Scott,
*The severed snake: Matrilineages, making place, and a Melanesian Christianity
in Southeast Solomon Islands* (Durham, NC: Carolina Academic Press, 2007).

23. See White, *Identity through history*, 32–44, for a similar description of
walking through the forests of Santa Isabel.

24. Hannah Haas et al., "Archaeological reconnaissance and the first radiocarbon dates from Simbo Island, Western Province, Solomon Islands," *Journal
of Pacific Archaeology* 9, no. 1 (2018).

25. A. M. Hocart, "Warfare in Eddystone of the Solomon Islands," *Journal of
the Royal Anthropological Institute of Great Britain and Ireland* 61 (1931): 302.

26. Harold Scheffler, "Kindred and kin groups in Simbo Island social structure," *Ethnology* 1, no. 2 (1962), recorded a similar story in 1961.

27. Instead of previously being inhabited by people, northern Narovo is known
as the dwelling place of specific spirit entities known as *tuturu*. See A. M. Hocart, "The cult of the dead in Eddystone of the Solomons," *Journal of the Royal
Anthropological Institute of Great Britain and Ireland* 52 (1922): 264. These existents were spirits (tomate) of madness or simply "madmen" that haunted the
forests and ate wild rather than human foods. The only evidence of their existence today are a number of stunning petroglyph sites dotting the northern half
of Narovo. The shallow etched lines of the petroglyphs adorn large, dark, volcanic boulders and depict abstract shapes as well as zoomorphic and anthropomor-
phic designs. One of the most impressive petroglyphs, a 2-meter-high boulder
called Tobulu, sits overlooking the Tapurai beach site.

28. Jeannette Mageo, "Continuity and shape shifting: Samoan spirits in culture history," in *God, spirits, and history: A theoretical perspective*, ed. Jeannette
Mageo and Alan Howard (New York: Routledge, 1996).

29. Scott, *Severed snake*, 176.

30. Dureau, "Mixed blessings," 138.

31. Harwood, "Christian Fellowship Church."

32. The SDA congregation on Simbo has a much more dismissive stance on
ancestor spirits, and they openly proclaim that their faith nullifies the influence
of pre-Christian forces. Indeed, the SDA village called Tuku was established on
a piece of land previously known as *tuku* ("closed"). I was told that the land was
formerly a graveyard for the bones of women and newborns who died in child-
birth and was dangerous for settlement due to the presence of malevolent ancestral spirits. By establishing their village on that particular piece of land the SDA
were demonstrating the power of their faith to neutralize the ancestral spirits
and build a successful village. See Dureau, "Mixed blessings," 242.

33. Bennett, *Wealth of the Solomons*, 127.

34. Judith A. Bennett, *Pacific forest: A history of resource control and contest
in the Solomon Islands c. 1800–1997* (Cambridge, UK: White Horse Press, 2000).

35. Edvard Hviding and Tim Bayliss-Smith, *Islands of rainforest: Agroforestry, logging and eco-tourism in Solomon Islands* (Aldershot: Ashgate, 2000).

36. Edvard Hviding, "Indigenous essentialism? Simplifying customary land ownership in New Georgia, Solomon Islands," *Bijdragen tot de Taal-, Land- en Volkenkunde* 149, no. 4 (1993).

37. Scheffler, "Kindred and kin groups."

38. Christine Dureau, "Keeping and giving, keeping for keeping: Christian property taboo on Simbo, Solomon Islands," in *A polymath anthropologist: Essays in honour of Ann Chowning*, ed. Claudia Gross et al. (Auckland, NZ: Department of Anthropology, University of Auckland, 2005), 140.

39. Deborah B. Gewertz and Frederick Karl Errington, *Cheap meat: Flap food nations in the Pacific Islands* (Berkeley: University of California Press, 2010).

40. Strathern, *Gender of the gift*.

41. Strathern, *Gender of the gift*; and Roy Wagner, "The fractal person," in *Big men and great men: Personifications of power in Melanesia*, ed. M. Godelier and M. Strathern (Cambridge: Cambridge University Press, 1991).

42. Akin and Robbins, *Money and modernity*; and Maurice Bloch and Jonathan Parry, eds., *Money and the modernity of exchange* (Cambridge: Cambridge University Press, 1989).

43. Nicholas Thomas, "Substantivization and anthropological discourse: The transformation of practices into institutions in neotraditional Pacific societies," in *History and tradition in Melanesian anthropology*, ed. James G. Carrier (Berkeley: University of California, 1992), 80.

44. Foster, *Social reproduction and history in Melanesia*, 244.

45. Joel Robbins and David Akin, "An introduction to Melanesian currencies: Agency, identity, and social reproduction," in *Money and modernity: State and local currencies in Melanesia*, ed. David Akin and Joel Robbins (Pittsburgh, PA: University of Pittsburgh Press, 1999), 14–15.

46. Matthew Lauer, "Calamity, kastom, and modernity: Local interpretations of vulnerability in the western Pacific," *Environmental Hazards* 13, no. 4 (2014).

47. Some of the survivors told me that the Japanese scientists who visited Simbo just after the tsunami talked about the possibility of another large tsunamigenic quake. Indeed, geologists have documented that the Solomon Islands region is unique for its earthquake "doublets," large seismic events that occur in closely related pairs that are separated sometimes by a few hours and at other times by a few days or years. See Thorne Lay and Hiroo Kanamori, "Earthquake doublets in the Solomon Islands," *Physics of the Earth and Planetary Interiors* 21, no. 4 (1980). In fact, a second large-magnitude (7.1) earthquake struck again on January 3, 2010, creating a 7-meter tsunami that inundated the southern shore of Rendova Island. See Andrew V. Newman et al., "The energetic 2010 MW 7.1 Solomon Islands tsunami earthquake," *Geophysical Journal International* 186, no. 2 (2011). The epicenter was 20 kilometers to the southwest of the

2007 quake, and luckily tsunami waves did not reach Simbo. Simboans were terrified when they felt the large quake, and everyone ran to high ground, sleeping there for several days.

48. As described by Rickie Burman, "Time and socioeconomic change on Simbo, Solomon Islands," *Man* 16, no. 2 (1981), the ripening of canarium nuts is central to time constructs on Simbo. The year is divided into two seasons or "years," *auro vino* and *auro ngari*. In this context the word *auro*, which also glosses as "nut grove," translates as "year." The two nut seasons are marked by the two major wind patterns of *ragi* (southeast trades) and peja (northwesterlies) and are associated with specific planting, fishing, and other important subsistence activities.

49. Tim Ingold, *The perception of the environment: Essays on livelihood, dwelling and skill* (London: Routledge, 2000).

50. See Debra McDougall, *Engaging with strangers: Love and violence in the rural Solomon Islands* (New York: Berghahn Books, 2016), for a similar concept on nearby Ranongga Island.

51. There is a specific taboo known as *meke* that focuses on these kinds of property. The owner of a resource like a fruit tree will place a small wood placard near it with the words "Meke Minister" and a number painted on it. The placard is thought to protect the resource from theft and to cause any thieves or their close kin to fall ill. In addition to this contemporary Indigenous Christian property taboo there is an older form known as *kejo*, which serves the same purpose, but instead of a placard it is an upright stick, split at the top, where a specific leaf or other token is wedged.

52. Jacka, *Alchemy in the rainforest.*

CHAPTER 5. ASSEMBLING RECONSTRUCTION

1. See Solomon Islands Government, *Special audit report: Tsunami and earthquake relief fund* (Honiara: Office of the Auditor-General, 2008). This report revealed an enormous amount of corruption and mismanagement of donated and government funds.

2. Anthony Oliver-Smith, *The martyred city: Death and rebirth in the Andes* (Albuquerque: University of New Mexico Press, 1986).

3. Oliver-Smith, *Martyred city*, 78.

4. Lamont Lindstrom, *Cargo cult: Strange stories of desire from Melanesia and beyond* (Honolulu: University of Hawaii Press, 1993), 162.

5. Ben Burt, "Land in Kwara'ae and development in Solomon Islands," *Oceania* 64, no. 4 (1994); Edvard Hviding, "Indigenous essentialism? Simplifying customary land ownership in New Georgia, Solomon Islands," *Bijdragen tot de Taal-, Land- en Volkenkunde* 149, no. 4 (1993); Debra McDougall, "The

unintended consequences of clarification: Development, disputing, and the dynamics of community in Ranongga, Solomon Islands," *Ethnohistory* 52, no. 1 (2005); and Michael Scott, *The severed snake: Matrilineages, making place, and a Melanesian Christianity in Southeast Solomon Islands* (Durham, NC: Carolina Academic Press, 2007).

6. James F. Weiner and Katie Glaskin, *Customary land tenure and registration in Australia and Papua New Guinea: Anthropological perspectives*, vol. 3 (Canberra: Australia National University Press, 2007); Jamon Alex Halvaksz, *Gardens of gold: Place-making in Papua New Guinea* (Seattle: University of Washington Press, 2020); Hufanga Okusitino Māhina, "Ta, va, and moana: Temporality, spatiality, and indigeneity," *Pacific Studies* 33, no. 2 (2010); James J. Fox, "Place and landscape in comparative Austronesian perspective," in *The poetic power of place: Comparative perspectives on Austronesian ideas of locality*, ed. James J. Fox (Canberra: Australian National University, 1997); and James Leach, *Creative land: Place and procreation on the Rai Coast of Papua New Guinea* (New York: Berghahn Books, 2003).

7. Annemarie Mol, *The body multiple: Ontology in medical practice* (Durham, NC: Duke University Press, 2002).

8. Mario Blaser et al., "Ontological conflicts and the stories of peoples in spite of Europe: Toward a conversation on political ontology," *Current Anthropology* 54, no. 5 (2013); Marisol de la Cadena, "Indigenous cosmopolitics in the Andes: Conceptual reflections beyond 'politics,'" *Cultural Anthropology* 25, no. 2 (2010); and Tim Ingold, "One world anthropology," *Hau: Journal of Ethnographic Theory* 8, nos. 1/2 (2018).

9. Tim Ingold, *Being alive: Essays on movement, knowledge and description* (London: Routledge, 2011); Bruno Latour, *Reassembling the social: An introduction to actor-network-theory* (Oxford: Oxford University Press, 2005); Donna Haraway, *When species meet* (Minneapolis: University of Minnesota Press, 2008); and Gilles Deleuze and Felix Guattari, *A thousand plateaus*, trans. B. Massumi (1980; Minneapolis: University of Minnesota Press, 1987).

10. Ilaitia S. Tuwere, *Vanua: Towards a Fijian theology of place* (Suva: University of South Pacific, 2002), 35.

11. Nicholas Blomley, "Performing property: Making the world," *Canadian Journal of Law & Jurisprudence* 26, no. 1 (2013).

12. Tania Murray Li, *Land's end: Capitalist relations on an indigenous frontier* (Durham, NC: Duke University Press, 2014).

13. Karl Polanyi, *The great transformation* (Boston: Beacon Press, 1944).

14. Halvaksz, *Gardens of gold*, 2020; and Donna Haraway, *The companion species manifesto: Dogs, people, and significant otherness* (Chicago: Prickly Paradigm Press, 2003). I employ "human/nonhuman collectives" in Latour's analytically agnostic sense that collectives are free to collect and relate to anyone or any entity without necessarily adhering to the modernist scheme of nature (singular)

and cultures (plural). See Bruno Latour, *Facing Gaia: Eight lectures on the new climatic regime* (Cambridge, UK: Polity, 2017), 121.

15. Regis Tove Stella, *Imagining the other: The representation of the Papua New Guinean subject* (Honolulu: University of Hawaii Press, 2007), 29.

16. Tuwere, *Vanua*, 42.

17. A. M. Hocart, "Katapana—Bush People—Iliganigani" (unpublished manuscript, n.d.).

18. Jully Makini, ed., *Na buka vivinei malivi pa zinama Roviana* (Roviana custom stories book) (Solomon Islands: Western Province Government, 1995).

19. For example, Debra McDougall, *Engaging with strangers: Love and violence in the rural Solomon Islands* (New York: Berghahn Books, 2016), 68.

20. At the request of the elders who told me these stories I have intentionally changed the narratives as well as the specific place and person names.

21. Scott, *Severed snake*; and Mary Salmond, *Aphrodite's island: The European discovery of Tahiti* (Berkeley: University of California Press, 2009), 22.

22. Fox, "Place and landscape in comparative Austronesian perspective."

23. Rickie Burman, "Time and socioeconomic change on Simbo, Solomon Islands," *Man* 16, no. 2 (1981).

24. Simon Foale and Martha Macintyre, "Dynamic and flexible aspects of land and marine tenure at West Nggela: Implications for marine resource management," *Oceania* 71, no. 1 (2000); Geofrey M. White, *Identity through history: Living stories in a Solomon Islands society*, Cambridge studies in social and cultural anthropology (Cambridge: Cambridge University Press, 1991); and Scott, *Severed snake*.

25. The term "bubutu," however, is polysemous and today many Simboans employ the Pijin terms traeb (tribe) and laen (line) or the English word "community" as synonyms for bubutu.

26. Roger M. Keesing, "Descent, residence, cultural codes," in *Anthropology in Oceania: Essays presented to Ian Hogbin*, ed. Lester Richard Hiatt and C. Fayawardena (London: Angus and Robertson, 1971).

27. Margaret Rodman, *Masters of tradition: Consequences of customary land tenure in Longana, Vanuatu* (Vancouver: University of British Columbia Press, 1987), 35.

28. Pei-yi Guo, "Law as discourse: Land disputes and the changing imagination of relations among the Langalanga, Solomon Islands," *Pacific Studies* 34, no. 2 (2011); and Harold Scheffler and Peter Larmour, "Solomon Islands: Evolving a new custom," in *Land tenure in the Pacific*, ed. Selwyn Arutangai and R. G. Crocombe (Suva, Fiji: University of the South Pacific, 1987).

29. Tania Murray Li, "What is land? Assembling a resource for global investment," *Transactions of the Institute of British Geographers* 39, no. 4 (2014): 589.

30. K. B. Jackson, "Tie hokara, tie vaka, black man, white man: A history of the New Georgia Group to 1925" (PhD diss., Australian National University, 1978), 383.

31. Similar cognates of bubutu are found in many languages across the New Georgia Group: Roviana and Kubokota (Ranongga), *butubutu*; Nduke (Kolombangara), *bubutu*. McDougall, *Engaging with strangers*; and Ian Alexander Scales, "The social forest: Landowners, development conflict and the state in Solomon Islands" (PhD diss., Australian National University, 2003).

32. Joel Robbins, *Becoming sinners: Christianity and moral torment in a Papua New Guinea society*, vol. 4 (Berkeley: University of California Press, 2004).

33. Here I am drawing on Scales, "Social forest." Some scholars have argued that bubutu are long-standing rather than repurposed social categories. See Edvard Hviding, "Disentangling the butubutu of New Georgia," in *Oceanic socialities and cultural forms: Ethnographies of experience*, ed. Ingjerd Hoëm and Sidsel Roalkvam (New York: Berghahn Books, 2003), who followed Harold W. Scheffler, "Simbo Island social structure," *Ethnology* 1, no. 2 (1962).

34. Hocart, "Chieftainship."

35. Harold W. Scheffler, *Choiseul Island social structure* (Berkeley: University of California Press, 1965).

36. Scheffler, "Kindred and kin groups."

37. For similar examples of this in the region, see Burt, "Land in Kwara'ae"; and White, *Identity through history.*

38. Takashi Tomita et al., "Joint report for tsunami field survey for the Solomon Islands earthquake of April 1, 2007," *Tsunami Engineering Report of Research* (2008).

39. Hermann M. Fritz and Nikos Kalligeris, "Ancestral heritage saves tribes during 1 April 2007 Solomon Islands tsunami," *Geophysical Research Letters* 35, no. L01607 (2008).

40. Michele Ruth Gamburd, *The golden wave: Culture and politics after Sri Lanka's tsunami disaster* (Bloomington: Indiana University Press, 2013), reported the opposite reaction among Sri Lankans who survived the 2004 Indian Ocean tsunami. There, beachside residents' relationship with the ocean shifted, and the ocean became a major source of fear and uncertainty.

41. Some of the most educated, literate Simboans had some familiarity with the concepts of vulnerability and disasters prior to the tsunami. In fact, one of my closest interlocutors, Nickson Sione, had been trained in disaster assessment prior to the tsunami.

42. John Wagner and Malia Talakai, "Customs, commons, property, and ecology: Case studies from Oceania," *Human Organization* 66, no. 1 (2007); and Keir Martin, *The death of the big men and the rise of the big shots: Custom and conflict in East New Britain* (New York: Berghahn Books, 2013).

43. Many of the most acrimonious disputes that end up in court are between clans who have ancestral attachments to the same district. In these cases, unlike the case of Tapurai and their attempt to build the grammar school, a clan has much more difficulty asserting full control over land, and the disputes usually end up in the local courts for adjudication.

44. Paul Nadasdy, "The gift in the animal: The ontology of hunting and human–animal sociality," *American Ethnologist* 34, no. 1 (2007).

45. Matthew Lauer et al., "Globalization, Pacific Islands, and the paradox of resilience," *Global Environmental Change* 23, no. 1 (2013).

46. C. L. Birrell, L. J. McCook, and B. L. Willis, "Effects of algal turfs and sediment on coral settlement," *Marine Pollution Bulletin* 51, nos. 1–4 (2005).

47. S. Albert, J. Udy, and I. R. Tibbetts, "Responses of algal communities to gradients in herbivore biomass and water quality in Marovo Lagoon, Solomon Islands," *Coral Reefs* 27, no. 1 (2008).

48. Quoted from Tim Ingold, *The life of lines* (New York: Routledge, 2015), 38.

49. Here I am following Timothy Mitchell's brilliant analysis of expertise in *Rule of experts* (Berkeley: University of California Press, 2002).

CHAPTER 6. VULNERABLE ISLES?

1. UNDP, "Eleven years after deadly tsunami, Simbo Island in the Solomons welcomes evacuation drills in schools," April 20, 2018,www.asia-pacific.undp .org/content/rbap/en/home/presscenter/articles/2018/04/20/devastated-by-the -2007-tsunami-simbo-island-in-the-solomon-islands-welcomes-emergency -evacuation-drill.html.

2. UNDP, "Eleven years after deadly tsunami."

3. Christopher B. Field and Vicente R. Barros, *Climate change 2014—Impacts, adaptation and vulnerability: Regional aspects* (Cambridge: Cambridge University Press, 2014); and Nobuo Mimura et al., "Small islands," in *Climate Change 2007: Impacts, adaptation and vulnerability; Contribution of working group II to the fourth assessment report of the Intergovernmental Panel on Climate Change*, ed. M. L. Parry et al. (Cambridge: Cambridge University Press, 2007).

4. Field and Barros, *Climate change 2014*, 1618.

5. UNDP, *Human development report* (New York: UNDP, 2020).

6. Sophie Webber, "Performative vulnerability: Climate change adaptation policies and financing in Kiribati," *Environment and Planning A* 45, no. 11 (2013); and Heather Lazrus, "Sea change: Island communities and climate change," *Annual Review of Anthropology* 41 (2012).

7. Kenneth Hewitt, ed., *Interpretations of calamity from the viewpoint of human ecology* (Boston: Allen & Unwin, 1983).

8. Carl Folke, "Resilience: The emergence of a perspective for social-ecological systems analyses," *Global Environmental Change* 16 (2006). Other important texts include B. H. Walker and David Salt, *Resilience thinking: Sustaining ecosystems and people in a changing world* (Washington, DC: Island Press, 2006); and Lance H. Gunderson and C. S. Holling, *Panarchy: Understanding transformations in human and natural systems* (Washington, DC: Island Press, 2002).

9. Kathleen Tierney, *The social roots of risk: Producing disasters, promoting resilience* (Palo Alto, CA: Stanford University Press, 2014), 6.

10. See Kevin Grove, *Resilience* (New York: Routledge, 2018).

11. C. S. Holling, "Resilience and stability of ecological systems," *Annual Review of Ecology and Systematics* 4 (1973).

12. See, for example, Eugene P. Odum, "The strategy of ecosystem development," *Science* 164, no. 3877 (1969).

13. I. Scoones, "New ecology and the social sciences: What prospects for a fruitful engagement?," *Annual Review of Anthropology* 28 (1999).

14. C. S. Holling, "Understanding the complexity of economic, ecological, and social systems," *Ecosystems* 4, no. 5 (2001).

15. Fikret Berkes, Carl Folke, and Johan Colding, *Linking social and ecological systems: Management practices and social mechanisms for building resilience* (Cambridge: Cambridge University Press, 1998); Folke, "Resilience"; Gunderson and Holling, *Panarchy*; and Walker and Salt, *Resilience thinking*.

16. W. Neil Adger, "Vulnerability," *Global Environmental Change* 16, no. 3 (2006).

17. Adger, "Vulnerability," 268.

18. Christopher B. Field et al., eds., *Managing the risks of extreme events and disasters to advance climate change adaptation: Special report of the Intergovernmental Panel on Climate Change* (Cambridge: Cambridge University Press, 2012).

19. Kevin J. Grove, "From emergency management to managing emergence: A genealogy of disaster management in Jamaica," *Annals of the Association of American Geographers* 103, no. 3 (2013).

20. Roberto E. Barrios, "Resilience: A commentary from the vantage point of anthropology," *Annals of Anthropological Practice* 40, no. 1 (2016); Katrina Brown, "Global environmental change I: A social turn for resilience?," *Progress in Human Geography* 38, no. 1 (2014); and Marc Welsh, "Resilience and responsibility: Governing uncertainty in a complex world," *Geographical Journal* 180, no. 1 (2013).

21. Roy A. Rappaport, *Pigs for the ancestors: Ritual in the ecology of a New Guinea people* (New Haven, CT: Yale University Press, 1984).

22. Barrios, "Resilience."

23. Tierney, *Social roots of risk*; Muriel Cote and Andrea J. Nightingale, "Resilience thinking meets social theory: Situating social change in socio-ecological systems (SES) research," *Progress in Human Geography* 36, no. 4 (2012); and Michael Dillon and Julian Reid, *The liberal way of war: Killing to make life live* (New York: Routledge, 2009).

24. David Harvey, *A brief history of neoliberalism* (New York: Oxford University Press, 2005).

25. Christine J. Walley, *Exit zero: Family and class in postindustrial Chicago* (Chicago: University of Chicago Press, 2013).

26. Mario Blaser et al., "Ontological conflicts and the stories of peoples in spite of Europe: Toward a conversation on political ontology," *Current Anthropology*

54, no. 5 (2013): 11; and Marisol de la Cadena and Mario Blaser, *A world of many worlds* (Durham, NC: Duke University Press, 2018).

27. See John Law, *After method: Mess in social science research* (London: Routledge, 2004); and Li, "What is land? Assembling a resource for global investment," *Transactions of the Institute of British Geographers* 39, no. 4 (2014): 589–602.

28. Even in cases where land alienation is rejected, capitalist relations may take hold in insidious ways. See Li, *Land's end: Capitalist relations on an indigenous frontier* (Durham, NC: Duke University Press, 2014) for a case in which Sulawesi highlanders unintentionally individualized their own land rights when they planted cash-earning tree crops.

29. Elizabeth K. Marino and A. J. Faas, "Is vulnerability an outdated concept? After subjects and spaces," *Annals of Anthropological Practice* 44, no. 1 (2020).

30. Kenneth Hewitt, "The idea of calamity in a technocratic age," in *Interpretations of calamity from the viewpoint of human ecology*, ed. Kenneth Hewitt (Boston: Allen & Unwin, 1983); and Karen O'Brien et al., "What's in a word? Conflicting interpretations of vulnerability in climate change research," *Climate Policy* 7 (2004).

CHAPTER 7. SENSING DISASTER COMPOSITIONS

1. Elizabeth Povinelli, "Routes/worlds," *e-flux journal* 27 (2011): 1.

2. Eduardo Kohn, *How forests think: Toward an anthropology beyond the human* (Berkeley: University of California Press, 2013); Philippe Descola, *Beyond nature and culture*, trans. Janet Lloyd (Chicago: University of Chicago Press, 2013); and Martin Holbraad and Morten Axel Pedersen, *The ontological turn: An anthropological exposition* (Cambridge: Cambridge University Press, 2017).

3. Eduardo Viveiros de Castro, "Zeno and the art of anthropology: Of lies, beliefs, paradoxes, and other truths," *Common Knowledge* 17, no. 1 (2011).

4. Hermann M. Fritz and Nikos Kalligeris, "Ancestral heritage saves tribes during 1 April 2007 Solomon Islands tsunami," *Geophysical Research Letters* 35 (2008); and Brian G. McAdoo, Andrew Moore, and Jennifer Baumwoll, "Indigenous knowledge and the near field population response during the 2007 Solomon Islands tsunami," *Natural Hazards* 48, no. 1 (2009).

5. Anthony Davis and Kenneth Ruddle, "Constructing confidence: Rational skepticism and systematic enquiry in local ecological knowledge research," *Ecological Applications* 20, no. 3 (2010): 893.

6. Davis and Ruddle, "Constructing confidence," 881.

7. Michel Foucault, ed., *"Society must be defended": Lectures at the Collège de France, 1975–1976* (New York: Picador, 2003), 180.

8. Susan A. Crate, "Gone the bull of winter? Grappling with the cultural implications of and anthropology's role(s) in global climate change," *Current Anthropology* 49, no. 4 (2008): 570.

9. Crate, "Gone the bull of winter?," 570.

10. Peter Rudiak-Gould, "'We have seen it with our own eyes': Why we disagree about climate change visibility," *Weather, Climate, and Society* 5, no. 2 (2013).

11. Rudiak-Gould, "'We have seen it with our own eyes.'"

12. Harold C. Conklin, "The relation of Hanunóo culture to the plant world" (PhD diss., Yale University, 1954); Robert E. Johannes, *Words of the lagoon: Fishing and marine lore in the Palau District of Micronesia* (Berkeley: University of California Press, 1981).

13. Arun Agrawal, "Dismantling the divide between indigenous and scientific knowledge," *Development and Change* 26 (1995).

14. Michael Howes and Robert Chambers, "Indigenous technical knowledge: Analysis, implications and issues," in *Indigenous knowledge systems and development*, ed. David Brokensha, Dennis M. Warren, and Oswald Werner (Washington, DC: University Press of America, 1980), 330.

15. Andrew Pickering, *Science as practice and culture* (Chicago: University of Chicago Press, 1992); and Bruno Latour and Steve Woolgar, *Laboratory life: The construction of scientific facts*, 2nd ed. (Princeton, NJ: Princeton University Press, 1986 [1979]).

16. Donna Haraway, "Situated knowledges: The science question in feminism and the privilege of partial perspective," *Feminist Studies* 14, no. 3 (1988).

17. Bruno Latour, *Science in action: How to follow scientists and engineers through society* (Cambridge, MA: Harvard University Press, 1987).

18. Arun Agrawal, "Why 'indigenous' knowledge?," *Journal of the Royal Society of New Zealand* 39, no. 4 (2009): 157.

19. For a brilliant discussion of absolutisms and their deployment in US popular and political culture, see Stanley Fish's, *There's no such thing as free speech* (Oxford: University of Oxford Press 1994).

20. For an excellent exposition of this argument, see Naomi Oreskes, *Why trust science?* (Princeton, NJ: Princeton University Press, 2019).

21. Kim TallBear, *Native American DNA: Tribal belonging and the false promise of genetic science* (Minneapolis: University of Minnesota Press, 2013), 204.

22. James C. Scott, *Seeing like a state: How certain schemes to improve the human condition have failed* (New Haven, CT: Yale University Press, 1998).

23. Julie Cruikshank, *Do glaciers listen? Local knowledge, colonial encounters, and social imagination* (Vancouver: University of British Columbia Press, 2005).

24. Bill Cooke and Uma Kothari, *Participation: The new tyranny?* (London: Zed Books, 2001).

25. Fikret Berkes, *Sacred ecology: Traditional ecological knowledge and resource management*, 3rd ed. (New York: Routledge, 2012).

26. C. S. Holling and Gary K. Meffe, "Command and control and the pathology of natural resource management," *Conservation Biology* 10, no. 2 (1996): 328.

27. Jessica Mercer et al., "Framework for integrating indigenous and scientific knowledge for disaster risk reduction," *Disasters* 34, no. 1 (2010).

28. Walter V. Reid, Fikret Berkes, and Thomas J. Wilbanks, *Bridging scales and knowledge systems: Concepts and applications in ecosystem assessment* (Washington, DC: Island Press, 2006).

29. Maria Tengö et al., "Connecting diverse knowledge systems for enhanced ecosystem governance: The multiple evidence base approach," *Ambio* 43, no. 5 (2014).

30. Jean Baudrillard, *For a critique of the political economy of the sign*, trans. Charles Levin (Candor, NY: Telos Press Publishing, 2019).

31. UNDP, *Durie, the tsunami teacher* (Bangkok: UNDP, 2021).

32. UNDP, "Surviving the 2007 Tsunami in the Solomon Islands, Durie Hickie's Story," May 4, 2018, https://undpasiapac.medium.com/surviving-the -2007-tsunami-in-the-solomon-islands-durie-hickies-story-6c1e071420c7.

33. Helen Verran, "Engagements between disparate knowledge traditions: Toward doing difference generatively and in good faith," in *Contested ecologies: Dialogues in the South on nature and knowledge*, ed. Lesley Green (Cape Town, South Africa: HSRC Press, 2013), 156; and John Law and Solveig Joks, "Luossa and laks: Salmon, science and LEK," *Revue d'Anthropologie des Connaissances* 11, no. 2 (2017).

34. Elizabeth A Povinelli, *Geontologies: A requiem to late liberalism* (Durham, NC: Duke University Press, 2016).

35. Here I am following the work of Esther Turnhout et al., "Listen to the voices of experience," *Nature* 488, no. 7412 (2012); and David Turnbull, "Reframing science and other local knowledge traditions," *Futures* 29, no. 6 (1997).

36. Foucault, *"Society must be defended."*

37. Kenneth Hewitt, "The idea of calamity in a technocratic age," in *Interpretations of calamity from the viewpoint of human ecology*, ed. Kenneth Hewitt (Boston: Allen & Unwin, 1983), 12.

38. Susanna M. Hoffman and Roberto E. Barrios, *Disaster upon disaster: Exploring the gap between knowledge, policy and practice* (New York: Berghahn Books, 2019), 2:3.

39. P. O'Keefe et al., "Taking the 'naturalness' out of 'natural disaster,'" *Nature* 260 (1976): 566–67.

40. Immanuel Wallerstein, "The rise and future demise of the world capitalist system: Concepts for comparative analysis," in *The capitalist world-economy* (Cambridge: Cambridge University Press, 1979); Jonathan Friedman, "Marxism, structuralism, and vulgar materialism," *Man* 9, no. 3 (1974); and Eric Wolf, *Europe and the people without history* (Berkeley: University of California Press, 1982).

41. Aletta Biersack and James B. Greenberg, *Reimagining political ecology* (Durham, NC: Duke University Press, 2006).

42. Anthony Oliver-Smith, *The martyred city: Death and rebirth in the Andes* (Albuquerque: University of New Mexico Press, 1986).

43. J. H. Steward, *Basin-plateau aboriginal sociopolitical groups* (Washington, DC: Bureau of American Ethnology Bulletin, 1938).

44. Bradley B. Walters et al., eds., *Against the grain: The Vayda tradition in human ecology and ecological anthropology* (Lanham, MD: AltaMira Press, 2008).

45. Here I am following Philippe Descola's little but mighty book, *The ecology of others* (Chicago: Prickly Paradigm Press, 2013).

46. Hufanga Okusitino Māhina, "Food me'akai and body sino in traditional Tongan society: Their theoretical and practical implications for health policy," *Pacific Health Dialog* 6, no. 2 (1999): 281.

47. Christina Toren, "Seeing the ancestral sites: Transformations in Fijian notions of the land," in *The anthropology of landscape: Perspectives on place and space*, ed. Eric Hirsch and Michael O'Hanlon (Oxford: Oxford University Press, 1995), 163.

48. Marisol de la Cadena, "Indigenous cosmopolitics in the Andes: Conceptual reflections beyond 'politics,'" *Cultural Anthropology* 25, no. 2 (2010); and Mario Blaser et al., "Ontological conflicts and the stories of peoples in spite of Europe: Toward a conversation on political ontology," *Current Anthropology* 54, no. 5 (2013).

49. A. J. Faas and Roberto E. Barrios, "Applied anthropology of risk, hazards, and disasters," *Human Organization* 74, no. 4 (2015); and Roberto E. Barrios, "What does catastrophe reveal for whom? The anthropology of crises and disasters at the onset of the Anthropocene," *Annual Review of Anthropology* 46 (2017).

50. Anthony Oliver-Smith, "Anthropological research on hazards and disasters," *Annual Review of Anthropology* 25, no. 1 (1996): 304.

51. Irus Braverman, *Coral whisperers: Scientists on the brink*, vol. 3 (Oakland: University of California Press, 2018).

52. Adrian Franklin, "A choreography of fire: A posthumanist account of Australians and eucalyptus," in *The mangle in practice: Science, society, and becoming*, ed. Andrew Pickering et al. (Durham, NC: Duke University Press, 2009).

53. Zoe Todd, "An indigenous feminist's take on the ontological turn: 'Ontology' is just another word for colonialism," *Journal of Historical Sociology* 29, no. 1 (2016).

54. Todd J. Braje and Matthew Lauer, "A meaningful Anthropocene? Golden spikes, transitions, boundary objects, and anthropogenic seascapes," *Sustainability* 12, no. 16 (2020).

55. Gillian R. Foulger et al., "Global review of human-induced earthquakes," *Earth-Science Reviews* 178 (2018); and Bill McGuire, *Waking the giant: How a*

changing climate triggers earthquakes, tsunamis, and volcanoes (Oxford: Oxford University Press, 2013).

56. ChiChing Liu, Alan T. Linde, and I. Selwyn Sacks, "Slow earthquakes triggered by typhoons," *Nature* 459, no. 7248 (2009).

57. Patricia L. Corcoran, Charles J. Moore, and Kelly Jazvac, "An anthropogenic marker horizon in the future rock record," *GSA Today* 24, no. 6 (2014).

58. Timothy Morton, *Hyperobjects: Philosophy and ecology after the end of the world* (Minneapolis: University of Minnesota Press, 2013).

59. Amelia Moore, "Anthropocene anthropology: Reconceptualizing contemporary global change," *Journal of the Royal Anthropological Institute* 22, no. 1 (2016).

60. Dipesh Chakrabarty, "The climate of history: Four theses," *Critical Inquiry* 35, no. 2 (2009).

61. Clive Hamilton, *Defiant earth: The fate of humans in the anthropocene* (Cambridge, UK: Polity, 2017).

62. Jason W. Moore, *Capitalism in the web of life: Ecology and the accumulation of capital* (London: Verso Books, 2015); and Donna Haraway, "Anthropocene, capitalocene, plantationocene, Chthulucene: Making kin," *Environmental Humanities* 6, no. 1 (2015).

63. David Chandler, *Ontopolitics in the Anthropocene: An introduction to mapping, sensing and hacking* (London: Routledge, 2018).

64. Chandler, *Ontopolitics in the Anthropocene*, 20.

65. Anthony Oliver-Smith, "Theorizing disasters," in *Catastrophe and culture: The anthropology of disaster*, ed. Susanna M. Hoffman and Anthony Oliver-Smith (Santa Fe, NM: School of American Research Press, 2002), 39.

66. Descola, *Beyond nature and culture*, 19.

67. Blaser et al., "Ontological conflicts."

68. Viveiros de Castro, "Zeno and the art of anthropology."

69. Kohn, *How forests think*.

70. Bruno Latour, *We have never been modern* (Cambridge, MA: Harvard University Press, 1993).

71. Ulrich Beck, *Risk society: Towards a new modernity* (1986; London: Sage, 1992).

72. Anna Lowenhaupt Tsing et al., eds., *Arts of living on a damaged planet: Ghosts and monsters of the Anthropocene* (Minneapolis: University of Minnesota, 2017).

73. Todd, "Indigenous feminist's take."

74. Arthur Maurice Hocart, *The life-giving myth* (1952; London: Routledge, 2004), 23.

75. Epeli Hau'ofa, "Our sea of islands," in *A new Oceania: Rediscovering our sea of islands*, ed. Vijay Naidu and Eric Waddell (Suva: School of Social and Economic Development, University of the South Pacific, 1993), 15.

Bibliography

Adger, W. Neil. "Vulnerability." *Global Environmental Change* 16, no. 3 (2006): 268–81.

Adger, W. Neil, Nigel W. Arnell, and Emma L. Tompkins. "Adapting to climate change: Perspectives across scales." *Global Environmental Change* 15, no. 2 (2005): 75–76.

Agrawal, Arun. "Dismantling the divide between indigenous and scientific knowledge." *Development and Change* 26 (1995): 413–39.

———. *Environmentality: Technologies of government and the making of subjects.* Durham, NC: Duke University Press, 2005.

———. "Why 'indigenous' knowledge?" *Journal of the Royal Society of New Zealand* 39, no. 4 (2009): 157–58.

Agrawal, Arun, and Clark C. Gibson. "Enchantment and disenchantment: The role of community in natural resource management." *World Development* 27, no. 4 (1999): 629–49.

Akin, David, and Joel Robbins, eds. *Money and modernity: State and local currencies in Melanesia.* Pittsburgh, PA: University of Pittsburgh Press, 1999.

Akin, David W. *Colonialism, Maasina rule, and the origins of Malaitan kastom.* Honolulu: University of Hawaii Press, 2013.

Albert, S., J. Udy, and I. R. Tibbetts. "Responses of algal communities to gradients in herbivore biomass and water quality in Marovo Lagoon, Solomon Islands." *Coral Reefs* 27, no. 1 (2008): 73–82.

Allen, Melinda S. "Three millennia of human and sea turtle interactions in remote Oceania." *Coral Reefs* 26, no. 4 (2007): 959–70.

Arunotai, Narumon. "Saved by an old legend and a keen observation: The case of Moken Sea nomads in Thailand." In *Indigenous knowledge for disaster risk reduction: Good practices and lessons learned from experiences in the Asia-Pacific Region*, edited by Rajib Shaw, Noralene Uy, and Jennifer Baumwoll, 73–78. New Delhi: United Nations International Strategy for Disaster Reduction–Asia Pacific, 2008.

Aswani, Shankar. "Changing identities: The ethnohistory of Roviana predatory headhunting." *Journal of the Polynesian Society* 109 (2000): 39–70.

Aswani, Shankar, and Richard J. Hamilton. "Integrating indigenous ecological knowledge and customary sea tenure with marine and social science for conservation of bumphead parrotfish (*Bolbometopon muricatum*) in Roviana Lagoon, Solomon Islands." *Environmental Conservation* 31 (2004): 69–83.

Aswani, Shankar, and Matthew Lauer. "Incorporating fishers' local knowledge and behavior into geographical information systems (GIS) for designing marine protected areas in Oceania." *Human Organization* 65, no. 1 (2006): 80–101.

———. "Indigenous people's detection of rapid ecological change." *Conservation Biology* 28, no. 3 (2014): 820–28.

Aswani, Shankar, Matthew Lauer, Pam Weiant, Leen Geelen, and Stan Herman. *The Roviana and Vonavona marine resource management project, final report, 2000–2004*. Santa Barbara: University of California, Department of Anthropology, 2004.

Atwater, Brian F. *Surviving a tsunami—Lessons from Chile, Hawaii, and Japan*. Denver, CO: United States Geological Survey, 1999.

Barrios, Roberto E. "Resilience: A commentary from the vantage point of anthropology." *Annals of Anthropological Practice* 40, no. 1 (2016): 28–38.

———. "What does catastrophe reveal for whom? The anthropology of crises and disasters at the onset of the Anthropocene." *Annual Review of Anthropology* 46 (2017): 151–66.

Baudrillard, Jean. *For a critique of the political economy of the sign*. Translated by Charles Levin. Candor, NY: Telos Press Publishing, 2019.

Bayliss-Smith, Tim, and Richard G. Feachem. *Subsistence and survival: Rural ecology in the Pacific*. New York: Academic Press, 1977.

BBC News. "Saved by tsunami folklore." Accessed March 10, 2007. http://news .bbc.co.uk/2/hi/programmes/from_our_own_correspondent/6435979.stm.

Beck, Ulrich. *Risk society: Towards a new modernity*. London: Sage, 1992. First published 1986.

Becker, Julia, David Johnston, Heather Lazrus, George Crawford, and Dave Nelson. "Use of traditional knowledge in emergency management for tsunami hazard: A case study from Washington State, USA." *Disaster Prevention and Management* 17, no. 4 (2008): 488–502.

Bennett, Judith A. *Pacific forest: A history of resource control and contest in the Solomon Islands c. 1800–1997*. Cambridge, UK: White Horse Press, 2000.

———. *Wealth of the Solomons: A history of a Pacific archipelago, 1800–1978*. Honolulu: University of Hawaii Press, 1987.

Berkes, Fikret. *Sacred ecology: Traditional ecological knowledge and resource management*. New York: Routledge, 2012.

———. "Traditional ecological knowledge in perspective." In *Traditional ecological knowledge concepts and cases*, edited by Julian Inglis, 1–10. Ottawa, ON: International Program on Traditional Ecological Knowledge: International Development Research Centre, 1993.

Berkes, Fikret, Johan Colding, and Carl Folke. "Rediscovery of traditional ecological knowledge as adaptive management." *Ecological Applications* 10, no. 5 (2000): 1251–62.

Berkes, Fikret, Carl Folke, and Johan Colding. *Linking social and ecological systems: Management practices and social mechanisms for building resilience*. Cambridge: Cambridge University Press, 1998.

Biersack, Aletta, and James B. Greenberg. *Reimagining political ecology*. Durham, NC: Duke University Press, 2006.

Bird, Deanne K., Catherine Chagué-Goff, and Anna Gero. "Human response to extreme events: A review of three post-tsunami disaster case studies." *Australian Geographer* 42, no. 3 (2011): 225–39.

Bird-David, Nurit. "'Animism' revisited: Personhood, environment, and relational epistemology." *Current Anthropology* 40, no. S1 (1999): S67–S91.

Birrell, C. L., L. J. McCook, and B. L. Willis. "Effects of algal turfs and sediment on coral settlement." *Marine Pollution Bulletin* 51, nos. 1–4 (2005): 408–14.

Bishop, Paul, David Sanderson, Jim Hansom, and Niran Chaimanee. "Age-dating of tsunami deposits: Lessons from the 26 December 2004 tsunami in Thailand." *Geographical Journal* 171, no. 4 (2005): 379–84.

Blaser, Mario, Claudia Briones, Anders Burman, Arturo Escobar, Lesley Green, Martin Holbraad, Helen Verran, and Mario Blaser. "Ontological conflicts and the stories of peoples in spite of Europe: Toward a conversation on political ontology." *Current Anthropology* 54, no. 5 (2013): 547–68.

Bloch, Maurice, and Jonathan Parry, eds. *Money and the modernity of exchange*. Cambridge: Cambridge University Press, 1989.

Blomley, Nicholas. "Performing property: Making the world." *Canadian Journal of Law & Jurisprudence* 26, no. 1 (2013): 23–48.

Bohensky, Erin L., and Yiheyis Maru. "Indigenous knowledge, science, and resilience: What have we learned from a decade of international literature on 'integration'?" *Ecology and Society* 16, no. 4 (2011): 6.

Bowen, Elenore Smith. *Return to laughter*. New York: Doubleday, 1964.

Braje, Todd J., and Matthew Lauer. "A meaningful Anthropocene? Golden spikes, transitions, boundary objects, and anthropogenic seascapes." *Sustainability* 12, no. 16 (2020): 6459.

Brandenstein, Carl Georg von. *Names and substance in the Australian subsection system.* Chicago: University of Chicago Press, 1982.

Braverman, Irus. *Coral whisperers: Scientists on the brink.* Oakland: University of California Press, 2018.

Brown, Katrina. "Global environmental change I: A social turn for resilience?" *Progress in Human Geography* 38, no. 1 (2014): 107–17.

Bryant, Raymond L. "Political ecology: An emerging research agenda in Third-World studies." *Political Geography* 11, no. 1 (1992): 12–36.

Bubandt, Nils. "Anthropocene uncanny: Nonsecular approaches to environmental change." In *A non-secular Anthropocene: Spirits, specters and other nonhumans in a time of environmental change*, edited by Nils Bubandt, 2–15. Aarhus: Aarhus University Research on the Anthropocene (AURA), 2018.

Bulmer, Ralph C. "Why is the cassowary not a bird? A problem of zoological taxonomy among the Karam of the New Guinea Highlands." *Man* 2, no. 1 (1967): 5–25.

Burman, Rickie. "Time and socioeconomic change on Simbo, Solomon Islands." *Man* 16, no. 2 (1981): 251–67.

Burt, Ben. "Land in Kwara'ae and development in Solomon Islands." *Oceania* 64, no. 4 (1994): 317–35.

Butler, Judith, and Athena Athanasiou. *Dispossession: The performative in the political.* Cambridge, UK: Polity, 2013.

Callon, Michel, Pierre Lascoumes, and Yannick Barthe, eds. *Acting in an uncertain world: An essay on technical democracy.* Cambridge, MA: MIT Press, 2009. First published 2001.

Cepek, Michael L. "There might be blood: Oil, humility, and the cosmopolitics of a Cofán petro-being." *American Ethnologist* 43, no. 4 (2016): 623–35.

Chakrabarty, Dipesh. "The climate of history: Four theses." *Critical Inquiry* 35, no. 2 (2009): 197–222.

———. *Provincializing Europe: Postcolonial thought and historical difference.* Princeton, NJ: Princeton University Press, 2000.

Chandler, David. "Beyond neoliberalism: Resilience, the new art of governing complexity." *Resilience* 2, no. 1 (2014): 47–63.

———. *Ontopolitics in the Anthropocene: An introduction to mapping, sensing and hacking.* London: Routledge, 2018.

Chen, Ting, Andrew V. Newman, Lujia Feng, and Hermann M. Fritz. "Slip distribution from the 1 April 2007 Solomon Islands earthquake: A unique image of near-trench rupture." *Geophysical Research Letters* 36, no. 16 (2009). https://doi.org/10.1029/2009GL039496.

Cheyne, Andrew. *The trading voyages of Andrew Cheyne, 1841–1844.* Honolulu: University of Hawaii Press, 1971.

Clark, Nigel. *Inhuman nature: Sociable life on a dynamic planet*. London: Sage, 2011.

Conklin, Harold C. "The relation of Hanunóo culture to the plant world." PhD diss., Yale University, 1954.

Cooke, Bill, and Uma Kothari. *Participation: The new tyranny?* London: Zed Books, 2001.

Corcoran, Patricia L., Charles J. Moore, and Kelly Jazvac. "An anthropogenic marker horizon in the future rock record." *GSA Today* 24, no. 6 (2014): 4–8.

Cote, Muriel, and Andrea J. Nightingale. "Resilience thinking meets social theory: Situating social change in socio-ecological systems (SES) research." *Progress in Human Geography* 36, no. 4 (2012): 475–89.

Crate, Susan A. "Gone the bull of winter? Grappling with the cultural implications of and anthropology's role(s) in global climate change." *Current Anthropology* 49, no. 4 (2008): 569–95.

Cruikshank, Julie. *Do glaciers listen? Local knowledge, colonial encounters, and social imagination*. Vancouver: University of British Columbia Press, 2005.

Davis, Anthony, and Kenneth Ruddle. "Constructing confidence: Rational skepticism and systematic enquiry in local ecological knowledge research." *Ecological Applications* 20, no. 3 (2010): 880–94.

Davis, Karen. *A grammar of the Hoava language, Western Solomons*. Canberra: Australian National University, Pacific Linguistics, Research School of Pacific and Asian Studies, 2003.

de la Cadena, Marisol. "Indigenous cosmopolitics in the Andes: Conceptual reflections beyond 'politics.'" *Cultural Anthropology* 25, no. 2 (2010): 334–70.

de la Cadena, Marisol, and Mario Blaser. *A world of many worlds*. Durham, NC: Duke University Press, 2018.

Deleuze, Gilles, and Felix Guattari. *A thousand plateaus*. Translated by B. Massumi. Minneapolis: University of Minnesota Press, 1987. First published 1980.

Denver Post. "Tsunami wiped out entire island village." April 4, 2007. www.denverpost.com/2007/04/04/tsunami-wiped-out-entire-island-village/.

Descola, Philippe. *Beyond nature and culture*. Translated by Janet Lloyd. Chicago: University of Chicago Press, 2013.

———. *The ecology of others*. Chicago: Prickly Paradigm Press, 2013.

Díaz, Sandra, Sebsebe Demissew, Julia Carabias, Carlos Joly, Mark Lonsdale, Neville Ash, Anne Larigauderie, et al. "The IPBES conceptual framework—connecting nature and people." *Current Opinion in Environmental Sustainability* 14 (2015): 1–16.

Dillon, Michael, and Julian Reid. *The liberal way of war: Killing to make life live*. New York: Routledge, 2009.

Dove, Michael R. "Indigenous people and environmental politics." *Annual Review of Anthropology* 35 (2006): 191–208.

Dureau, Christine. "Keeping and giving, keeping for keeping: Christian property taboo on Simbo, Solomon Islands." In *A polymath anthropologist: Essays in*

honour of Ann Chowning, edited by Claudia Gross, Harriet Lyons, Dorothy
Ayers Counts, and Ann Chowning, 139–45. Auckland, NZ: Department of
Anthropology, University of Auckland, 2005.

———. "Mixed blessings: Christianity and history in women's lives on Simbo,
Western Solomon Islands." PhD diss., Macquarie University, 1994.

———. "Recounting and remembering 'first contact' on Simbo." In *Cultural
Memory: Reconfiguring History and Identity in the Postcolonial Pacific*,
edited by Jeannette Marie Mageo, 130–62. Honolulu: University of Hawaii
Press, 2001.

———. "Skulls, mana and causality." *Journal of the Polynesian Society* 109, no. 1
(2000): 71–97.

Durkheim, Émile. *The elementary forms of religious life*. Translated by
Karen E. Fields. New York: Free Press, 1995. First published 1915.

———. "Review of Antonio Labriola, Essays on the materialist conception of
history" (1897). In *Readings from Émile Durkheim*, rev. ed., edited by
Kenneth Thompson. New York: Taylor & Francis Group, 2004.

Ellen, Roy, Peter Parkes, and Alan Bicker, eds. *Indigenous environmental
knowledge and its transformations: Critical anthropological perspectives*.
Amsterdam: Harwood Academic Publishers, 2000.

Ellen, Roy F., ed. *Modern crises and traditional strategies: Local ecological
knowledge in island Southeast Asia*. New York: Berghahn Books, 2007.

Escobar, Arturo. "After nature: Steps to an anti-essentialist political ecology."
Current Anthropology 40, no. 1 (1999): 1–30.

———. *Designs for the pluriverse: Radical interdependence, autonomy, and the
making of worlds*. Durham, NC: Duke University Press, 2018.

Faas, A. J. "Disaster vulnerability in anthropological perspective." *Annals of
Anthropological Practice* 40, no. 1 (2016): 14–27.

Faas, A. J., and Roberto E. Barrios. "Applied anthropology of risk, hazards, and
disasters." *Human Organization* 74, no. 4 (2015): 287–95.

Feld, Steven, and Keith H. Basso. *Senses of place*. Santa Fe, NM: School of
American Research Press 1996.

Ferguson, James. *The anti-politics machine: "Development", depoliticization,
and bureaucratic power in Lesotho*. Cambridge: Cambridge University
Press, 1990.

Field, Christopher B., Vicente Barros, Thomas F. Stocker, Qin Dahe, David Jon
Dokken, Gian-Kasper Plattner, Kristie L. Ebi, et al., eds. *Managing the risks of
extreme events and disasters to advance climate change adaptation: Special
report of the Intergovernmental Panel on Climate Change*. Cambridge:
Cambridge University Press, 2012.

Field, Christopher B., and Vicente R. Barros. *Climate change 2014—Impacts,
adaptation and vulnerability: Regional aspects*. Cambridge: Cambridge
University Press, 2014.

Fish, Stanley. *There's no such thing as free speech: And it's a good thing, too.* Oxford: Oxford University Press, 1994.

Foale, Simon, and Martha Macintyre. "Dynamic and flexible aspects of land and marine tenure at West Nggela: Implications for marine resource management." *Oceania* 71, no. 1 (2000): 30–45.

Folke, Carl. "Resilience: The emergence of a perspective for social-ecological systems analyses." *Global Environmental Change* 16 (2006): 253–67.

Foster, Robert J. "Commoditization and the emergence of *Kastam* as a cultural category: A New Ireland case in comparative perspective." *Oceania* 62, no. 4 (1992): 284–94.

Foster, Robert John. *Social reproduction and history in Melanesia: Mortuary ritual, gift exchange, and custom in the Tanga Islands.* Cambridge: Cambridge University Press, 1995.

Foucault, Michel. *The history of sexuality.* New York: Vintage Books, 1990.

——, ed. *"Society must be defended": Lectures at the Collège de France, 1975–1976.* New York: Picador, 2003.

Foulger, Gillian R., Miles P. Wilson, Jon G. Gluyas, Bruce R. Julian, and Richard J. Davies. "Global review of human-induced earthquakes." *Earth-Science Reviews* 178 (2018): 438–514.

Fox, James J. "Place and landscape in comparative Austronesian perspective." In *The poetic power of place: Comparative perspectives on Austronesian ideas of locality*, edited by James J. Fox, 1–21. Canberra: Australian National University, 1997.

Frake, Charles O. "Cultural ecology and ethnography." *American Anthropologist* 64, no. 1 (1962): 53–59.

Franklin, Adrian. "A choreography of fire: A posthumanist account of Australians and eucalyptus." In *The mangle in practice: Science, society, and becoming*, edited by Andrew Pickering, Keith Guzik, Barbara Herrnstein Smith, E. Roy Weintraub, and Adrian Franklin, 17–45. Durham, NC: Duke University Press, 2009.

Friedman, Jonathan. "Marxism, structuralism, and vulgar materialism." *Man* 9, no. 3 (1974): 444–69.

Fritz, Hermann M., and Nikos Kalligeris. "Ancestral heritage saves tribes during 1 April 2007 Solomon Islands tsunami." *Geophysical Research Letters* 35 (2008). https://doi.org/10.1029/2007GL031654.

Furlong, Kevin P., Thorne Lay, and Charles J. Ammon. "A great earthquake rupture across a rapidly evolving three-plate boundary." *Science* 324, no. 5924 (2009): 226–29.

Gamburd, Michele Ruth. *The golden wave: Culture and politics after Sri Lanka's tsunami disaster.* Bloomington: Indiana University Press, 2013.

Garcia-Acosta, Virginia. "Historical disaster research." In *Catastrophe and culture: The anthropology of disaster*, edited by Susanna Hoffman and

Anthony Oliver-Smith, 49–66. Santa Fe, NM: School of American Research Press, 2002.

Gegeo, David Welchman. "Cultural rupture and indigeneity: The challenge of (re)visioning 'place' in the Pacific." *Contemporary Pacific* 13, no. 2 (2001): 491–507.

Gewertz, Deborah B., and Frederick Karl Errington. *Cheap meat: Flap food nations in the Pacific Islands.* Berkeley: University of California Press, 2010.

———. *Emerging class in Papua New Guinea: The telling of difference.* Cambridge: Cambridge University Press, 1999.

Goff, James, Yuichi Ebina, Kazuhisa Goto, and James Terry. "Defining tsunamis: Yoda strikes back?" *Earth-Science Reviews* 159 (2016): 271–74.

Gregg, Chris E., Bruce F. Houghton, Douglas Paton, Roy Lachman, Janet Lachman, David M. Johnston, and Supin Wongbusarakum. "Natural warning signs of tsunamis: Human sensory experience and response to the 2004 great Sumatra earthquake and tsunami in Thailand." *Earthquake Spectra* 22, no. 3 (2006): 671–91.

Grove, Kevin. *Resilience.* New York: Routledge, 2018.

Grove, Kevin J. "From emergency management to managing emergence: A genealogy of disaster management in Jamaica." *Annals of the Association of American Geographers* 103, no. 3 (2013): 570–88.

Gunderson, Lance H., and C. S. Holling. *Panarchy: Understanding transformations in human and natural systems.* Washington, DC: Island Press, 2002.

Guo, Pei-yi. "Law as discourse: Land disputes and the changing imagination of relations among the Langalanga, Solomon Islands." *Pacific Studies* 34, no. 2 (2011): 223–49.

Gupta, Akhil. *Postcolonial developments: Agriculture in the making of modern India.* Durham, NC: Duke University Press, 1998.

Haas, Hannah, Todd J. Braje, Matthew Lauer, Scott M. Fitzpatrick, Lawrence Kiko, and Grinta Ale'eke. "Archaeological reconnaissance and the first radiocarbon dates from Simbo Island, Western Province, Solomon Islands." *Journal of Pacific Archaeology* 9, no. 1 (2018): 63–69.

Halvaksz, Jamon Alex. *Gardens of gold: Place-making in Papua New Guinea.* Seattle: University of Washington Press, 2020.

Hamilton, Clive. *Defiant earth: The fate of humans in the Anthropocene.* Cambridge, UK: Polity, 2017.

Haraway, Donna. "Anthropocene, capitalocene, plantationocene, Chthulucene: Making kin." *Environmental Humanities* 6, no. 1 (2015): 159–65.

———. *The companion species manifesto: Dogs, people, and significant otherness.* Chicago: Prickly Paradigm Press, 2003.

———. "Situated knowledges: The science question in feminism and the privilege of partial perspective," *Feminist Studies* 4, no. 3 (1988): 575–99.

———. *When species meet.* Minneapolis: University of Minnesota Press, 2008.

Harvey, David. *A brief history of neoliberalism*. New York: Oxford University Press, 2005.

Harvey, Graham. *Animism: Respecting the living world*. New York: Columbia University Press, 2005.

Harwood, Frances. "The Christian Fellowship Church: A revitalization movement in Melanesia." PhD diss., University of Chicago, 1971.

Hau'ofa, Epeli. "Our sea of islands." In *A new Oceania: Rediscovering our sea of islands*, edited by Vijay Naidu and Eric Waddell, 2–16. Suva: School of Social and Economic Development, University of the South Pacific, 1993.

———. *We are the ocean: Selected works*. Honolulu: University of Hawaii Press, 2008.

Hewitt, Kenneth. "The idea of calamity in a technocratic age." In *Interpretations of calamity from the viewpoint of human ecology*, edited by Kenneth Hewitt, 3–32. Boston: Allen & Unwin, 1983.

———, ed. *Interpretations of calamity from the viewpoint of human ecology*. Boston: Allen & Unwin, 1983.

Hilliard, David L. *God's gentlemen: A history of the Melanesian mission, 1849–1942*. St Lucia: University of Queensland Press, 1978.

———. "Protestant missions in the Solomon Islands." PhD diss., Australian National University, 1966.

Hobart, Mark. *An anthropological critique of development: The growth of ignorance*. London: Routledge, 1993.

Hocart, A. M. "The canoe and the bonito in Eddystone Island." *Journal of the Royal Anthropological Institute of Great Britain and Ireland* 65 (1935): 97–111.

———. "Chieftainship." Unpublished manuscript, n.d.

———. "The cult of the dead in Eddystone of the Solomons, part I." *Journal of the Royal Anthropological Institute of Great Britain and Ireland* 52 (1922): 259–305.

———. "The cult of the dead in Eddystone of the Solomons, part II." *Journal of the Royal Anthropological Institute of Great Britain and Ireland* 52 (1922): 71–112.

———. "Katapana—Bush people—Iliganigani." Unpublished manuscript, n.d.

———. "Medicine and witchcraft in Eddystone of the Solomons." *Journal of the Royal Anthropological Institute of Great Britain and Ireland* 55 (1925): 229–70.

———. "Trade and money." Unpublished manuscript, n.d.

———. "Warfare in Eddystone of the Solomon Islands." *Journal of the Royal Anthropological Institute of Great Britain and Ireland* 61 (1931): 301–24.

———. "White men." Unpublished manuscript, n.d.

Hocart, Arthur Maurice. *The life-giving myth*. London: Routledge, 2004. First published 1952.

Hoffman, Susanna, and Anthony Oliver-Smith, eds. *Catastrophe and culture: The anthropology of disaster.* Santa Fe, NM: School of American Research Press, 2002.

Hoffman, Susanna M., and Roberto E. Barrios. *Disaster upon disaster: Exploring the gap between knowledge, policy and practice.* New York: Berghahn Books, 2019.

Hoffman, Susanna M., and Anthony Oliver-Smith. "Introduction to the second edition of *The Angry Earth*: From introduction to widespread reception." In *The angry earth: Disaster in anthropological perspective*, edited by Anthony Oliver-Smith and Susanna M. Hoffman, 14–25. New York: Routledge, 2020.

Holbraad, Martin, and Morten Axel Pedersen. *The ontological turn: An anthropological exposition.* Cambridge: Cambridge University Press, 2017.

Holland, Dorothy C., and Naomi Quinn. *Cultural models in language and thought.* Cambridge: Cambridge University Press, 1987.

Holling, C. S. "Resilience and stability of ecological systems." *Annual Review of Ecology and Systematics* 4 (1973): 1–23.

———. "Understanding the complexity of economic, ecological, and social systems." *Ecosystems* 4, no. 5 (2001): 390–405.

Holling, C. S., and Gary K. Meffe. "Command and control and the pathology of natural resource management." *Conservation Biology* 10, no. 2 (1996): 328–37.

Howes, Michael, and Robert Chambers. "Indigenous technical knowledge: Analysis, implications and issues." In *Indigenous knowledge systems and development*, edited by David Brokensha, Dennis M. Warren, and Oswald Werner, 329–40. Washington, DC: University Press of America, 1980.

Hviding, Edvard. "Disentangling the butubutu of New Georgia." In *Oceanic socialities and cultural forms: Ethnographies of experience*, edited by Ingjerd Hoëm and Sidsel Roalkvam, 71–113. New York: Berghahn Books, 2003.

———. *Guardians of Marovo Lagoon: Practice, place, and politics in maritime Melanesia.* Honolulu: University of Hawaii Press, 1996.

———. "Indigenous essentialism? Simplifying customary land ownership in New Georgia, Solomon Islands." *Bijdragen tot de Taal-, Land- en Volkenkunde* 149, no. 4 (1993): 802–24.

Hviding, Edvard, and Tim Bayliss-Smith. *Islands of rainforest: Agroforestry, logging and eco-tourism in Solomon Islands.* Aldershot: Ashgate, 2000.

Hviding, Edvard, and Cato Berg, eds. *The ethnographic experiment: A. M. Hocart and W. H. R. Rivers in Island Melanesia, 1908.* New York: Berghahn Books, 2014.

Ingold, Tim. *Being alive: Essays on movement, knowledge and description.* London: Routledge, 2011.

———. "Epilogue: Towards a politics of dwelling." *Conservation and Society* 3, no. 2 (2005): 501–8.

———. *The life of lines.* New York: Routledge, 2015.

———. "One world anthropology." *Hau: Journal of Ethnographic Theory* 8, nos. 1/2 (2018): 158–71.

———. *The perception of the environment: Essays on livelihood, dwelling and skill.* London: Routledge, 2000.

Ingold, Tim, and Gisli Palsson. *Biosocial becomings: Integrating social and biological anthropology.* Cambridge: Cambridge University Press, 2013.

Jacka, Jerry. *Alchemy in the rainforest: Politics, ecology, and resilience in a New Guinea mining area.* Durham, NC: Duke University Press, 2015.

Jackson, K. B. "Tie hokara, tie vaka, black man, white man: A history of the New Georgia Group to 1925." PhD diss., Australian National University, 1978.

Jasanoff, Sheila. *States of knowledge: The co-production of science and the social order.* London: Routledge, 2004.

Johannes, R. E. "Traditional marine conservation methods in Oceania and their demise." *Annual Review of Ecology and Systematics* 9, no. 1 (1978): 349–64.

Johannes, Robert E. *Words of the lagoon: Fishing and marine lore in the Palau District of Micronesia.* Berkeley: University of California Press, 1981.

Jourdan, Christine, and Ellen Maebiru. *Pijin: A trilingual cultural dictionary: Pijin-Inglish-Franis, Pijin-English-French, Pijin-Anglais-Français.* Pacific Linguistics, 526. Canberra: Pacific Linguistics Research School of Pacific and Asian Studies, Australian National University, 2002.

Keesing, Roger M. "Descent, residence, cultural codes." In *Anthropology in Oceania: Essays presented to Ian Hogbin*, edited by Lester Richard Hiatt and C. Fayawardena, 121–38. London: Angus and Robertson, 1971.

———. "Rethinking 'Mana.'" *Journal of Anthropological Research* 40, no. 1 (1984): 137–56.

Keremama, Milton Galokale. "Ethno-meteorological knowledge: Local indicators and perceptions of weather and seasons from Choiseul, Solomon Islands." PhD diss., University of South Pacific, 2019.

Knudson, Kenneth E. "Titiana: A Gilbertese community in the Solomon Islands." PhD diss., University of Oregon, 1964.

Kohn, Eduardo. *How forests think: Toward an anthropology beyond the human.* Berkeley: University of California Press, 2013.

Krajick, Kevin. "Tracking myth to geological reality." *Science* 310, no. 5749 (2005): 762–64.

Kuper, Adam. "The return of the native." *Current Anthropology* 44, no. 3 (2003): 389–403.

Lanyon-Orgill, Peter A. *The language of Eddystone Island (Western Solomon Islands).* Balmains, Stanley, Perthshire, Scotland: Crichton Press, 1969.

Latour, Bruno. *Facing Gaia: Eight lectures on the new climatic regime.* Cambridge, UK: Polity, 2017.

———. *Pandora's hope: Essays on the reality of science studies.* Cambridge, MA: Harvard University Press, 1999.

———. *Reassembling the social: An introduction to actor-network-theory.* Oxford: Oxford University Press, 2005.

———. *Science in action: How to follow scientists and engineers through society.* Cambridge, MA: Harvard University Press, 1987.

———. *We have never been modern.* Cambridge, MA: Harvard University Press, 1993.

Latour, Bruno, and Steve Woolgar. *Laboratory life: The construction of scientific facts.* Princeton, NJ: Princeton University Press, 1986. First published 1979.

Lauer, Matthew. "Calamity, kastom, and modernity: Local interpretations of vulnerability in the Western Pacific." *Environmental Hazards* 13, no. 4 (2014): 281–97.

———. "Changing understandings of local knowledge in island environments." *Environmental Conservation* 44, no. 4 (2017): 336–47.

———. "State-led democratic politics and emerging forms of indigenous leadership among the Ye'kwana of the Upper Orinoco." *Journal of Latin American Anthropology* 11, no. 1 (2006): 51–108.

Lauer, Matthew, Simon Albert, Shankar Aswani, Benjamin S. Halpern, Luke Campanella, and Douglas La Rose. "Globalization, Pacific Islands, and the paradox of resilience." *Global Environmental Change* 23, no. 1 (2013): 40–50.

Lauer, Matthew, and Shankar Aswani. "Indigenous ecological knowledge as situated practices: Understanding fishers' knowledge in the Western Solomon Islands." *American Anthropologist* 111, no. 3 (2009): 317–29.

———. "Indigenous knowledge and long-term ecological change: Detection, interpretation, and responses to changing ecological conditions in Pacific Island communities." *Environmental Management* 45, no. 5 (2010): 985–97.

———. "Integrating indigenous ecological knowledge and multi-spectral image classification for marine habitat mapping in Oceania." *Ocean and Coastal Management* 51, no. 6 (2008): 495–504.

Lauer, Matthew, and Jaime Matera. "Who detects ecological change after catastrophic events? Indigenous knowledge, social networks, and situated practices." *Human Ecology* 44, no. 1 (2016): 33–46.

Lave, Jean. *Cognition in practice: Mind, mathematics, and culture in everyday life.* Cambridge: Cambridge University Press, 1988.

———. "The practice of learning." In *Understanding practice: Perspectives on activity and context,* edited by Seth Chaiklin and Jean Lave, 3–32. Cambridge: Cambridge University Press, 1993.

Law, John. *After method: Mess in social science research.* London: Routledge, 2004.

Law, John, and Solveig Joks. "Luossa and laks: Salmon, science and LEK." *Revue d'Anthropologie des Connaissances* 11, no. 2 (2017). http://journals.openedition.org/rac/2198.

Lawrence, David Russell. *The naturalist and his "beautiful islands": Charles Morris Woodford in the Western Pacific*. Canberra: Australia National University Press, 2014.

Lay, Thorne, and Hiroo Kanamori. "Earthquake doublets in the Solomon Islands." *Physics of the Earth and Planetary Interiors* 21, no. 4 (1980): 283–304.

Lazrus, Heather. "Sea change: Island communities and climate change." *Annual Review of Anthropology* 41 (2012): 285–301.

Leach, James. *Creative land: Place and procreation on the Rai Coast of Papua New Guinea*. New York: Berghahn Books, 2003.

Lee, Kai N. *Compass and gyroscope: Integrating science and politics for the environment*. Washington, DC: Island Press, 1994.

Leung, Rebecca. "Sea gypsies see signs in the waves: How Moken people in Asia saved themselves from deadly tsunami." *CBS News*, March 18, 2005. www.cbs news.com/news/sea-gypsies-saw-signs-in-the-waves/2/.

Li, Tania Murray. "Articulating indigenous identity in Indonesia: Resource politics and the tribal slot." *Comparative Studies in Society and History* 42, no. 1 (2000): 149–79.

———. "Indigeneity, capitalism, and the management of dispossession." *Current Anthropology* 51, no. 3 (2010): 385–414.

———. *Land's end: Capitalist relations on an indigenous frontier*. Durham, NC: Duke University Press, 2014.

———. "What is land? Assembling a resource for global investment." *Transactions of the Institute of British Geographers* 39, no. 4 (2014): 589–602.

Lindstrom, Lamont. *Cargo cult: Strange stories of desire from Melanesia and beyond*. Honolulu: University of Hawaii Press, 1993.

LiPuma, Edward. *Encompassing others: The magic of modernity in Melanesia*. Ann Arbor: University of Michigan Press, 2000.

Liu, ChiChing, Alan T. Linde, and I. Selwyn Sacks. "Slow earthquakes triggered by typhoons." *Nature* 459, no. 7248 (2009): 833–36.

Lubis, Ashar Muda, and Nobuhiro Isezaki. "Shoreline changes and vertical displacement of the 2 April 2007 Solomon Islands earthquake Mw 8.1 revealed by Alos Palsar images." *Physics and Chemistry of the Earth, Parts A/B/C* 34, no. 6 (2009): 409–15.

Mageo, Jeannette. "Continuity and shape shifting: Samoan spirits in culture history." In *God, spirits, and history: A theoretical perspective*, edited by Jeannette Mageo and Alan Howard, 29–54. New York: Routledge, 1996.

Māhina, Hufanga 'Okusitino. "Food me'akai and body sino in traditional Tongan society: Their theoretical and practical implications for health policy." *Pacific Health Dialog* 6, no. 2 (1999): 276–87.

———. "Ta, va, and moana: Temporality, spatiality, and indigeneity." *Pacific Studies* 33, no. 2 (2010): 168.

Majnep, Ian Saem, and Ralph N. H. Bulmer. *Birds of my Kalam country*. Auckland: Auckland University Press, 1977.

Makini, Jully, ed. *Na buka vivinei mulivi pa zinama Roviana (Roviana custom stories book)*. Solomon Islands: Western Province Government, 1995.

Malinowski, Bronislaw. *The sexual life of savages*. London: George Routledge & Sons, 1932.

Malinowski, Bronislaw C. "Fishing in the Trobriand Islands." *Man* 18 (1918): 87–92.

———. "Magic, science and religion." In *Science, religion and reality*, edited by Joseph Needham, 19–86. New York: Macmillan, 1925.

Marino, Elizabeth K., and A. J. Faas. "Is vulnerability an outdated concept? After subjects and spaces." *Annals of Anthropological Practice* 44, no. 1 (2020): 33–46.

Martin, Keir. *The death of the big men and the rise of the big shots: Custom and conflict in East New Britain*. New York: Berghahn Books, 2013.

Mathews, Andrew S. "Anthropology and the Anthropocene: Criticisms, experiments, and collaborations." *Annual Review of Anthropology* 49, no. 1 (2020): 67–82.

McAdoo, B. G., L. Dengler, G. Prasetya, and V. Titov. "*Smong*: How an oral history saved thousands on Indonesia's Simeulue Island during the December 2004 and March 2005 tsunamis." *Earthquake Spectra* 22 (2006): S661–69.

McAdoo, Brian G., Hermann Fritz, Kelly L. Jackson, Nikos Kalligeris, Jens Kruger, Michael Bonte-Grapentin, Andrew L. Moore, et al. "Solomon Islands tsunami, one year later." *EOS, Transactions—American Geophysical Union* 89, no. 18 (2008): 18.

McAdoo, Brian G., Andrew Moore, and Jennifer Baumwoll. "Indigenous knowledge and the near field population response during the 2007 Solomon Islands tsunami." *Natural Hazards* 48, no. 1 (2009): 73–82.

McDougall, D., I. Barry, and S. Pio. *Disaster and recovery on Ranongga: Six months after the earthquake in the Western Solomons*. Perth: Bergen Pacific Studies Group Initiative, 2008.

McDougall, Debra. *Engaging with strangers: Love and violence in the rural Solomon Islands*. New York: Berghahn Books, 2016.

———. "Paths of Pinauzu: Captivity and social reproduction in Ranongga." *Journal of the Polynesian Society* 109, no. 1 (2000): 99–113.

———. "The unintended consequences of clarification: Development, disputing, and the dynamics of community in Ranongga, Solomon Islands." *Ethnohistory* 52, no. 1 (2005): 81–109.

McGuire, Bill. *Waking the giant: How a changing climate triggers earthquakes, tsunamis, and volcanoes*. Oxford: Oxford University Press, 2013.

McKinnon, J. M. "Tomahawks, turtles and traders: A reconstruction of the circular causation of warfare in the New Georgia Group." *Oceania* 45, no. 4 (1975): 290–307.

Mercer, Jessica, Ilan Kelman, Lorin Taranis, and Sandie Suchet-Pearson. "Framework for integrating indigenous and scientific knowledge for disaster risk reduction." *Disasters* 34, no. 1 (2010): 214–39.

Miller, Daniel. *Report of the national sites survey, 1976–1978: Solomon Islands.* Honiara: National Museum, 1978.

Mimura, Nobuo, Leonard Nurse, Roger McLean, John Agard, Lino Briguglio, Penehuro Lefale, Rolph Payet, and Graham Sem. "Small islands." In *Climate change 2007: Impacts, adaptation and vulnerability; Contribution of Working Group II to the fourth assessment report of the Intergovernmental Panel on Climate Change,* edited by M. L. Parry, O. F. Canziani, J. P. Palutikof, P. J. van der Linden, and C. E. Hanson, 687–716. Cambridge: Cambridge University Press, 2007.

Misra, Neelesh. "Stone age cultures survive tsunami waves." Associated Press, January 2005. www.msnbc.msn.com/id/6786476/ns/world_news-tsunami_a _year_later/.

Mitchell, Timothy. *Rule of experts.* Berkeley: University of California Press, 2002.

Mol, Annemarie. *The body multiple: Ontology in medical practice.* Durham, NC: Duke University Press, 2002.

Moore, Amelia. "Anthropocene anthropology: Reconceptualizing contemporary global change." *Journal of the Royal Anthropological Institute* 22, no. 1 (2016): 27–46.

Moore, Jason W. *Capitalism in the web of life: Ecology and the accumulation of capital.* London: Verso Books, 2015.

Morton, Timothy. *Hyperobjects: Philosophy and ecology after the end of the world.* Minneapolis: University of Minnesota Press, 2013.

Mosse, David. *Cultivating development: An ethnography of aid policy and practice.* London: Pluto Press, 2005.

Nadasdy, Paul. "Adaptive co-management and the gospel of resilience." In *Adaptive co-management: Collaboration, learning, and multilevel governance,* edited by D. Armitage, F. Berkes, and N. Doubleday. Vancouver: University of British Columbia Press, 2007.

———. "The gift in the animal: The ontology of hunting and human–animal sociality." *American Ethnologist* 34, no. 1 (2007): 25–43.

———. "How many worlds are there?" *American Ethnologist* 48, no. 4 (2021): 357–69.

———. *Hunters and bureaucrats: Power, knowledge, and aboriginal-state relations in the Southwest Yukon.* Vancouver: University of British Columbia Press, 2003.

National Geographic News. "Did island tribes use ancient lore to evade tsunami?" January 24, 2005.

Nazarea, Virginia D. "Local knowledge and memory in biodiversity conservation." *Annual Review of Anthropology* 35 (2006): 317–35.

Newman, Andrew V., Lujia Feng, Hermann M. Fritz, Zachery M. Lifton, Nikos Kalligeris, and Yong Wei. "The energetic 2010 Mw 7.1 Solomon Islands tsunami earthquake." *Geophysical Journal International* 186, no. 2 (2011): 775–81.

Nunn, P. D. "On the convergence of myth and reality: Examples from the Pacific Islands." *Geographical Journal* 167, no. 2 (2001): 125–38.

Nunn, Patrick D., and Ronna Pastorizo. "Geological histories and geohazard potential of Pacific Islands illuminated by myths." *Geological Society* 273, no. 1 (2007): 143–63.

Nunn, Patrick D., Mary Baniala, Morris Harrison, and Paul Geraghty. "Vanished islands in Vanuatu: New research and a preliminary geohazard assessment." *Journal of the Royal Society of New Zealand* 36, no. 1 (2006): 37–50.

O'Brien, Karen, Siri Eriksen, Ane Schjolden, and Lynn Nygaard. "What's in a word? Conflicting interpretations of vulnerability in climate change research." CICERO Working Paper 2004:04, Center for International Climate and Environmental Research, Oslo, Norway.

Odum, Eugene P. "The strategy of ecosystem development." *Science* 164, no. 3877 (1969): 262–70.

O'Keefe, P., et al. "Taking the 'naturalness' out of 'natural disaster.'" *Nature* 260 (1976): 566–67.

Oliver-Smith, Anthony. "Anthropological research on hazards and disasters." *Annual Review of Anthropology* 25, no. 1 (1996): 303–28.

———. *The martyred city: Death and rebirth in the Andes.* Albuquerque: University of New Mexico Press, 1986.

———. "Peru's five-hundred-year earthquake: Vulnerability in historical context." In *The angry earth: Disaster in anthropological perspective*, edited by Anthony Oliver-Smith and Susanna M. Hoffman, 74–88. New York: Routledge, 1999.

———. "Theorizing disasters." In *Catastrophe and culture: The anthropology of disaster*, edited by Susanna M. Hoffman and Anthony Oliver-Smith, 23–47. Santa Fe, NM: School of American Research Press, 2002.

Oliver-Smith, Anthony, and Susanna M. Hoffman. *The angry earth: Disaster in anthropological perspective.* New York: Routledge, 1999.

Ong, Aihwa. *Spirits of resistance and capitalist discipline: Factory women in Malaysia.* Albany: State University of New York Press, 2010.

Oreskes, Naomi. *Why trust science?* Princeton, NJ: Princeton University Press, 2019.

Phillip, Arthur. *The voyage of Governor Phillip to Botany Bay.* Compiled by John Stockdale. London: Printed for John Stockdale, Piccadilly, 1789.

Pickering, Andrew. *The mangle of practice: Time, agency, and science.* Chicago: University of Chicago Press, 1995.

———. *Science as practice and culture.* Chicago: University of Chicago Press, 1992.

Polanyi, Karl. *The great transformation.* Boston: Beacon Press, 1944.

Pouillon, Jean. "Remarks on the verb 'to believe.'" Translated by John Leavitt. In *Between belief and transgression: Structuralist essays in religion, history and myth*, edited by Michel Izard and Pierre Smith, 9–23. Chicago: Chicago University Press, [1979] 1982.

Povinelli, Elizabeth. "Routes/worlds." *e-flux journal* 27 (2011): 1–12.

Povinelli, Elizabeth A. *Geontologies: A requiem to late liberalism.* Durham, NC: Duke University Press, 2016.

Rappaport, Roy A. *Pigs for the ancestors: Ritual in the ecology of a New Guinea people.* New Haven, CT: Yale University Press, 1984.

Redford, Kent H. "The ecologically noble savage." *Orion Nature Quarterly* 9, no. 3 (1990): 153–71.

Reeve, R. "Recent work on the prehistory of the Western Solomons, Melanesia." *Bulletin of the Indo-Pacific Prehistory Association* 9 (1989): 44–67.

Reid, Walter V., Fikret Berkes, and Thomas J. Wilbanks. *Bridging scales and knowledge systems: Concepts and applications in ecosystem assessment.* Washington, DC: Island Press, 2006.

Richards, Paul. "Agriculture as a performance." In *Farmer first: Farmer innovation and agricultural research*, edited by R. G. Chambers, A. Pacey, and L. A. Thrupp, 39–43. London: Intermediate Technology Publications, 1989.

Robbins, Joel. *Becoming sinners: Christianity and moral torment in a Papua New Guinea society.* Berkeley: University of California Press, 2004.

Robbins, Joel, and David Akin. "An introduction to Melanesian currencies: Agency, identity, and social reproduction." In *Money and modernity: State and local currencies in Melanesia*, edited by David Akin and Joel Robbins, 1–40. Pittsburgh, PA: University of Pittsburgh Press, 1999.

Robertson, A. F. "Primitive society." In *International encyclopedia of the social & behavioral sciences*, edited by N. J. Smelser and P. B. Baltes, 12046–50. Oxford: Elsevier, 2004.

Rodman, Margaret. *Masters of tradition: Consequences of customary land tenure in Longana, Vanuatu.* Vancouver: University of British Columbia Press, 1987.

Ruddle, Kenneth. "Introduction to the collected works of R. E. Johannes: Publications on marine traditional knowledge and management." *SPC Traditional Marine Resource Management and Knowledge Information Bulletin* 23 (2008): 13–24.

Rudiak-Gould, Peter. "'We have seen it with our own eyes': Why we disagree about climate change visibility." *Weather, Climate, and Society* 5, no. 2 (2013): 120–32.

Sahlins, Marshall. "What is anthropological enlightenment? Some lessons of the twentieth century." *Annual Review of Anthropology* 28, no. 1 (1999): i–xxiii.

Said, Edward. *Orientalism.* New York: Vintage Books, 1979.

Salmond, Mary. *Aphrodite's island: The European discovery of Tahiti.* Berkeley: University of California Press, 2009.

Scales, Ian Alexander. "The social forest: Landowners, development conflict and the state in Solomon Islands." PhD diss., Australian National University, 2003.

Scheffler, Harold, and Peter Larmour. "Solomon Islands: Evolving a new custom." In *Land tenure in the Pacific*, edited by Selwyn Arutangai and R. G. Crocombe, 303–23. Suva, Fiji: University of the South Pacific, 1987.

Scheffler, Harold W. *Choiseul Island social structure*. Berkeley: University of California Press, 1965.

———. "Kindred and kin groups in Simbo Island social structure." *Ethnology* 1, no. 2 (1962): 135–57.

Schuermann, Savanna, and Matthew Lauer. "Disaster recovery in the Western Pacific: Scale, vulnerability, and traditional exchange practices." *Natural Hazards* 84, no. 2 (2016): 1287–306.

Schuller, Mark. *Killing with kindness: Haiti, international aid, and Ngos*. Rutgers, NJ: Rutgers University Press, 2012.

Schwarz, Anne-Maree, Christain Ramofafia, James G. Bennett, Delvene Notere, Alexander Tewfik, Cletus Oengpepa, Bruno Manele, and Nelly Kere. *After the earthquake: An assessment of the impact of the earthquake and tsunami on fisheries-related livelihoods in coastal communities of Western Province, Solomon Islands*. Gizo, Solomon Islands: WorldFish Center-Solomon Islands, WorldFish Center-Penang, WWF-Solomon Islands Program, Western Province Fisheries, 2007.

Scoones, I. "New ecology and the social sciences: What prospects for a fruitful engagement?" *Annual Review of Anthropology* 28 (1999): 479–507.

Scott, James C. *Seeing like a state: How certain schemes to improve the human condition have failed*. New Haven, CT: Yale University Press, 1998.

Scott, Michael. *The severed snake: Matrilineages, making place, and a Melanesian Christianity in Southeast Solomon Islands*. Durham, NC: Carolina Academic Press, 2007.

Sheppard, P. J., R. Walter, and T. Nagaoka. "The archaeology of head-hunting in Roviana Lagoon, New Georgia." *Journal of the Polynesian Society* 109, no. 1 (2000): 9–37.

Shineberg, Dorothy. *The trading voyages of Andrew Cheyne, 1841–1844*. Canberra: Australian National University Press, 1971.

Smith, Linda Tuhiwai. *Decolonizing methodologies: Research and indigenous peoples*. London: Zed Books, 1999.

Solomon Islands Government. *Special audit report: Tsunami and Earthquake Relief Fund*. Honiara: Office of the Auditor-General, 2008.

Stella, Regis Tove. *Imagining the other: The representation of the Papua New Guinean subject*. Honolulu: University of Hawaii Press, 2007.

Steward, Julian Haynes. *Basin-Plateau aboriginal sociopolitical groups*. Washington, DC: Bureau of American Ethnology Bulletin, 1938.

Strathern, Marilyn. *The gender of the gift: Problems with women and problems with society in Melanesia*. Berkeley: University of California Press, 1988.

Sukrung, Karnjariya. "Andaman sea gypsies heeded pre-tsunami signs." *Bangkok Post*, January 17, 2005. www.rense.com/general62/pretsn.htm.

Sutherland, Janice. *Tsunami: Caught on camera*. Video. Darlow Smithson Productions, 2009.

Tabe, Tammy. "*Ngaira Kain Tari*—'We are people of the sea': A study of the Gilbertese resettlement to Solomon Islands." PhD diss., University of Bergen, 2016.

Taipei Times. "Oral history saved islanders from tsunami." March 2, 2005. www.taipeitimes.com/News/world/archives/2005/03/02/2003225170.

TallBear, Kim. *Native American DNA: Tribal belonging and the false promise of genetic science*. Minneapolis: University of Minnesota Press, 2013.

Taylor, Frederick W., Richard W. Briggs, Cliff Frohlich, Abel Brown, Matt Hornbach, Alison K. Papabatu, Aron J. Meltzner, and Douglas Billy. "Rupture across arc segment and plate boundaries in the 1 April 2007 Solomons earthquake." *Nature Geoscience* 1, no. 4 (2008): 253–57.

Telford, J., J. Cosgrave, and R. Houghton. *Joint evaluation of the international response to the Indian Ocean tsunami: Synthesis report*. London: Tsunami Evaluation Coalition, 2006.

Tengö, Maria, Eduardo S. Brondizio, Thomas Elmqvist, Pernilla Malmer, and Marja Spierenburg. "Connecting diverse knowledge systems for enhanced ecosystem governance: The multiple evidence base approach." *Ambio* 43, no. 5 (2014): 579–91.

Thomas, Nicholas. "Substantivization and anthropological discourse: The transformation of practices into institutions in neotraditional Pacific societies." In *History and tradition in Melanesian anthropology*, edited by James G. Carrier, 64–85. Berkeley: University of California, 1992.

Thomas, Tim, Peter Sheppard, and Richard Walter. "Landscape, violence and social bodies: Ritualized architecture in a Solomon Islands society." *Journal of the Royal Anthropological Institute* 7, no. 3 (2001): 545–72.

Thomas, Timothy. "Axes of entanglement in the New Georgia Group, Solomon Islands." *Terra Australis* 51 (2019): 103–16.

———. "Shrines in the landscape of New Georgia." In *Monuments and people in the Pacific*, edited by Helene Martinsson-Wallin and Timothy Thomas, 47–76. Uppsala, Sweden: Uppsala Universitet, Department of Archaeology and Ancient History, 2014.

Thompson, Kenneth, ed. *Readings from Émile Durkheim*. New York: Taylor & Francis, 2004.

Tierney, Kathleen. *The social roots of risk: Producing disasters, promoting resilience*. Palo Alto, CA: Stanford University Press, 2014.

Todd, Zoe. "An indigenous feminist's take on the ontological turn: 'Ontology' is just another word for colonialism." *Journal of Historical Sociology* 29, no. 1 (2016): 4–22.

Tomita, Takashi, Taro Arikawa, D. Tatsumi, K. Honda, H. Higashino, K. Watanabe, Y. Nishimura, et al. "Joint report for tsunami field survey for the Solomon Islands earthquake of April 1, 2007." *Tsunami Engineering Report of Research* (2008): 173.

Toren, Christina. "Seeing the ancestral sites: Transformations in Fijian notions of the land." In *The anthropology of landscape: Perspectives on place and space*, edited by Eric Hirsch and Michael O'Hanlon, 163–83. Oxford: Oxford University Press, 1995.

Tryon, D. T., and B. D. Hackman. *Solomon Islands languages: An internal classification*. Canberra: Australian National University, 1983.

Tsing, Anna Lowenhaupt. *Friction: An ethnography of global connection*. Princeton, NJ: Princeton University Press, 2005.

Tsing, Anna Lowenhaupt, Nils Bubandt, Elaine Gan, and Heather Anne Swanson, eds. *Arts of living on a damaged planet: Ghosts and monsters of the Anthropocene*. Minneapolis: University of Minnesota, 2017.

Turnbull, David. *Masons, tricksters and cartographers: Comparative studies in the sociology of scientific and indigenous knowledge*. Amsterdam: Harwood Academic, 2000.

———. "Reframing science and other local knowledge traditions." *Futures* 29, no. 6 (1997): 551–62.

Turnhout, Esther, Bob Bloomfield, Mike Hulme, Johannes Vogel, and Brian Wynne. "Listen to the voices of experience." *Nature* 488, no. 7412 (2012): 454–55.

Tuwere, Ilaitia S. *Vanua: Towards a Fijian theology of place*. Suva: University of South Pacific, 2002.

Tyler, Stephen A. *Cognitive anthropology*. New York: Holt Rinehart and Winston, 1969.

Tylor, Edward Burnett. *Primitive culture: Researches into the development of mythology, philosophy, religion, art and custom*, volume 2. London: John Murray, 1871.

United Nations Development Programme (UNDP). *Durie, the tsunami teacher*. Bangkok: UNDP, 2021.

———. "Eleven years after deadly tsunami, Simbo Island in the Solomons welcomes evacuation drills in schools." April 20, 2018. www.asia-pacific.undp .org/content/rbap/en/home/presscenter/articles/2018/04/20/devastated-by -the-2007-tsunami-simbo-island-in-the-solomon-islands-welcomes -emergency-evacuation-drill.html.

———. *Human development report*. New York: UNDP, 2020.

———. "Surviving the 2007 Tsunami in the Solomon Islands, Durie Hickie's story." May 4, 2018. https://undpasiapac.medium.com/surviving-the-2007 -tsunami-in-the-solomon-islands-durie-hickies-story-6c1e071420c7.

United Nations International Strategy for Disaster Reduction (UNISDR). "Leaders of Indonesia's Simeulue Community receive a prestigious United Nations award." 2005. www.unisdr.org/news/v.php?id=5602.

United Nations Office for Disaster Risk Reduction (UNDRR). *The human cost of disasters: An overview of the last 20 years (2000–2019).* New York: UNDRR, 2020.

Verran, Helen. "Engagements between disparate knowledge traditions: Toward doing difference generatively and in good faith." In *Contested ecologies: Dialogues in the South on nature and knowledge,* edited by Lesley Green, 141–61. Cape Town, South Africa: HSRC Press, 2013.

Viveiros de Castro, Eduardo. "Cosmological deixis and Amerindian perspectivism." *Journal of the Royal Anthropological Institute* 4, no. 3 (1998): 469–89.

———. "Zeno and the art of anthropology: Of lies, beliefs, paradoxes, and other truths." *Common Knowledge* 17, no. 1 (2011): 128–45.

Wagner, John, and Malia Talakai. "Customs, commons, property, and ecology: Case studies from Oceania." *Human Organization* 66, no. 1 (2007): 1–10.

Wagner, Roy. "The fractal person." In *Big men and great men: Personifications of power in Melanesia,* edited by M. Godelier and M. Strathern, 159–73. Cambridge: Cambridge University Press, 1991.

Walker, B. H., and David Salt. *Resilience thinking: Sustaining ecosystems and people in a changing world.* Washington, DC: Island Press, 2006.

Wallerstein, Immanuel. "The rise and future demise of the world capitalist system: Concepts for comparative analysis." In *The capitalist world-economy.* Cambridge: Cambridge University Press, 1979.

Walley, Christine J. *Exit zero: Family and class in postindustrial Chicago.* Chicago: University of Chicago Press, 2013.

Walter, Richard, Tim Thomas, and Peter Sheppard. "Cult assemblages and ritual practice in Roviana Lagoon, Solomon Islands." *World Archaeology* 36, no. 1 (2004): 142–57.

Walters, Bradley B., Bonnie McCay, Paige West, and Susan Lees, eds. *Against the grain: The Vayda tradition in human ecology and ecological anthropology.* Lanham, MD: AltaMira Press, 2008.

Waterhouse, J. H. Lawry. *A Roviana and English dictionary, with English-Roviana index and list of natural history objects.* Guadalcanal: Melanesian Mission Press, 1928.

———. *A Roviana and English dictionary, with English-Roviana index and list of natural history objects and appendix of old customs.* Revised and enlarged by L. M. Jones. Sydney: Epworth Printing and Publishing House, 1949.

Webber, Sophie. "Performative vulnerability: Climate change adaptation policies and financing in Kiribati." *Environment and Planning A* 45, no. 11 (2013): 2717–33.

Weiner, James. "Between a rock and a non-place: Towards a contemporary anthropology of place." *Reviews in Anthropology* 31, no. 1 (2002): 21–27.

Weiner, James F., and Katie Glaskin. *Customary land tenure and registration in Australia and Papua New Guinea: Anthropological perspectives.* Canberra: Australia National University Press, 2007.

Welsh, Marc. "Resilience and responsibility: Governing uncertainty in a complex world." *Geographical Journal* 180, no. 1 (2013): 15–26.

West, Paige. *Conservation is our government now: The politics of ecology in Papua New Guinea.* New ecologies for the twenty-first century. Durham, NC: Duke University Press, 2006.

———. *Dispossession and the environment: Rhetoric and inequality in Papua New Guinea.* New York: Columbia University Press, 2016.

White, Geoffrey M. *Identity through history: Living stories in a Solomon Islands society.* Cambridge studies in social and cultural anthropology. Cambridge: Cambridge University Press, 1991.

Wisner, Benjamin. *At risk: Natural hazards, people's vulnerability, and disasters.* London: Routledge, 2004.

Wolf, Eric. *Europe and the people without history.* Berkeley: University of California Press, 1982.

Wynne, Brian. "May the sheep safely graze? A reflexive view of the expert-lay knowledge divide." In *Risk, environment and modernity: Towards a new ecology*, edited by Scott Lash, Bronislaw Szerszynski, and Brian Wynne, 44–79. London: Sage, 1996.

Yogaswara, Herry, and Eko Yulianto. *Smong, local knowledge of tsunami among the Simeulue Community, Nangroe Aceh Darusallam.* Jakarta, Indonesia: Jakarta Tsunami Information Centre, 2008.

Zelenietz, Martin. "The end of headhunting in New Georgia." In *The pacification of Melanesia*, edited by Margaret Rodman and Matthew Cooper, 91–108. Ann Arbor: University of Michigan Press, 1979.

Index

Founded in 1893,
UNIVERSITY OF CALIFORNIA PRESS
publishes bold, progressive books and journals
on topics in the arts, humanities, social sciences,
and natural sciences—with a focus on social
justice issues—that inspire thought and action
among readers worldwide.

The UC PRESS FOUNDATION
raises funds to uphold the press's vital role
as an independent, nonprofit publisher, and
receives philanthropic support from a wide
range of individuals and institutions—and from
committed readers like you. To learn more, visit
ucpress.edu/supportus.

Printed in Great Britain
by Amazon